UNDERSTANDING CHILD ABUSE

David N Jones qualified as a social worker after graduating from Oxford University and was appointed Leader of the Nottinghamshire and NSPCC Special Unit in 1979. He is an active member of the British Association of Social Workers, serving as chairman of the BASW working party on child abuse registers (1976–8) and subsequently as a member of the Social Policy Committee, and presented papers at the Second International Congress on Child Abuse and Neglect.

John Pickett qualified as a psychiatric social worker and is now Principal Social Work Manager for the NSPCC. He was responsible for setting up the first NSPCC Special Unit in 1973, and has served on two committees of enquiry into child deaths. Margaret Oates is Consultant Psychiatrist and Senior Lecturer in Psychiatry at the University of Nottingham, and honorary Consultant Psychiatrist to the NSPCC. She has a special interest in disorders associated with childbirth, and is involved in training midwives and health visitors as well as medical students. Peter Barbor is Consultant Paediatrician at the University Hospital, Nottingham, and a member of the NSPCC Central Executive and Professional Advisory Committees.

TEACH YOURSELF BOOKS

UNDERSTANDING CHILD ABUSE

David N Jones (Editor)
John Pickett
Margaret R Oates
Peter R H Barbor

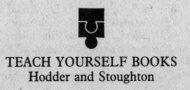

TEACH YOURSELF BOOKS
Hodder and Stoughton

First printed 1982

Copyright © 1982
David N Jones

All rights reserved. No part of this publication may be
reproduced or transmitted in any form or by any means,
electronic or mechanical, including photocopy, recording, or any
information storage and retrieval system, without permission in
writing from the publisher.

British Library Cataloguing in Publication Data

Understanding child abuse.
1. Child abuse
I. Jones, David N
362.7′044   HV721

ISBN 0 340 26818 2

Phototypeset in Linotron 202 Plantin by
Western Printing Services Ltd, Bristol.
Printed and bound in Great Britain
for Hodder and Stoughton Educational,
a division of Hodder and Stoughton Ltd,
Mill Road, Dunton Green, Sevenoaks, Kent
by Richard Clay (The Chaucer Press) Ltd, Bungay, Suffolk.

Contents

ference; Preparation for the conference; The conference agenda;
Chairmanship of conferences; Decision-making; Subsequent co-
ordination; Recording; Pre-requisites for effective case conferences.

Foreword
by the Director of the NSPCC

Wordsworth wrote:

> A simple child,
> That lightly draws its breath,
> And feels its life in every limb,
> What should it know of death?
> (We are Seven, 1815)

Where such a death results from abuse or neglect on the part of a child's parents, or others with parental responsibility, it is not surprising that there should be a strong emotional reaction from the public generally, and from their informants in the news media in particular.

There are, too, lesser 'deaths'. A number of children have lifelong disabilities of mind or body because of physical injury incurred at home, with the genteel classification 'non-accidental'; however loving the care, some are condemned to what can be managed as life in hospitals for the mentally disabled. For these, the results of mental and physical handicap are there to see. For countless others, the inward scars of emotional deprivation or abuse, the battered souls from sexually perverted practices, are just as real. They can lead to lifelong deprivation, bizarre relationships, disturbed and anti-social adolescence and adulthood. All such distorted experience – above all the emptiness of existence without love, or warmth, or even simple fun – are ready vehicles for carrying on the cycle of abuse.

Some aspects of this scene are met with disbelief; more generally there is revulsion, and if public response is seen as more punitive than supportive, there is a genuineness of concern that must be heeded. In that it ensures a priority for professional work in this field, well and good. There are negative consequences as well, however, and they too require attention.

It saddens me so often to receive morally indignant messages condemning cruelty to children from those who claim to have brought up families without stress, misgivings or mistakes. To them I would commend this book, which demonstrates how child abuse occurs – not to challenge their condemnation of the outcome, nor condone abusive acts, but to increase understanding of the underlying causes, such as inadequate upbringing, distorted expectation and intolerance to stress. With understanding can come support. Support for families – because those low in self-esteem, and lacking social skills, are ready targets for being shunned within their neighbourhood; such isolation compounds their problems, whereas good neighbourliness of itself could break the cycle of feeling rejected and inadequate. Support too for social workers and other caring practitioners, and understanding of the hazardous path they follow.

Probably the most damaging effect of public outcry when child abuse results in death is in the collective demoralisation of professional workers at one of their number being a scapegoat – pilloried for taking a wrong decision, 'wrong', that is, as judged with others' hindsight, and perhaps with imperfect knowledge of the facts. Negligent or incompetent practice cannot be condoned; nor should it be assumed, for, in any activity related to human problems, decisions however carefully and conscientiously reached are bound from time to time to be proved wrong by subsequent events. Over-reaction and the pillory do not encourage better practice, but rather lead to defensiveness – such as unnecessary removal into care, to a child's unnecessary distress – or indecisiveness.

For this is the area of social work that supremely concentrates, for all practitioners, the hazards of intervention into family life. If . . . When . . . How . . . to interfere? The fear of lost rapport with the parents, and of emotional trauma to the child, if it be removed from an allegedly abusing home. The anxiety of what abuse – or death – may happen if it be not removed. The prospect of professional martyrdom if the decision is later seen as 'wrong'. The risk of physical violence if aggressive parents feel that they have been 'wronged'. Consciousness that unnecessary distress can result from a false assumption of wilful injury. The constant awareness that a child's or children's whole future well-being can depend upon making the right assessment, and taking the right action, when the only information available may be incomplete – and inconclusive.

To members of an emergent profession, still feeling out its role – and unlike its elder sisters having to do so at speed and in the light of instant publicity that is often less than sympathetic – confrontation with cases of child abuse can concertina stress on stress. So many others in the community have such a range of social needs, but public pressure ensures priority for abused or neglected children. For the generic worker, trying to balance conflicting demands for time and resources, the imperiousness of this priority, and the hazards of involvement, can result in almost a masochistic feast of stressfulness. There must be adequate knowledge of the natural history, familiarity with the procedures, self-confidence in investigation, and competence in the variety of techniques of management that relate to child abuse and neglect. Insecurity over responding adequately will be compounded unless there is understanding supervision and support. To any who so feel, this book is an essential resource that should never be out of reach.

The authors rightly stress the importance of supervision. Whatever the skill and confidence of the practitioner, there can be a cumulative stress factor in dealing with child abuse cases which, if it is not to result in professional burn-out, needs to be anticipated, shared and properly managed. This may not be the occasion to develop the proposition that all investigation and management should be the responsibility of specialised teams, backed by multidisciplinary support, although both within the NSPCC and in other agencies the effectiveness of such provision has been demonstrated. One of the significant features of this book, which I believe to be fundamental to its effectiveness, is that it has been written by a group of professionals from different disciplines who are experienced in managing child abuse as members of a multidisciplinary team.

It has given me much pleasure to read their manuscript. It is an honour to have been asked to add this small contribution. It is a source of pride that the authors are all, in their various ways, associated with the work of the NSPCC. I believe that they have produced a masterly handbook that will become a standard work of reference. They write with the assurance and understanding of those who are masters of their subject; who know the stresses and anxieties and hazards of the work; who care for families in distress or disarray; who have a day-by-day contact with reality.

To those who may have misgivings about how to proceed, they demonstrate the necessity of timely and comprehensive investigation; the importance of focusing upon the needs of the child without neglecting the parents; the confidence in relationships which can come from an honesty of approach, from use of authority without being authoritarian; the confidence that can be established in a family through the practitioner's own self-confidence; the need to be consistent in purpose whilst flexible in approach. They write simply, without over-statement, as thorough-going professionals. The result is a work that will inform, guide, encourage and sustain all those whose professional work brings them into contact with child abuse in its various forms; it will provide essential reading for their supervisors, managers and trainers; it will be invaluable in its presentation and content to that wider audience of informed commentators and citizens who seek better understanding of this subject.

Alan Gilmour
NSPCC, October 1981

Acknowledgements

A book of this kind inevitably reflects the ideas, practice and experience of many people. We wish to express our appreciation of the support, friendship and stimulation of our colleagues in many different professions – especially in Nottinghamshire and Greater Manchester and in the NSPCC – and in particular our immediate colleagues, Sydney Brandon (Professor of Psychiatry, Leicester University), Celia Doyle (Unit Member, Nottinghamshire and NSPCC Special Unit), David Hull (Professor of Child Health, Nottingham University) and Andy Maton (former Unit Leader, Manchester Special Unit).

We are particularly grateful to Alan Gilmour (Director, NSPCC) for numerous helpful comments, Ann Fillmore for permission to quote from her paper on abused children as survivors, Fred Hedley (Legal Executive, NSPCC) for advice on child care law, Roy McClean (Chief Superintendent, Nottinghamshire Constabulary) for advice on certain police matters, and David Spicer (Barrister, Nottinghamshire County Council) for advice and guidance on the law and court proceedings. Extracts from DHSS Maria Colwell, LASSL 74(25), 1974, are reproduced on pp. 53–4 with the permission of the Controller of Her Majesty's Stationery Office. The quotation from E Baher *et al.* (1976) *At Risk: An Account of the Battered Child Research Department, NSPCC* (p. 105) is reproduced by permission of Routledge and Kegan Paul Ltd. Drawings in Chapter 5 are by Geoff Lyth (Medical Artist, Nottingham University) and the index was compiled by Thea Jones, to whom our thanks.

Christine Smakowska (Librarian, NSPCC National Advisory Service, tel. 01–580–8812) provides an invaluable public service in lending and advising on literature relating to child care and child abuse. We are especially grateful for her assistance.

Helen Leighton and Vicky Stevenson completed the final typescript with much appreciated speed and efficiency.

All names and identifying information in case material have been changed.

Writing a book whilst fully engaged in the routine of normal work has proved far more demanding than we had anticipated – this perhaps explains why more practitioners do not write about their work. I am personally grateful to my three co-authors for their stimulating and good-natured co-operation and to their families for their forbearance. Although we share authorship, as editor I must take final responsibility for the balance and style of the book and for any errors or omissions.

Members of my own family have suffered an almost intolerable invasion of our family time: Rebecca and Anna have discovered that authorship is a previously unrecognised form of child abuse, whilst Rachel, my wife, has patiently read all the drafts and proofs, advised on grammar and style, and tolerated many trials and tribulations. My very special affection and thanks are reserved for them.

David N Jones

Introduction

'Children are universally predisposed to the fear of infanticide by both their physical and their psychological stage of development . . . the intensity of that fear depends on the incidence of traumatic events and on the degree of love they have experienced' (Bloch). The suggestion that at some time we have all experienced the fear of being killed by our parents probably seems as unreal and outrageous to most people today as Freud's ideas about childhood sexuality seemed to the Victorians: 'surely parents love and care for their children?'. The idea is only a hypothesis, but on reflection it does seem to be grounded in experience. Children are small, defenceless, demanding and dependent, and all parents have times of frustration, irritability and anger with their offspring, however loving and caring they are. The children experience these parental emotions together with their own feelings of anger, rage and fear; the child's life is not a blissful state of immediate satisfaction. However strenuously we strive to deny it by retreat into our romantic idealisation of happy families, we all live in a world of ambivalent relationships and powerful, often violent emotions: the drive to survive presupposes the fear of destruction.

The reality of this fear of parent figures is perhaps seen in the abiding popularity of many children's stories: the cruel stepmother in Cinderella and the murderous stepmother in

Snow White, the fearsome grandmother turned wolf in Red Riding Hood and the cannibalistic witch in Hansel and Gretel. Some nursery rhymes betray the insecurity of childhood, for example The Old Woman who lived in a Shoe, and the favourite lullaby Rock-a-bye Baby, which ends with the cradle crashing to the ground. Religious stories and ancient myths also echo this theme: Romulus and Remus, the mythical founders of Rome, were abandoned as babies and found and brought up by a wolf, whilst the Bible is full of violent family feuds and Abraham is depicted as being willing to sacrifice his son. The powerful Greek legend of Oedipus, the latter part of which was used by Freud to illustrate his view of the human condition, includes his parents' attempt to kill him:

Oedipus: She gave it to you . . . To what purpose?
Shepherd: To be destroyed.
Oedipus: The child she bore!
Shepherd: Yes master. They said t'was on account of some wicked spell.
Oedipus: What spell?
Shepherd: Saying the child would kill its father.
Messenger: I found you (as a baby) in a wooded hollow in Cithaeron. . . . The infirmity in your ankles tells the tale. . . . Your ankles were rivetted, and I set you free. . . . To it you owe your present name.

(King Oedipus – transl. E F Watling)

If it is true that all parents have occasional murderous thoughts about their children, which need to be powerfully controlled, and that all children may sometimes fear destruction by their parents or caregivers, it is hardly surprising that the subject of overt child abuse arouses such strong public feeling. Whenever we talk on this subject to professional audiences or other interested people, a comment such as 'of course we all experience really angry feelings with our children at times' almost always generates an embarrassed and relieved wave of laughter. Yet reported cases of ill-treatment always stimulate expressions of shock, horror and disbelief, with demands for harsher penalties for the perpetrators.

Child abuse may be nearer to us all than we care to admit, but in practice the vast majority of parents and children learn to control and overcome primitive feelings of fear and violence: the 'degree of love' which is given and received far outweighs the 'incidence of traumatic events'. The hypothesis of murderous impulses is irrelevant to the daily lives of most people, although the romantic dream of happy families may be very necessary to sustain parents through wakeful nights and difficult times. But for some children and their parents the primitive fear becomes a frightening reality in the guise of physical or sexual assault, neglect, deprivation and emotional onslaught. Over one hundred children a year are killed in England and Wales alone (see Chapter 2).

This book is concerned with this small minority of families where the parent's negative feelings have become a reality for the child. We use the term *child abuse* throughout the text in a generic way to embrace all forms of unacceptable treatment of children by their parents or caregivers, including inflicted injury, neglect, deprivation, sexual and emotional ill-treatment. More precise legal definitions do exist (see Chapter 14), but these are limited in scope and interpreted according to changing ideas and attitudes. Agencies working with the problem may require a clear boundary to the area of their concern, and these have been attempted (e.g. BASW 1978, DHSS 1980), but for the purposes of this book we have assumed the problem of unacceptable parental behaviour without more precise definition. The main focus is on children physically injured by their parents, but much will be equally relevant to other forms of child abuse.

Our objective in writing this book has been to satisfy the need of those from many different professions who are working with abused children and their families for clear, concise and useable guidance about day-to-day practice, and also to provide a commentary on the problem for interested members of the public. We write primarily from our own daily experience of working with these families and their problems, although informed by the work and writing of others, and we report what we have found so far to be helpful. However, as we shall show later, knowledge about child abuse in particular and human behaviour in general is extremely partial, despite the vast outpouring of research and opinion in recent years. Workers in this complex field of human emotion must therefore proceed with caution, remaining open to the influence of new research, ideas and methods. This may sound like a recipe for vacillating inactivity and self-doubt, and there are those whose work reveals these characteristics. Yet the paradox remains that families in trouble desperately need a worker with confidence, self-respect, assurance, flexibility and humanity. The resolution of the paradox presents a new challenge with each new family the worker meets.

Individual chapters have not been ascribed to a specific author. The authors started by drafting those sections within the specialism of each. Each was given an opportunity to comment on the work of the others then, following discussion, the editor rewrote the whole, aiming at a coherent structure and jargon-free style which would be accessible to all. Thus, although each chapter is mainly the work of one or two people, all four are co-authors of the whole. This seemed the only honest approach, given the multidisciplinary nature of the subject, and it reflects the method of working with abused children and their families which is advocated in the book.

For ease of reading, references have not been included within the text except where there is a quotation or mention of a specific research finding. A list of authors is provided for each chapter at the end of the book, indicating material referred to in the text or otherwise relevant to the subject of the chapter, or worth further reading. This must be read in conjunction with the bibliography.

By aiming at simplicity and clarity in presentation, there is a danger that we will seem to have reduced the problem to a misleading generality. A small book can only hope to provide an overview of a subject, but we trust that it will enthuse readers to explore more detailed studies of the many issues we discuss, and such studies are cited in the bibliography.

The book should be read as guidance to support the individual assessment and management of each unique family situation and not as a universal prescription. Specific problems in work with a family should always be discussed with a supervisor or colleague. This work is complex, requiring the marriage of research and the experience of others with informed intuition and hope. Despite the complexity and uncertainty, it is possible to help abused children and their families, but no worker is omniscient and tragedies will still occur. There is no guarantee of success and the public has no right to expect it of those who necessarily take risks in undertaking the attempt.

To define child abuse as unacceptable parental treatment of a child assumes knowledge of what is normal and acceptable. The book therefore opens with a general discussion of parenting in Western society, before moving on to consideration of the abnormal and unacceptable and what to do about it when it first comes to light and thereafter.

PART I

Child Abuse: An Overview

I

Parenting

In Western society children are recognised as potential citizens with rights and duties, but deserving special protection because of their vulnerability. Parents have to provide adequate care and control, and only when parental standards are judged inadequate is it seen to be right for outsiders to intervene between parent and child. Few would argue with this, but in our discussion of 'normal' child rearing it is important to acknowledge that other societies past and present have different attitudes and standards and thus that the definition of good and bad child care necessarily implies a moral judgement.

Many different attitudes to children can be found. In many cultures in the past young children were not considered people, perhaps an acknowledgement of high childhood mortality, which allowed an unwanted child to be disposed of without the parent being guilty of the crime of murder. Some societies defined children as the property of the parent, to be done with as he willed, a view still sometimes expressed today: 'What right have you to interfere in my family life?'. Some cultures place great emphasis on the role of the extended family or community in caring for the child, with parents playing only a limited role. Scarring, piercing and circumcision during maturity rituals, and even mutilation, are acceptable to some; and children have been legitimate objects for ritual sacrifice. Protection of children from harm by their parents (as we understand it) has not been and is not seen in all cultures as a moral imperative. Ideas about what is good and bad treatment of children will vary, which creates problems when two or more cultures have to coexist.

Social trends affecting parenting

In our own society great emphasis is placed on parental responsibility not only for caring for children, including exercise of discipline, but also for their wrong-doing. Parents frequently feel judged on the performance and behaviour of their children and thus have a powerful investment in their successful development. There is now a plethora of books and other advice to parents on how to bring up their children and some have argued that this deluge of advice has served only to confuse and undermine self-confidence. There is undoubtedly a widespread demand for such advice, but in the end each family has to discover its own unique approach. This diversity creates a daily dilemma for those whose work is in helping parents; at what point does a difference of outlook or morals become child abuse?

In comparison with earlier generations, parents today have fewer children, move house more often and have less intense contact with their extended family. It is now rare for parents to have grown up learning about child and baby care by observation at close quarters.

There is increasing concern about the personal and financial cost of the rise in the number of marriages which break up, and there are many more single parent families, partly the result of these marital breakdowns and partly also the result of increased social acceptance of unmarried parenthood. There is no authoritative study of the impact of marital breakdown on children, but clinical experience suggests that arguments, bitterness and eventual separation frequently cause deep harm; many children feel torn by powerful divided loyalties and these children feature disproportionately in referrals to social and psychiatric agencies. The problems are no less intense for the parents and step-parents. There is no guarantee that a successful adult relationship can be extended to embrace step-children, and step-fathers figure disproportionately in child abuse statistics. Single parents also face many problems, in particular the care of their children whilst they are at work.

The quality of the physical environment significantly affects the quality of child care. Inner-city studies show that parents there have the same moral standards and aspirations for their children as others, yet the inner-city environment inhibits them from providing the care and control they believe to be right. If there are no open spaces, for example, children play on the street or stay at home. If at home, proximity generates conflict; if on the street, children are at risk in many ways, including contact with the police over some prank or misdemeanour which would have gone unnoticed in a more spacious suburb. This presents an insoluble parental dilemma which is bound to generate conflict and family stress.

Poor housing makes it difficult to maintain high standards of hygiene and warmth; the consequences can be interpreted as neglect. There is also some evidence that high lead levels in the polluted atmosphere of the city may cause behavioural problems, including heightened irritability and aggression in children and adults alike. The problems of young families in high-rise flats are now well documented, as are the problems of social isolation on new estates. Many parents would provide better care for their children if they lived in a more favourable environment.

The multi-racial character of our society also brings a variety of child care problems. For the children of many immigrants there is a clash between parental expectations derived from their original cultural background and the cultural environment in which they now live. This can generate conflict and occasionally results in child abuse.

Recent reports on child health services have demonstrated

beyond question unjustifiable differences in the standards of health care and other services for children between different regions and social classes, with the areas of greatest need often receiving the worst services. These disparities and other problems discussed in this section do not directly cause child abuse, but they are major contributory factors.

It is beyond the scope of this book to present a detailed critique of current attitudes towards children and families. An understanding of child abuse can only grow from an appreciation of the circumstances of all children and if this book dwells on services to individuals and families in trouble, it is not to deny the vital importance of policy and action to promote family welfare in general.

Responsibilities of parenthood

We now consider what happens in most families as children are born and grow up. Every family is unique and has to find its own approach to living together successfully but there are similarities which enable us to define a broad range of behaviours which we can call 'normal'. There will be wide variations within this norm, but we must try to define it if we are to talk about the abnormal or pathological.

In our culture parents have the prime responsibility for ensuring that their children grow into secure and productive members of society. This includes meeting basic physical needs of shelter and food, care in illness, protecting the child from danger, but also fostering independence and inquisitiveness (the balance changing as the child grows older) and providing for emotional, intellectual, spiritual and personality development, with an ability to make constructive relationships with others. The parents obviously share most of these responsibilities with others, but the influence of the home is seen as paramount. Most parents know something about the normal development of children. It is important that they do since, as we shall see later, misunderstanding of normal development and unrealistic expectations can lead parents into trouble.

Pregnancy and childbirth

This is a time of very significant physical and social change. The arrival of the first child is probably the most profound social event that most people experience. It is a time of heightened emotion for all involved and many couples feel in retrospect that it detracts from the happiness of their relationship. The ability to come to terms with all that happens will lay the foundation for the future security of the family and development of the child.

Physical and emotional changes in the woman start from the moment of conception and continue for some months after birth. Understanding these normal processes is essential when diagnosing emotional disturbance or mental illness. Many women experience morning sickness, tingling breasts and other discomfort during the first three months of pregnancy but these usually subside and most experience good health at least until the last three or four weeks. Parents have to come to terms with the pregnancy and, for first time parents, the transition to parenthood. For some this adjustment began with the decision to try to conceive, but for others the reality is a shock, perhaps unwanted, possibly even involving consideration of abortion. For most there is an initial excitement which often changes into a feeling of interminable waiting.

During the second trimester the pregnancy becomes visible to others and the foetus' movements are felt. The woman increasingly assumes a pregnant 'status'; significant emotional adjustments continue. Most parents start giving the foetus a personality, naming it, talking and worrying about it, and treating it as already part of the family. Most women and many men develop fears, fantasies and phobias associated with the baby and superstition assumes a powerful significance. They are anxious to know that all is going well and are easily upset by even the smallest problem – hypochondriasis projected on to the baby is very common.

All women are advised to attend ante-natal clinic during pregnancy, in order to screen for abnormalities which are more easily corrected if diagnosed early and to monitor the health and development of mother and baby. The operation of these clinics often presents both the woman and staff with considerable problems, not least of a large number of people to be seen in a short time in inadequate surroundings. Most women cope with these without apparent ill-effect and attendance is associated with a much lower risk of the baby dying before or just after birth. Going to clinic has become a part of the ritual of pregnancy.

Maternity services are the one part of the health service with which we are all likely to be involved at some stage, and it is therefore hardly surprising that they attract particular public scrutiny. Ante-natal services have been strongly criticised by some groups and, without entering that debate, it seems relevant here to note that the operation of the clinics and other support services may be of crucial preventative importance for the anxious and ambivalent mother, who may be at risk of abusing her baby. Long waits, perhaps without clothes, only very brief direct contact with doctors and nurses, use of medical terms and shorthand which are not explained, seeing different people each visit who give different advice, all heighten anxiety and confusion and tend to demoralise and alienate the vulnerable mother. She may then fail to attend or, if she continues, feel unable to share her problems and worries. It is important that such women are identified early and, if possible, a more personal service provided. The community midwife or health visitor may be best placed to make this assessment.

Pregnancy is a time of considerable anxiety and powerful emotions which can surprise even the most stable personalities. Throughout the latter stages, the woman is increasingly prone to emotional upset; she is less able to cope with life-changing crises, such as the death of a near relative (especially a parent). Many couples move house at this time too because more space is needed for the baby, but this can significantly disturb emotional stability.

Physical changes accelerate as the confinement approaches, particularly during the last four to two weeks. All physical and mental processes slow down, including speed of reaction, ability to concentrate, retention of recent memory and intellectual ability; optimistic plans of things to do come unstuck.

The woman often becomes more placid, although the man may appear increasingly agitated. Anxiety about the birth changes to impatience to get it all over with, and there is increasing preoccupation with preparations for the arrival (the 'nest building syndrome'). Some couples become socially withdrawn and introspective. Immediately before the birth the woman experiences significant physical and emotional changes – often a sudden increase in appetite for food and sex.

For most parents, however well prepared, the hard work and pain involved in labour come as a shock. Some argue that the birth experience itself is crucial in determining the future quality of the parent–child relationship. This can be over-emphasised since many parents have successfully reared children without the benefit of the most recent theories and practices. However, it is probably significant for the vulnerable or marginal mother. A sensitive handling of labour in her case can make the difference between laying a successful foundation for the future and precipitating a lifetime of relationship problems.

During the last few years in Britain, the vast majority of fathers have attended the birth of their children. This has been a comparatively recent trend and is in marked contrast to other cultures where men are excluded from childbirth. The pattern may reflect the increasing involvement of men in caring for very young children. There is some evidence that those present during or immediately after the birth more easily develop a close 'bond' with the baby (see p. 144). For this reason fathers should be encouraged to attend and, when there, made to feel meaningfully involved rather than a peripheral observer. This is not to argue that absence will inevitably create problems later on: millions of children have grown up happily without their father having been present at the birth. Indeed, paternal involvement may be impossible because of work or family demands. A positive reluctance to be present is now unusual, however, and may be significant. Paternal involvement may need careful preparation and, when the time comes, the parents' wishes must be respected.

The first eight hours after birth are usually a time of contagious euphoria; the opposite reaction suggests problems to come. Some parents react initially with shock and horror at the sight of the baby and outright rejection occasionally follows. The initial professional response should be reassurance and careful explanation about the strange transitory appearance of some babies. A powerful adverse reaction to the baby's sex indicates that major problems may develop. Some parents rapidly recover equilibrium and 'take to' the baby, but in others rejection or a marked ambivalence contine. This should be taken seriously and sometimes a case conference should be called to assess future risk to the child and services available to the family. The parents' reaction must not be blocked or ignored; there is always a danger that 'jollying along' and cheerful remarks by nurses that 'Of course its OK – he's a beautiful baby' simply compound the problem and prevent discussion of deeper feelings. If rejection persists, even after skilled counselling, the parents' request for adoption should be respected.

During this first eight hour period, both mother and baby are very awake and alert. It is the optimum time for them to get to know each other, and fathers, brothers and sisters should be involved. This 'bonding' process is now recognised and it is accepted that separation of mother and child at this time, and probably also exclusion of the father, may adversely affect their relationship, particularly with 'vulnerable' parents (see Chapters 6 and 11).

Although not essential, it seems that allowing this 'getting to know' process to happen naturally, in a family context, does give the best start, and for the 'marginal' parent can make the difference between success and failure. Birth in hospital certainly offers physical safeguards, but adjustment of the hospital routine to meet the individual emotional needs of mother and child may be difficult.

The first three days form a 'latent' period, with continued euphoria (for most) and the excitement of a rush of social contacts. The parents feel proud and special. Baby is usually quiet and sleeps. Most women experience a sudden change of mood after the third day ('fourth day blues') (80 per cent of first time mothers and 60 per cent of others). This is due to physical and emotional exhaustion and major hormonal adjustments, coupled with a growing realisation of the demands of the new 'normality' involving repeated feeding and changing. The special moment has come and gone forever and the routine has to begin. There are dramatic fluctuations in mood: one word out of place and the floodgates open. There is not much warning given and this usually comes as a great shock to both parents. The best treatment is reassurance and help with practical tasks, but if symptoms persist, expert advice is needed.

The first eight weeks after birth, known as the puerperium, see a gradual return to emotional stability and normal speed of reaction. Most women remain thin skinned and experience restless tension, inability to relax and feelings of inadequacy. Many have persistent unpleasant thoughts or images of harm coming to the baby and some become over concerned about hygiene. Even the most confident seek advice and reassurance only to be upset with those who give it. It is surprising how often first-time mothers are taken aback by the demands of motherhood: 'Nobody told me how tired I would feel, how worried I would be, it would be like this, how much there is to do', perhaps partly because they are unlikely to have learnt by observation.

Many first-time mothers experience full-time life at home for the first time when a baby is born and frequently have a strong sense of isolation and loneliness, especially if they have left a satisfying job or career, and there is nobody to turn to if new to the area and away from the extended family. Informal neighbourhood contacts, mother and baby clubs, midwives, health visitors and clinics have a helpful role to play in assisting these women to develop new relationships and also to provide essential emotional and practical support.

The arrival of the baby demands a total change in outlook and life-style, especially for the mother who has to contend with conflicting societal expectations that she will be a perfect mother devoted to her children (as idealised in TV adverts) on the one hand and a 'liberated' working mother on the other. Few can sustain both roles successfully and many come to feel trapped by the baby. This may be a legitimate reflection of social circumstances and/or a reflection of personality problems. People who feel trapped usually react with extreme emotions, either an angry desire to escape, or depressed resignation. There is evidence of increasing stress and mild depression in this group and many women are prescribed tranquillisers, sedatives or sleeping tablets. This in itself can be dangerous as we discuss below (see Chapter 15).

Most families take these upheavals in their stride and establish themselves as successful parents, but almost one-fifth of women will develop some persistent emotional disturbance. The vast majority do not require formal treatment and recover, although the experience is very unpleasant for the family. Symptoms include extreme tiredness, headaches, depression, irritability and loss of sexual interest, and can last several weeks. The best treatment is support from family and friends with reassurance and practical advice from doctor and health visitor. If symptoms continue or worsen, psychiatric treatment should be considered.

It is very easy in a book such as this to dwell on the problems of pregnancy and childbirth to the exclusion of the normal experience of most parents. In fact most women come through pregnancy with no significant difficulty and, in retrospect at least, see it as a positive period in their life. Childbirth is undoubtedly one of the most memorable and significant events in life and is usually recalled with pleasure and pride.

The first year

The newborn baby is more than a passive recipient of experience. From the first moment of life he not only reacts to his environment but takes initiatives within it, involving give and take on both sides. All relationships involve demand and response, a process of negotiation, but the more profound the issue the higher the stakes and the more likely the conflict. The baby is totally dependent on his caregiver for survival and development and at times most parents feel trapped and dominated by this dependency. For them, too, the early years often feel like a battle for survival as an independent personality. Survival is fundamental and so it is not surprising that there is tension and conflict in family life. As a rule, the closer the relationship and the greater the dependency, the more the potential for conflict; it is statistically safer to walk through the inner city at night than to sit in your own front room.

During the first months the baby needs food, warmth, cleanliness, sufficient sleep, freedom from discomfort, social contact and love, and he will actively seek them out by crying and other increasingly sophisticated communications. He cannot want something that is bad for him; wants and needs coincide. Many parents feel that responding immediately to his demands will produce a naughty, 'spoilt' child and for some the fear of spoiling is central to their problems with their children. It is groundless. Babies who are fed on demand, picked up when they cry, and played with when lonely are usually easier to manage as they grow up than those for whom life has been a sequence of conflicts from the outset. Of course the demands can be erratic, inconvenient and extremely wearing for the parent, but it is important to recognise that whilst this may be a problem for the parent it is definitely not the fault of the child. For the sake of both a compromise must be sought; however, this may take time to evolve.

The child's physical needs are immediate and difficult to ignore; it is easier to overlook emotional, intellectual and psychological needs. Yet from the moment of birth, babies need and seek social contact. At first his facial expression appears blank and can be unnerving; the eye can only focus at about one foot, exactly the distance from eye to eye when held in arms. Yet the baby can differentiate between parents and others within hours of birth, by sight, sound and smell and there are signs of recognition even in the early days. The first smile at around six weeks is a major event for most parents, symbolising a break-through in the relationship. The baby's needs for company and stimulation (things to do and think about) are present during these early weeks and gradually increase. Many parents do not realise that during the first six months babies are awake on average eight hours a day, which is a lot of 'free time' to fill. He will respond to eye contact, talking and music, and will enjoy pictures in cot and pram, mobiles and television. Above all he needs to be cuddled, rocked and touched. Physical contact is as essential as food and is probably the main way in which he experiences the love of his parents. Spending time with him is essential. Gradually he will learn to occupy himself for longer periods and this grows easier when he can sit unaided (six to seven months). Crawling (nine to ten months) and walking unaided (twelve to fifteen months) mark the first stages on the path to independence.

The appropriate age to expect children to abide by rules and routine is debatable but certainly during the first twelve to eighteen months it is inappropriate. The parent should be working towards a regular pattern of sleeping and eating, for example, but need not get upset when the baby does not stick to it. Punishment, especially smacking or beating, is not only dangerous but also pointless. Smacking a crying baby will usually make the crying worse, unless he freezes in terror. It will not resolve the reason for the crying. Smacking a crawling baby for exploring where he should not go is equally futile: better to remove the child and distract him with something harmless.

Most parents probably feel like smacking their small babies, especially at times of stress. The Newsons' study of 700 Nottingham children (Newson and Newson 1963) found that most knew this to be inappropriate, but many think it safe to 'give him a good shaking up'. Paradoxically this is far more dangerous than smacking (see Chapter 5). These angry feelings say more about the parent than the needs of the child. Smacking a child under one year should be avoided.

Problems associated with crying, feeding, sleeping and spoiling are discussed in a later chapter, but at this point it is sufficient to conclude that until the first birthday or thereabouts the baby will only cry when there is something wrong (i.e. his basic needs are not being met) and the best way to stop the crying is to satisfy that need. As a result of regular and predictable satisfaction of basic needs the baby not only grows physically but, just as important, he also develops a sense of inner security and trust which is the necessary foundation for subsequent personality development. Many parents who abuse their children have never developed this basic trust; a sense of insecurity and mistrust learnt in the first year of life is seldom lost.

One to five

This is a period of rapid physical and intellectual development, marked by increasing assertion of independence. He will constantly challenge the parent's view of the world; 'Why?' is perhaps his most common word. It is a time of open conflict between parent and child, but also a time when there is a need for reassurance, security and order. It is also an exciting time for both, with the child's intense interest in the world around him, rapid learning and infectious enthusiasm.

In terms of physical development, most children will be able to run and jump around the age of two and will increasingly set out to explore. They will be able to use a potty by the age of two but are unlikely to be dry at night before 2½–3 years, or even later.

Potty training may be a major source of conflict at this time. There is very little anybody can do to speed up bowel and bladder control, but there is a lot that can be done to delay it. Most toilet training problems are caused by parents who have unrealistic expectations of their children and try to force the pace. The child will always retain ultimate control over use of the potty, so parents are well advised to avoid a confrontation they are bound to lose.

At one year most children mimic voice intonation but have only two recognisable words, 'Mama' and 'Dada'. By the age of two they may have a vocabulary of fifty or more words, and it will continue increasing rapidly. Language acquisition allows development of fantasy and this is seen increasingly in play, at first alone, then alongside other children. By about three the child may be beginning to play with other children in a coherent way, perhaps entering a shared fantasy.

Most toddlers seem self-centred, negative and stubborn for much of the time. Between eighteen months and three years they will probably have more than one temper tantrum a week either because they are incapable of doing something or because the parent prevents it. Parents have a duty to protect their children from danger and help them learn the limits of acceptable behaviour. There is no point in prolonging arguments at this age, the younger child has too little control over his feelings to learn from experience, but it is equally inappropriate to accept his every demand. Conflict and tantrums are therefore inevitable, but it is all too easy to become preoccupied with arguments and prohibitions to the exclusion of shared enjoyable experiences, thus making life miserable for all. Small children are often frightened by the force of their own rage and need reassurance, when it is over, that their anger has not destroyed their parents' love for them.

Food is a common source of conflict. Many parents expect their toddler to have a 'proper mixed diet' and are infuriated by a reluctance or refusal to eat. Many parents feel rejection of food is tantamount to rejection of parental love. Yet if the child is gaining weight and is normal for his age there is no need to worry. Table manners become more important around four or five, but it is foolish to try to introduce knives and forks and sitting still before the age of three. Choice of food, clothes and playthings is a pointless battlefield, yet many parents fear that allowing the child to assert his own wishes means that the parent has lost control or 'given in' and the child has 'won' or is boss. This is unjustified. Parents need to decide what is really important, for example playing with dangerous objects or in dangerous places, and take a firm and consistent stand, whilst avoiding conflict over inessentials. Fighting on all fronts at once is not only exhausting but also counter-productive.

Most children under five live most of the time in the care of their mother, but a few are left with day nurseries or childminders, occasionally because the parent feels unable to cope with full-time care, but more frequently because of the need or wish to go out to work. From the age of three a greater number attend playgroups or nursery school. These facilities undoubtedly provide parents with respite from the constant demands of the young child and, at best, the child can benefit from companionship and developmental stimulation. Who cares for the young child seems not to be particularly important provided that there is a consistent parent-figure at home, arrangements are routine and predictable and the child receives sufficient individual attention during the day (see Chapter 17).

Smacking reaches its peak during these years; at the age of four, 75 per cent of the 700 children in the Nottingham study (Newson and Newson 1968) were smacked at least once a week, and 3 per cent were hit or actively threatened with an implement (stick, slipper, belt). Most parents disliked doing this and were upset by it. It is easy to see how smacking arises. The toddler is stubborn and demanding, with limited language skills and not open to reason. He is a constant challenge to parents and can be infuriating. No wonder that tolerance is sometimes pushed to the limit. Most parents use smacking to underline or emphasise a verbal prohibition, rather than force a child into submission by fear: 'It is a punctuation in the relationship, not an aversive stimulus' (Newson and Newson 1968). Of course, most parents keep the use of physical punishment under control, but many who injure their young children justify this by the need for discipline. They often sound like law-abiding citizens setting 'high moral standards' for their children and exercising firm control, or at least trying to. Our culture places considerable emphasis on the infliction of physical pain on children as a form of learning and control, far more than other European societies, but there is no evidence that it is successful in changing attitudes and behaviour. Indeed the opposite seems as likely.

It seems unlikely that the occasional smack with the hand on the leg or buttocks causes permanent harm to the child's development provided that it is within a loving parental relationship, but it is equally unclear whether it serves a positive purpose. Indiscriminate hitting out at a child in anger, especially to the head, has unpredictable physical and emotional consequences and could be viewed as child abuse. Repeated confrontations, shouting and smacking will either cow the child with fear or, more likely at this age, make him immune to it all; punishment becomes routine and so loses its significance.

Conflict is wearing, so many parents find these years trying and tiring. However, for the child, they are a time of uninhibited enthusiasm as well as uncontrollable anger. If parents can focus on these good times it is easier to survive the tantrums, because the child's basic need for love, affection and security remain unchanged. Despite all that happens he needs to know that he is still loved and wanted and if parents can give this feeling they will usually be rewarded with unconditional love – some of the time!

Five to eleven

Most injured children reported as suffering child abuse are under five and the younger the child the more likely is the injury to be serious. In the light of this we have decided not to discuss at such length the developmental stages and problems of children over five. However there is a trend to reporting more injuries to children in the older age groups, and thus they cannot be ignored. The age divisions chosen are of course arbitrary, related to usual school changes rather than individual child development; however they provide a basis for comparison. It must always be remembered that children develop at different paces. We must also be aware that this discussion relates to twentieth century Western society. Only 150 years ago, children of this age were expected to be out at work, as is still the case in many parts of the world.

The major difference between the toddler and the school age child is that perhaps for the first time he moves into a social world independent of his parents. As he grows older he will be allowed to leave the home territory on his own for the first time, a significant watershed for parent and child. At school he is subject to the influence of teachers and other children and he brings home new ideas and attitudes. Parents have to adjust to this and rigid insistence on the predominance of their influence above all else will lead to problems for child and parents. Entry into the social world also gives access to new contacts and friends; this is a period of groups, gangs and 'secret societies'. Children compare their parents and home with those of others and may draw unfavourable comparisons: 'Sarah's mum lets her watch "Dr Who", so why can't I?'

The child continues to develop physical, intellectual and relationship skills. His language grows in sophistication and breadth of vocabulary. The use of fantasy and imagination becomes more pronounced in play, writing and art. This enables him to imagine himself in the place of others and so be more aware of how others see him and how he affects them. This can be a worrying experience and will generate anxiety. However it is important not to over-rate his cognitive skills and ability to reason. Developed concepts of right and wrong do not usually emerge until later in this period.

Most parents expect their children to be dry and clean by the age of five, but a significant proportion of children still wet the bed for no obvious physical or emotional reason (10 per cent at five years and 5 per cent at ten). Parents should also expect occasional bowel accidents during the early part of this period, and 'messy eating'. As indicated in the previous section, an overly repressive or punitive parental response to these problems is more likely to lead to things getting worse rather than better.

Minor crises and arguments from time to time are inevitable in relationships between parents and children at this age; the Newsons comment that 'nagging appears to be normal on both sides'. Smacking also continues at a high rate; according to the Nottingham study (Newson and Newson 1976) 8 per cent of seven year olds are smacked once a day or more, a further 33 per cent at least once a week and 28 per cent at least monthly. Around one-third of children at seven are smacked less than once a month or not at all. This compares with 75 per cent of four year olds who were smacked at least once a week. It would therefore appear that the rate of smacking falls as the child grows older, although for some children the frequency will increase. Interestingly, the majority of mothers said they felt upset and guilty about smacking their child, even if they thought it the right thing to do. Just under a half approved of smacking in principle, whilst around a quarter saw it as unfortunate but necessary.

Whilst the rate of smacking seems to decline with age, the rate of beating with an implement (stick, cane, shoe, belt) seems to go up. 22 per cent of seven year olds had received a beating at some time, whilst a further 53 per cent had been threatened with, but not actually received, such punishment, indicating that three-quarters of Nottingham children (91 per cent of boys) live with the reality of corporal punishment in the home. The Newsons' data was collected some years ago and it is possible that parental attitudes have changed, but there seems little reason to doubt that use or active threat of corporal punishment with an implement in the home is as normal as not. The Newsons suggest that most parents wish to preserve the 'myth of invincibility', preferably by exercise of wisdom, experience and charisma, but if necessary by use of force.

Having acknowledged the times of stress, most parents enjoy their children at this age. They are absorbed in the pleasure of formal and informal learning. The tantrums of the toddler phase are past and the conflicts of adolescence are still to come. Relationships between parents and child are thus relatively uncluttered and pleasurable to both.

Adolescence

Our society tends to see adolescence as a time of major family conflict as the adolescent struggles to establish an independent adult identity. The period of conflict is probably prolonged by the lengthy, enforced dependency of the adolescent on his parents required by school attendance until sixteen, and is usually a source of ambivalence for all concerned. The adolescent grows more self-conscious and anxious about how others see him, particularly as awareness of the opposite sex develops. In mid-adolescence there is a tendency to move from groups of friends to pairs of the same or opposite sex.

This is also a period of major physical changes which are very obvious to everybody and which can be tiring for the adolescent. There is a need to come to terms with newly acquired sexual maturity in a social world which exerts considerable sexual pressures. The development of sexuality also affects the parents and their attitude to and feelings about their children. Feelings of sexual attraction towards their children are probably more common than is generally admitted, which is to say that this is normal rather than a problem.

Adolescence is also a time of considerable pressure to achieve. Those in school face public examinations which may determine their whole future. There are pressures to get a job and contribute to the family finances, and considerable problems for those who are unable or choose not to find work.

Parental attitudes to punishment change at this time, probably because the children are too big for the parent to threaten, but parents are also more aware, consciously or not, of the sexual dimension of hitting. They have to rely more on verbal punishments and persuasion, and hope that sufficient mutual respect has been established for their children to adhere to whatever rules are laid down, for example about coming home at night. The Nottingham study (Newson and Newson 1980) revealed that overall 12 per cent of children (19 per cent of boys) are beaten and a further 28 per cent

(30 per cent boys) threatened with a beating with an instrument at age eleven. However this does not seem to prevent further mischief or bad behaviour. The Newsons conclude,

> the old fashioned, simplistic adage 'spare the rod and spoil the child' is clearly not supported by this kind of statistical evidence in the context of contemporary child-rearing beliefs and practices. We are not justified in telling parents that if they punish their children more in the physical sense, this will necessarily prevent them from getting into trouble.

Most families experience varying degrees of turmoil during adolescence. It has been suggested that parents can do little except to hold on and weather the storm, in the hope that the relationship established in the early years will stand the test of time. It is perhaps not surprising that step-parents and other substitute caregivers, including foster parents and residential staff, who did not have the benefit of a relationship with the pre-adolescent child, have problems at this time.

Corporal punishment

The discussion so far has included passing references to different forms of punishment, but in a book on child abuse it is important to consider in more detail the use of pain and injury as forms of control and punishment. In a wide-ranging American study (see Chapter 2), David Gil concluded that 'culturally determined attitudes towards the use of physical force in child-rearing seem to constitute the common core of all physical abuse of children in American society', and he went on to recommend that a major part of any child abuse prevention programme should be a campaign to change such attitudes, including the development of appropriate sanctions against those who beat children. He also advocated the immediate banning of all corporal punishment in public institutions, arguing that 'so long as we condone corporal punishment of children, we must admit that we are also willing to place some children in danger of being hurt badly'.

Discussion of this issue is bedevilled by inadequate research, deep feeling and ingrained prejudice. Since it seems that most parents at some time beat or threaten their children with an implement, it is hardly surprising that any suggestion that this is harmful will generate a strong reaction. It is nevertheless very noticeable that parents who seriously injure their children, at whatever age and however seriously, more often than not relate the event to a concept of punishment, even when they accept that they went too far. There is no doubt that our society, more than most other European societies and other cultures, places a high premium on the infliction of pain as necessary or inevitable in the rearing of children; the United Kingdom and Eire are the only European States still to allow beatings in schools and State residential establishments for children. It seems probable that this creates a context in which child abuse is more likely.

Like Gil, we would argue that the use of corporal punishment in public institutions for children should be made illegal and would hope that a Member of Parliament would have sufficient courage to take up this issue in a Private Member's Bill. We also hope that, either by change in the law or decisions of the courts, the use of implements to hit children in the home will be made illegal.

Preparation for parenthood

Experience of living forms the basis of preparation for parenthood for most people, but there has been much emphasis in recent years on the need to supplement this by formal classes in schools and elsewhere, in part as a contribution to the prevention of child abuse. We see value in these classes as part of a general education about living and relationships, but are sceptical about the likely impact on the incidence of child abuse. There is evidence that the best time to stage such classes is during pregnancy, when there is an obvious relevance of the material and a heightened parental anxiety created by the impending birth. Many midwives and health visitors run such courses, although it would seem that many dwell exclusively on the birth experience itself and the immediate handling of the newborn, with less consideration of the needs and problems of older children.

To place faith in education for parenthood as the major preventive strategy for child abuse is to assume that the approach of parents to their role is conscious and open to cognitive change. It is our view that this may apply to some, but those parents who most seriously abuse their children have deep personality and relationship problems which cannot be resolved by participation in a class, learning what was being done wrong and going away and changing it. Preparation for parenthood classes in schools and pre-natal settings are helpful and worth promoting, but it should not be assumed that they will have a major impact on the incidence of ill-treatment of children.

Developmental summary – eight ages of man

One approach to the understanding of human development, which many have found illuminating and therapeutically useful, is that described by Erikson, a major figure in the 'ego-psychology' school. He argues that the human personality develops in common stages, each related to the others and all depending on progression through a systematic sequence. Each aspect exists in some form throughout life, but is particularly significant at a different time: 'each comes to its ascendance, meets its crisis, and finds its lasting solution . . . towards the end of the stages mentioned'. Erikson has conceptualised the framework as a sequence of opposites:

Year 1	Basic trust	v	Basic mistrust
1–3	Autonomy	v	Shame and doubt
3–5	Initiative	v	Guilt
5–11	Industry	v	Inferiority
Adolescence	Identity	v	Role confusion
Young adult	Intimacy	v	Isolation
Middle age	Generativity	v	Stagnation
Old age	Ego integrity	v	Despair

Erikson stresses that this framework does not represent an 'achievement scale', which would imply that basic trust is a goal to be attained, vanquishing all sense of basic mistrust forever. He argues that the positive and negative dimensions remain with the personality throughout, ebbing and flowing depending on circumstances.

The concept of establishing basic trust in babyhood has been discussed above. This grows out of the regular meeting of needs, and secure, caring relationships; 'the amount of trust derived from the earliest experience does not seem to depend on absolute quantities of food or demonstrations of love but rather on the quality of the maternal [and other] relationship[s]'.

In the next stage the child is learning conscious control of muscles and movement and is also more aware of his separateness. He needs to be aware of limits to acceptable behaviour, but yet allowed to explore his environment and his place within it. 'Denied the gradual and well-guided experience of the autonomy of free choice, or weakened by an initial loss of trust, the sensitive child may . . . over-manipulate himself, he will develop a precocious conscience.' As he becomes aware of the controlling power of his parents, he also needs to learn the pleasure of discovery and autonomy. Constant checking, punishing and controlling may create an abiding sense of shame and self-doubt and thus stunt his enjoyment of life, growth and development. Other children react by becoming oblivious to the feelings of others, seeing as evil only those who frustrate their desires.

At the next stage the child has mastered basic physical/muscular processes (sitting, walking, running) and is developing language skills and fantasy. He begins to imagine what it is like to be adult and watches to see which adult roles are worth copying. He becomes more defensive of himself and 'his', and jealous of others. Rivalry and anger are common as the child seeks to assert himself and establish a place in his society. In many of his endeavours he is doomed to inevitable failure, but how his parents and others react to his efforts will be important in determining whether he emerges disabled by a sense of guilt and failure or encouraged and hopeful, with a sense of confidence in his own initiative.

In the fourth stage the child is more adept at manipulating things and exploring the world in which he lives. He needs support and encouragement, but constant failure and criticism will result in a sense of inferiority, which may become a hallmark of his future personality. In the adolescent phase the young person has to rediscover himself and in some respects return to the emotional turmoil of early childhood in his quest for identity.

It is our experience that many of the parents who most seriously abuse their children have progressed along the negative side of this dichotomy. They experienced coldness, rejection, inconsistency and even cruelty from their parents and have learnt that any sense of trust is misplaced. Their childhood dependency on their parents was a source of fear and resentment and this is carried into their adult relationships, including that with the therapist. Erikson argues that 'only as a dependant does man develop conscience, that dependence on himself which makes him, in turn, dependable'. This book could be said to describe the process of helping abused children to discover 'dependable' parents.

2

Research

Introduction

The last two decades (1960–80) have seen a vast proliferation of research and other literature on child abuse. An international journal has been established (*Child Abuse and Neglect*) and many hundreds of new papers are published annually in the various professional and academic journals around the world. Most practitioners are too busy to keep pace with this outpouring, let alone to evaluate what it has to offer.

Yet despite all that has been written, our state of knowledge is not good. Many of the papers are very limited in scope, both of subject and case numbers; few seem to have principles of general application or to say anything new. There is a paucity of research into effective treatment and intervention methods and much of what exists is not easily transferable into routine agency settings.

This chapter will not attempt an exhaustive literature review; this can be found elsewhere. It does attempt to highlight some significant research findings which will be relevant to subsequent chapters.

The various studies have been divided into five groups:

defining the problem;

epidemiological studies (describing the extent of the problem and socio-demographic characteristics);

typological studies (dividing abusing families into types according to common characteristics);

therapeutic studies (describing work with families);

management studies (discussing the law, service delivery systems and inter-agency co-ordination).

Defining the problem

There is little disagreement about the identification of acts of gross child abuse – such as murder, sadistic ill-treatment, incest or gross neglect – but the boundary between inadequate parenting and minor forms of abuse is more difficult to determine. Studies of cohorts of children (Crellin, Newson, Pringle) give a baseline against which to attempt to judge the abnormal and unacceptable.

The first major survey of public attitudes to child abuse was conducted in the USA by Gil during 1965 and reported in 1970 and 1973. 1520 respondents, forming a national, balanced sample, were interviewed about knowledge of child abuse and related services, and their attitudes to the problem. 80 per cent knew something about child abuse, but a significant minority had no knowledge of services available to help those with such problems. 15.9 per cent reported having come near to abusing their own child, whilst 0.4 per cent admitted having once injured a child in their care, both probably under-reporting. 66.4 per cent favoured supervision and treatment for parents in the community, whilst 27.1 per cent thought parents should be jailed or otherwise punished.

In a later major survey of professional and public attitudes to child abuse in the USA, Giovannoni and Becerra (1979) found considerable agreement between police, social workers, doctors and lawyers on the definition and ranking of different forms of abuse: sexual abuse, physical injury, inadequate supervision/leaving alone, failure-to-provide, encouraging delinquency, emotional mistreatment, educational neglect, moral danger because of parental sexual mores, and parental drug/alcohol abuse. However other differences in attitude were evident – the strongest and most persistent being between the doctors and lawyers, and the social workers and police who are responsible for primary screening into the protective system and tend to see each form of abuse as more serious.

An important element in material by administrators and professionals attempting a working definition to guide practice is awareness of resource and service limitations. Early Department of Health and Social Security circulars focused on non-accidental injury and gross neglect, but have since expanded to embrace other forms of serious abuse, although not sexual abuse (DHSS, 1980). The recommendations for register criteria made by the British Association of Social Workers and British Paediatric Association Joint Working Party were also limited to serious forms of abuse, because it was known that the various agencies could not cope with a system of formal co-ordination which embraced many children with minor forms of neglect or emotional abuse (BASW, 1978).

Some argue that child abuse should embrace any maltreatment of children which prevents their attaining their full potential, be it in the home, school or world at large. By this definition, the vast majority of children in the world suffer child abuse, but it does not provide an operational basis for planning services for abused children.

Epidemiological studies

The two major studies of the incidence and characteristics of child abuse are by Gil (USA, 1973) and the NSPCC (UK, Rose 1976; Creighton, 1977 and 1980). Gil concluded that child abuse was not 'a major cause of mortality or morbidity in the USA'. Kempe *et al* (1978) argued that this is a serious underestimate since it was based only on reported incidents, taken during the earliest years of the child reporting laws (1965–9). They cite a ten-fold increase in reported incidents in California between 1968–72 and a leap from only ten cases to 30,000 in Florida in the same period.

The NSPCC study is based on returns from registers maintained by NSPCC Special Units, in most cases on behalf of all agencies in their area, covering 13 per cent of the under-fifteen population in 1976. The 1976 extrapolation of national incidence was 5147 children abused, including around 100 fatalities and 759 serious injuries, a reduction on the returns for both 1975 and 1974. This gave an annual rate of non-accidental injury to children of around 0.5 per 1000 under fifteen, compared with Kempe's report (1978) of the incidence of reported abuse of all types in the USA of 0.3 per 1000 total population.

The three NSPCC studies show a progressive decline in the number of serious injuries and deaths, but an increase in the number of moderate injuries reported. In 1976 81.5 per cent suffered soft tissue injuries only (Creighton, 1980), whilst 4 per cent suffered head injuries, including fractures, and brain and eye damage. The proportion of children under four registered with head injuries has declined from 1974 – 15 per cent, 1975 – 9.7 per cent and 1976 – 7 per cent; the absolute numbers also fell. This finding has been observed elsewhere. Kempe (1978) states 'not only are more cases being reported – they are of a milder nature, suggesting that families are being helped sooner. In Denver the number of hospitalised abused children who die from their injuries has dropped from twenty a year (1960–75) to less than one a year.'

There will be continuing debate over the true incidence, given the problems of collecting statistics and differing definitions of abuse.

Epidemiological studies have also identified a number of characteristics which occur more frequently in families where child abuse has occurred than would be expected by chance. The children as a group have been found to share the following features:

Younger age distribution than the national norm;
more likely to be premature/low birth weight;

boys more at risk than girls, except in adolescence when
  girls are more at risk;
the most serious injuries tend to be inflicted on the youngest children;
more injuries to older children being reported;
more likely to be illegitimate;
Not more likely to be ill or handicapped at birth.

None of these associations should be interpreted as indicating a causal relationship, for example low birth weight,
illegitimacy and young parents are all statistically related,
regardless of child abuse. However, it seems reasonable to
hypothesise that small babies are most at risk of serious
injury because of their physical vulnerability, and high dependence on and proximity to the parent.

Studies of families where abuse has occurred reveal the
following commonly observed features:

parents younger than average;
high mobility/frequent change of home;
larger than average family size;
atypical family structures (i.e. higher than average proportion of step-parents and other non-biological parents);
frequent marital discord (sometimes with violence);
low socio-economic status;
high unemployment rate;
high rate of general criminality.

These studies have distinguished abusing parents from the
total population, but the features are not significantly different from other groups of parents having problems with children (e.g. attenders at paediatric or child guidance clinics),
nor from other groups with personality or social problems
(e.g. overdoses, petty crime). The features are therefore
helpful in defining the population most at risk, but no help in
predicting which children will be abused, nor in establishing
the cause of child abuse; many families will share the same
characteristics but with little likelihood of major problems.
Similar child care difficulties are probably also experienced

by more advantaged members of society, but are either hidden behind a semblance of competence and respectability or solved before crises develop, using knowledge or resources not readily available to the less well-off, such as better use of the health services, sending the child to boarding school or employing a nanny or au pair.

There is a danger that this typical profile of a young, socially deprived and chaotic abusing parent becomes the dominant stereotype, with less common types being missed. It can also lead to an inappropriate, unitary mode of treatment/intervention. Qualitative studies of parental and family functioning are also necessary.

Typological studies

These studies attempt to categorise abusing families by such criteria as personality, psychopathology, psychosocial functioning or child's history, usually with a view to providing a basis for assessing risk and likely prognosis of intervention. The nature of the study means that the results are usually derived from comparatively small samples and open to the theoretical bias of the researcher.

Common features which have emerged from such studies include:

high incidence of personality disorders;
maternal/paternal deprivation in parental histories;
rigid parental attitudes to discipline;
distorted perception of the child;
ignorance of normal childhood behaviour and development;
impulsive parental behaviour/low tolerance of stress;
adverse social circumstances;
poor health;
low social class.

Although these studies enhance understanding of the parent, many of the features are not confined to abusing parents. Not all parents with personality disorders injure their children and maternal deprivation does not determine a propensity to lose control. Many normal mothers report occasional irrational and quasi-delusional ideas about their children that some writers have described as abnormal or even 'psychotic', for example the phenomenon of 'role reversal' described by Morris and Gould is not unique to abusing parents. So again, such studies can highlight areas of risk or significant features to watch for but cannot predict the likelihood of child abuse with any certainty.

The main British papers attempting to classify child abuse by method, motive and parental pathology have drawn on groups of parents who have killed a child (e.g. Scott, 1973). Inevitably they include a disproportionate number of male psychopaths and more seriously disturbed individuals, and are thus of little general applicability, except in alerting workers to the typical profile of a person who has killed a child, although Smith (1973; 1975) found a high incidence of serious personality disorder in the parents of a group of abused children seen at a British hospital. Scott defined the following common characteristics of the child murderer in the home:

male;
not the natural father;
recent imprisonment and criminal record usually including violence;
unemployed;
caring for a young child while mother is out at work;
previous convictions for dishonesty and violence.

Some attempts have been made by American authors (Boisvert; Zalba) to evolve classifications based on parental psychopathology and types of treatment. British readers need to be aware of the seductive similarity of the language which hides significant differences in the use of such terms as 'schizophrenic', 'psychotic' and 'sociopath'. The psychodynamic concepts used to differentiate the groups are also difficult to apply in practice.

Therapeutic studies

By their very nature, therapeutic studies describe the work of one person or team and tend to be drawn from specialist settings which makes direct comparison with more routine fieldwork settings very difficult. Two useful English studies, both by NSPCC specialist teams, describe and reflect on their work with abusing families, one in London from 1968–74 (Baher, 1976) and the other (involving one of the present authors) in Manchester from 1974–7 (Pickett, 1977). The London study (*At Risk*) is probably the most thorough analysis of social work and related issues in the British child abuse field. The publications of the Denver-based National Center for the Prevention and Treatment of Child Abuse and Neglect (C H Kempe, *et al.*) are also essential reading, although at times the American context inhibits direct comparison with British settings.

Therapeutic studies all demonstrate the long-term nature of therapy for many families, although some have claimed significant success for a shorter, behaviour modification approach (Reavley; Jeffrey). Intervention has to be multifaceted, involving:

 (i)   relationship therapy with parents, attempting to promote their emotional development;
 (ii) basic education about childcare skills, child development and sometimes homecraft;
 (iii) efforts to improve the family's social circumstances;
 (iv) direct work with the child;
 (v)   active communication with other agencies.

There is an obvious need for comparative studies of different forms of treatment/intervention, especially of the value of behaviour modification, group work and family therapy as elements in the process. A major consideration should be the relationship between therapeutic effectiveness and staff turnover.

Most therapeutic approaches are based on the relationship between family and worker, yet one study of 200 cases in

Nottinghamshire (Hill, 1980) found that over 75 per cent of families had at least one change of worker in the year following the incident because of departmental policy, staff turnover or change of address. A recent poll of clients found frequent changes of social worker to be the most significant area of dissatisfaction. If the workers primarily responsible for the 'therapy' are not involved long enough to form a viable 'therapeutic relationship' it seems to make a nonsense of attempting that approach (Kitchen, 1981).

Management studies

There is a considerable literature on the organisation of service delivery, much of it stressing the need for interagency, multidisciplinary co-ordination, but few studies of service organisation in practice. Two of the present authors were involved in a British study, completed during 1977, which found that there were very significant differences between different local authority areas in the organisation of their register systems and other aspects of policy (BASW, 1978; Jones, 1979a). The authors have also published studies of multidisciplinary co-ordination of services in Manchester and Nottingham (Pickett, 1976; 1979; Jones 1979a; 1979b). A study of the social work management of 200 cases in Nottinghamshire is in process (Hill, 1980).

The major US survey of service delivery systems and legal issues is by Sussman and Cohen, and presents research drawn on nationwide data as well as in-depth studies of four States. It contains perhaps the most thorough discussion of civil liberty issues associated with child abuse, including registers. A draft reporting law is suggested. The major conclusions are that:

(i)   too broad a definition of child abuse results in a swamping of the register system, making the pattern of coordination impossible;

(ii) follow-up services are unable to cope with the number of new cases reported;

(iii)   co-operation is better in small rural areas than larger conurbations;
(iv)   mandatory reporting to police reduces the rate of case identification;
(v)   registers were not being used as originally envisaged;
(vi)   there should be no further broadening of the scope of the system without money to increase resources.

There are also many studies of teamwork and multidisciplinary co-ordination in other parts of the health and social services, but surprisingly little cross-fertilisation of ideas (see Chapter 4).

A few studies have been published discussing the personal consequences of the stress of child abuse work: the term 'Burn Out' has been coined to describe the common reaction of workers. It seems clear that child abuse work does involve considerable personal stress, and that management, supervisors and workers themselves need to be aware of the risks and structure work patterns to minimise them. The rapid turnover of staff in all agencies, especially in inner-city areas, is said to be evidence of this problem. Awareness of this must be central to management style in any agency working with abusing families.

Future research needs

Child abuse has attracted considerable interest and substantial research funds over the last decade and some projects are only now coming to fruition. Nevertheless the following subjects seem ripe for further study:

the effectiveness of therapeutic models;
the impact of day nurseries/family centres on children and parents;
decision making (theory and practice);
consequences of legal intervention following child abuse;
definition, characteristics and incidence of neglect, emotional and sexual abuse;
long-term consequences of fostering and adoption.

Summary

There is no agreed definition of child abuse nor fully accurate ideas of its incidence. Epidemiological studies demonstrate that there are no unique demographic characteristics of abusing families; in almost every respect, non-abusing parents of similar social class share the same characteristics. Likewise, typological studies have identified certain personality traits which are frequently observed in abusing parents, but these too are commonly found in groups of non-abusing parents. Therapeutic studies are usually based on a small number of cases in specialist settings, making comparison difficult with routine agency services. They are nevertheless helpful in suggesting valuable approaches to work with families. None of the studies have identified causal or predictive factors of reliable significance.

The encouraging fact to emerge from these studies is the apparent decline in the incidence of serious injury to children, and also in the rate and seriousness of re-injury. There seems little doubt that concentration on child abuse in recent years has resulted in these measurable benefits. However, understanding has not developed to the point where workers can confidently expect their intervention to result in qualitative improvement in parenting ability. Such development does occur in individual cases, but predictive and prognostic skills and criteria are inadequate to generalise. This does not mean that research has nothing to offer the busy practitioner, but there is a real danger of creating an illusion of knowledge that does not exist.

3

Historical Perspective

Six major trends can be seen in recent social policy developments associated with child abuse.

1 Increasing recognition by public and professionals of the extent of inflicted injury involving children in the home, even when outwardly the standard of physical care appears good.

2 Increasing awareness in all professions of the need to provide appropriate intervention to protect abused children, in contrast to earlier reluctance to acknowledge the existence of child abuse.

3 Increased acceptance of the need for communication between agencies and professions and an awareness that past failures in communication in certain cases meant that the full extent of risk was never appreciated and the child was left unprotected.

4 Broadening of the definition of child abuse to include physical injury, neglect, emotional and sexual abuse of those up to sixteen years (or older).

5 Concern about prevention of child abuse and the ethics of

screening large populations, especially when research has not validated predictive criteria.

6 Legal and social trends recognising children as independent of their parents with their own rights as citizens.

This chapter reviews policy developments in the United Kingdom over the last century and the next discusses current policy on the organisation of services for abused children and their families.

Child cruelty

For many centuries it was considered necessary literally to beat good into children and punish them severely when they were naughty. Attitudes began to change in the twentieth century, some say associated with the reduction in the child mortality rate. In the mid-eighteenth century between 50–75 per cent of children died before reaching five years. By 1865 the infant mortality rate had fallen to 15.4 per cent and is now around 2 per cent, thanks to improved public health and sanitation, control of infectious diseases, improved diet and health care, and advances in obstetric and paediatric knowledge and practice. The late nineteenth century was a time of considerable social upheaval and numerous social 'crusades'. Lord Shaftesbury and others led campaigns to improve the working conditions of children, and Dickens and Kingsley wrote novels which aroused the national conscience. Voluntary bodies emerged, inspired by such figures as Dr Barnardo, to provide for the homeless, orphaned and destitute. Parliament took steps to provide universal, free education and as a consequence the length of the dependency of children on their parents grew longer, with some evidence of increasing family tensions as a result.

The scandal of Mary Ellen which occurred in 1874 was the first of a series of children whose tragic life and death led to public outcry and demands for action. She lived in a New York tenement with her adoptive parents, and neighbours were concerned that she was being ill-treated and neglected.

They contacted an organisation providing voluntary help to immigrants and a visit was made to the flat. She was found in a terrible state, neglected, beaten, and cut with scissors, but the parents refused to change their treatment of her and insisted that they could do as they wished. There were laws against ill-treatment of animals, but no similar laws to protect children, so it was decided to argue in court that Mary Ellen was a member of the animal kingdom for this purpose. The case was found proved and she was granted protection. The scandal resulted in the formation of the New York Society for the Prevention of Cruelty to Children which was the inspiration for the founding in Britain of the National Society for the Prevention of Cruelty to Children which received its Royal Charter in 1895. Nevertheless, it was still possible in 1892 for a defence barrister in England to argue, albeit unsuccessfully, that a Mrs Montague should not be convicted of the killing of her child who had suffocated when locked in a cupboard as a punishment, because parents had absolute rights over their children.

The apparent reluctance or unwillingness of professionals to accept the existence of violence to children can be seen in papers published by two London doctors – Athol Johnson and West – in the 1880s, describing an unusual pattern of multiple fractures in small children. These were attributed to bone disease (rickets), although it seemed strange that the bones healed normally; an abnormality would have been expected if there was a disease process. A review of these cases today suggests that most, if not all, were cases of inflicted injury, but the doctors refused or were unable to detect the obvious. We suggest later that such denial is associated with disbelief and horror at the thought of parental violence and perhaps suppressed personal fears of violent feelings to dependants.

There were obvious cases of cruelty nevertheless, and after campaigns by the NSPCC and others, Parliament recognised public concern by passing the Prevention of Cruelty Act, 1889 which, among other provisions, gave powers to magistrates to issue a warrant to permit the entering of a home if there was suspicion of ill-treatment, to the police to arrest those suspected of ill-treatment, and to courts to remove such children from their parents. The Children Act, 1908 codified, consolidated and extended previous legislation and for the first time established juvenile courts. The Children and Young Persons Act, 1932 raised the age limit for protection proceedings to seventeen years and introduced other provisions. These two Acts were consolidated in the Children and Young Persons Act, 1933, and extended in 1938 by the introduction of statutory supervision in the family home. The Infanticide Act, 1938 acknowledged that some mothers injure and occasionally kill newborn babies whilst suffering from a mental illness associated with childbirth. This saved such women from the gallows.

The next child whose death led to important changes in outlook and policy was Dennis O'Neill. He was a war evacuee and had been placed with foster parents who were later convicted of his murder. His case highlighted concern about the vulnerability of children living in substitute homes which had grown with the wartime experience of evacuation. The Government established the Curtis Committee to investigate these matters and its report led directly to the Children Act, 1948 which established Children's Departments, staffed by social workers known as child care officers, whose task was to look after the interests of children in local authority care. A further Act of 1952 made it possible to bring care proceedings without first prosecuting the parent. An awareness of the value of preventing admission to care, emphasised in the report of the Ingleby Committee, led to the Children and Young Persons Act, 1963 which laid an explicit duty on local authorities to promote the welfare of children and undertake work to prevent them coming into care.

The ability to diagnose violence to children advanced significantly following developments in radiology during the 1940s. It became possible to date fractures according to the stage of healing and thus to say that a child had suffered repeated violence. It was also possible to detect healing fractures not previously brought for treatment. In 1946 a radiologist named Caffey published a seminal paper describing a pattern of multiple fractures and subdural haematoma in small children. The origin of the injuries was then unclear although there was speculation that they could be the result of injury rather than disease. The paper attracted little attention and no real public interest. In 1953 Silverman suggested that the injuries might result from parental carelessness, and in 1955 Woolley and Evans first suggested the possibility of deliberate acts of injury by parents or caregivers.

Despite awareness of the existence of violence to children at home, the general view was that numbers were small and that problems of neglect, delinquency and multi-problem families were more widespread and needing more attention. In 1950 the Government recognised the need for co-ordination of services to 'problem families' and recommended the establishment of local co-ordinating committees to undertake this (in one sense the precursors of area review committees and case conferences): 'Without co-ordination, information may not reach the service which could be of most assistance until valuable time has been lost.' Very few professional papers were published discussing work with families where there had been violence to children.

Battered babies

The 1961 interdisciplinary presentation to the American Academy of Pediatrics by Dr C Henry Kempe and colleagues marks a significant watershed. The papers were published in 1962 entitled *The Battered Child Syndrome* and their influence cannot be over-stressed. Kempe says he deliberately chose emotive terms to arouse public indignation and attract professional attention in order to get something done. Part of the message was that many cases were being incorrectly diagnosed as accidents, with sometimes fatal consequences. There is no doubt that he succeeded. In 1963 a paper was published in Britain by Griffiths and Moynihan, orthopaedic surgeons with clinical experience of 'battered children'. They were also convinced that many cases were being incorrectly diagnosed and therefore wrongly treated, and were probably the first to use the term 'battered baby'. In 1966 the British Paediatric Association, with Government support, published a memorandum giving guidance to members about the management of these cases. Active interest was confined to very few, however. Despite the statutory responsibilities of social workers for the protection of children, there were very few papers published in the British social work journals before 1973.

Following contact between Henry Kempe and Arthur Morton (NSPCC Director), including a sabbatical visit by Kempe to the NSPCC, it was decided that the Society should undertake action research to test his theories and treatment models in an English context. The NSPCC Battered Child Research Team was subsequently established in 1968. They published numerous papers between 1969 and 1972 aiming to disseminate knowledge and arouse professional interest. An early publication in 1969 suggested that 60 per cent of a sample of children injured at home had received previous injuries which had not been detected. The team (Baher, *et al.*) published their conclusions in 1976.

Kempe and his colleagues have always accepted that their early work was restricted to only a small part of the whole range of child abuse, in particular to small babies with immature parents. They accepted that the personalities of some of the parents were so damaged that it was impossible to give sufficient help to enable the child to remain safe in their care. Such children should be removed to long-term substitute caregivers, but about 80 per cent were said to be accessible to help. It was argued that many parents had such bad experiences of their own parents that they were suspicious of all in authority and required sensitive handling if therapy was to be successful. They were said to be unable to form a trusting, therapeutic relationship with a person who was also acting towards them in a controlling manner which they saw as punitive. Thus wherever possible the therapist should not become involved in court proceedings. We do not share this approach and return to discuss the issue in more detail later.

In one major respect the work of Kempe had a very damaging effect on the attitudes of doctors, social workers and police in this country. In the absence of an all-inclusive theory or categorisation of child abuse, one school seemed to take Kempe's approach to excess and argued that all parents who injured their children needed tender loving care and none should ever be brought before an adult or juvenile court. There was a failure to recognise that child abuse is one symptom of many diverse family problems requiring different responses. An opposing school, including mainly police officers, argued that in all cases an offence had been committed and thus the offender should be brought to court. Some police spokesmen claimed that doctors, social workers and others were hiding criminals from justice. This battle provoked considerable argument, especially between police and social workers during the early 1970s, but it now seems that better relationships are emerging.

The response to Kempe's work in the USA has been rapid and widespread. By 1975 all States had enacted legislation compelling the reporting of suspected child abuse by professionals. Most States also operate a central register of confirmed or suspected cases, but despite these laws and public and professional concern, it seems that many registers are hardly used and there has been little change in professional practice.

Some Americans have expressed concern that there has been considerable investment in systems to identify and investigate cases of suspected abuse but insufficient time and money given to subsequent work with families. Some argue that there has been an over-reaction, with professionals tending to 'play safe' by removing too many children into care with insufficient follow-up. It is argued that care is rarely a satisfactory alternative to family life, even given family problems. Substitute caregivers frequently change, either through foster-home breakdown or change of residential care staff, so children are more at risk of inconsistent parenting in care than at home. Similar arguments have been advanced in Britain, and we share the concern. It is comparatively straightforward to remove an abused child from his parents but more difficult to secure a stable future for him elsewhere. Children should not be removed from parental care unless there is no viable alternative: this is the assumption of British child care law.

Neglect of neglect

It would seem that this sudden rush of interest in 'battered babies', and later inflicted injuries to children of all ages, diverted attention from neglecting or 'problem' families. There have been numerous studies of the incidence and characteristics of injured children, but little is known of the incidence of child neglect or the circumstances of the parents. Yet neglect is a chronic condition, resulting in retarded physical and emotional development. Recent cases subject to public enquiry (Brown, Chapman, Page, Gates – see next chapter) clearly demonstrate the potentially lethal consequences of neglect and also show the overlap between neglect and physical injury. The DHSS 1980 circular recommends the inclusion of neglect within the same procedural system as injury and it is to be hoped that this and other studies will measure the incidence of neglect and the resource implications for intervention. There is also a need to clarify the similarities and differences in family characteristics and treatment methods and to explore effective intervention strategies.

The Multidisciplinary approach

The explosion of knowledge in all aspects of human studies has lead to professional specialisation and increasing complexity in the organisation of health and social services. It is now common for most medical or social problems to be managed by a number of individuals, each responsible for an aspect of the treatment or service. The Court Report into child health services (1974) argued that, just as doctors, nurses and therapists must work together as a team in the health service, so the health service must work in partnership with the education and social services . . . The planning and development of an integrated health service must therefore be done in such a way as to facilitate at every level the closest possible working relationships with these other services.

Concern about child abuse has not developed in a vacuum so it is not surprising to find that the early literature on battered children devotes considerable attention to the importance of using a multidisciplinary approach and the problems associated with this. A list of those who may become involved illustrates the complexity of the problem of co-ordination:

Social Services Department: social worker
senior social worker
area officer (usually
   conference chairman)
residential adviser
officer-in-charge
   (community home)
fostering officer
courts officer
family aide/homemaker
day nursery matron
Education Department: head teacher
class teacher
education welfare officer
educational psychologist
Clerk's Department: solicitor
Health Authority: health visitor
nursing officer (community)
midwife
family doctor
consultants – paediatric
   – casualty
   – psychiatry
   – neurology

	– surgeon
	– orthopaedic
	hospital nurses
	hospital junior doctors
	community medical officers
	school/clinic nurse
Police:	inspector
	sergeant
	constable
Housing Department:	housing visitor
	arrears enforcement officer
NSPCC:	special unit team member
	inspector
Voluntary Agencies:	social worker
	volunteer
	clergyman
DHSS:	special case officer

It is an added complication that many of those involved in a given case may never have met before. Rather than a 'team', they constitute a 'network' whose only link may be the child in question. It takes time for any group to work effectively, yet in a child abuse case urgency requires immediate co-operation and effective decisions in a crisis atmosphere. We discuss practical difficulties and ways of overcoming them in a later chapter.

NSPCC Special Units

The NSPCC Battered Child Research Department established in 1968 had a considerable impact on professional awareness of child abuse, but the Society had to remain alert to further developments. During 1971 discussions began between the Society, Manchester Social Services Department and Manchester University Department of Child Health. The Professor of Paediatrics, then chairman of the Manchester child abuse policy committee, invited the submission of proposals,

> to provide a specialist service for helping the community services, both statutory and voluntary, deal adequately with families who

severely maltreat their children, as is seen in the clinical condition known as the battered child syndrome. The NSPCC Unit would be available for consultation and casework service where a child under the age of four was suspected of receiving injuries other than by accident.

The Unit opened in 1972 and soon after was given responsibility for the central register. The age range was later extended to sixteen.

The NSPCC has since opened eleven Special Units, most of which are modelled on the Manchester pattern, providing a mixture of direct casework to families, consultation on case management to other agencies, central administrative and co-ordinating services and teaching. Some work in conjunction with the NSPCC inspector in the area, who investigates allegations of ill-treatment and provides a supportive casework service, whilst others include these functions within their brief. Some local authorities have established their own internal services modelled on the NSPCC pattern.

Parents Anonymous

The last few years have seen a mushrooming of small, voluntary groups offering a telephone lifeline to parents who feel like injuring their children or who have other problems. Many run group sessions and social events for parents who make contact. They emphasise confidentiality and take anonymous calls and in this sense are similar to the Samaritans, who offer a confidential 'phone service to potential suicides.

Such groups are often based on a self-help philosophy and aim to involve parents who themselves have experienced difficulties with their children, in helping others to resolve their problems; the best help is felt to come from somebody who has experienced and solved the problem at first hand, rather than a paid professional. There is also a feeling that helping others with their problems is an effective way of working through your own. Some groups are hostile to the statutory services, seeing them as uncaring and bureaucratic, whilst others work closely with them.

The benefits of this approach from the parents' viewpoint is that the service is personal and non-threatening, with no sense of authority or State control. It is usually available outside office hours, as most groups offer an evening availability. The organisation is small and informal and therefore flexible. Such groups do face problems, however, not least the issue of confidentiality. Samaritans can argue that they talk with adults who are competent to make their own decisions about life and death so confidentiality and non-intervention can be guaranteed, but the argument is more complex with child abuse. The adult 'phoning Parents Anonymous may be harming a young baby or child; the focus is somebody other than the caller. Should the group keep silent about a serious threat to the life of a child if the parent insists on total confidentiality and refuses help? In most cases parents whose children are at grave risk when they 'phone are seeking help and can be easily persuaded to accept it from statutory services, but groups are well advised to form a policy on their response to this situation before opening for calls.

These groups are also limited by the usual constraints of voluntary bodies. They are often dependent on the enthusiasm of one person or a small group and so are vulnerable to changing circumstances and attitudes; they cannot guarantee a consistent service. They have very limited resources, if any, other than the time and commitment of volunteers, and do not have access to foster-homes and day nurseries, except through statutory services. They are also limited in what they can take on – only a small number of families compared with social services, for example. Finally they depend on client initiative in 'phoning or seeking help which is difficult for those without access to a 'phone, although the barrier may still be easier to overcome than an approach to a social services department. This effectively excludes the isolated and inarticulate parent who so often features in a child abuse case.

Existing Parents Anonymous groups have proved that there is a demand for a crisis 'phone service for parents and volunteers are coming forward to assist. There is also evidence that some parents are helped by involvement in a self-help group, although for others group work is too threatening. Many workers in statutory services advise parents to use Parents Anonymous when there are problems out of office hours. There is clearly plenty of room for statutory agencies and voluntary bodies to co-exist to their mutual benefit.

Summary

Neglect, ill-treatment and abuse of children has always been present in human society. It is only during the present century that general attitudes have changed and some children are now seen as being in need of protection from their parents. The first impetus in the UK came at the turn of the century with the founding of the NSPCC and passing of the Protection of Children Act, 1881. The scope of the law has since been progressively widened. The second impetus came in the 1960s with the work of Kempe: 'the battered child syndrome'. At the same time, increasing knowledge and professional specialisation in the health and social services have created communication problems in working with abusing families. One response to child abuse has been the founding of NSPCC Special Units and Parents Anonymous self-help groups.

4

Administrative Framework

Having put child abuse in its historical perspective, we turn now to consider the response of Government and statutory agencies. This discussion must start with consideration of the major enquiries into the deaths of certain children, and in particular that of Maria Colwell. We then outline the main points of the various circulars issued by the Department of Health and Social Security by way of guidance to local authorities and health authorities. After a brief discussion of child abuse registers we conclude by placing child abuse in the context of other work undertaken by statutory agencies.

Maria Colwell and the major enquiries

Maria Colwell was the third child whose tragic life and death resulted in national action and a change in policy. She was killed by her step-father in 1973, shortly after having been returned to the care of her mother from foster parents, with whom she had lived for five years, who were relatives of her natural father. She was aged eight years when she died, so emphasising that violence to children was not confined to 'battered babies'. Her death in Brighton attracted only local concern at first, but the decision by Sir Keith Joseph, then

Secretary of State for Health and Social Services, to set up a public enquiry into the events of her life and the circumstances of her death opened the case to unprecedented national interest. Her photograph was on the front page of popular newspapers and the social worker involved before her death was vilified in the press and physically assaulted in the street. There was considerable criticism of social workers in general and public feeling that emphasis on the blood tie between parent and child had contributed to Maria's death. She was not the first child to be killed by parents since the death of Dennis O'Neill around twenty years before, but her death proved significant; the time was ripe for 'scandal' and action.

We have already seen that there had been only a slow build-up of interest in child abuse, with a few papers in professional journals in the 1960s. There was some understanding of how to detect and even prevent such tragedies but it had not been disseminated. A small group of doctors, lawyers, social workers and others had recently come together to study the battered child syndrome and promote public and professional concern. They became known as the Tunbridge Wells Study Group and Sir Keith Joseph attended their first residential meeting only days before announcing the Colwell enquiry. The meeting was assisted by the Department of Health and Social Security which published and promoted its findings. For some time Sir Keith had been interested in services to multi-problem families, which he saw as a major drain on State resources; he was promoting the 'cycle of deprivation' theory, and child abuse seemed to support his thesis.

There had also been public concern for some time about the rights of foster parents and especially 'tug-of-love' cases involving the return to the natural parents of a child who had been a long time in foster care. The Houghton Committee published its official report on adoption in 1972 and this discussed the needs of children in long-term foster care. Dr David Owen MP was already promoting a Private Member's Bill at the time of the Colwell enquiry to give effect to many of Houghton's recommendations, so there was a ready parliamentary vehicle to pursue issues arising out of the case. The Bill became the Children Act, 1975 and was significantly influenced by the Colwell case.

The final ingredient creating the context for a scandal was the recent reorganisation of the social services of local authorities into a new social services department. This was an amalgam of the former children's departments (established in 1948), welfare departments (elderly and physically handicapped) and parts of the health department (services for the mentally ill and handicapped, day nurseries), and consumed on average 10 per cent of local authority expenditure. At the same time the duties of this new department had been vastly extended by the Health Services and Public Health Act, 1968, the Children and Young Persons Act, 1969 and the Chronic Sick and Disabled Persons Act, 1970. The health service reorganisation in 1972–4 had added further confusion. The extent of this upheaval in social work cannot be under-estimated and has been cited as a contributory factor in several child abuse tragedies. Many qualified and experienced social workers were promoted to managerial and supervisory roles, with many young, unqualified people being appointed as social workers in their place. There was considerable concern among doctors that mental health and welfare services were deteriorating and there has been public debate about this. Many were also concerned about the loss of specialist expertise in the demise of the former children's departments.

The Colwell enquiry report emphasised four main areas of concern:

1 Inexperience and lack of specialist knowledge of those professionally concerned with Maria's welfare, leading to errors of judgement.

2 'Maria fell through the welfare net . . . primarily because of communications failures', in particular between social services, education services, school medical services and NSPCC: 'It is inevitable that a considerable number of

agencies and persons will be involved in such cases. What is important is that their respective roles should be clearly defined and not overlap unnecessarily.'

3 'Social workers may reasonably expect that matters of concern about individual families or children will be passed on to them by other agencies whether or not they have already indicated their interest to them.' It was argued that social workers have a responsibility to seek out information about families of concern to them but others also have a responsibility not to withhold information about children at risk.

4 'Inaccuracies and deficiencies in the recording of visits and telephone messages played a part in the tragedy.' The report stressed 'the importance of recording the actual dates of visits', 'the importance of distinguishing between fact and impression', 'it is very important to make clear the source of information', and finally, 'when children are at physical risk, or in any other comparable "life and death" situation, the style and content of recording may well have to be more detailed and precise' than more routine work.

Since the Colwell enquiry there has been at least one major enquiry each year into a child death in the home (see Bibliography). Without exception, these have found evidence of failures in professional practice and in the co-ordination of services, whilst acknowledging that not all deaths can be avoided. Some of the reports have led to modifications to government guidance, but all have endorsed the system established in 1974 following the Colwell report (see below). These enquiries are inevitably expensive (Paul Brown cost £500,000 in direct costs alone, excluding individual legal representation), yet most of their recommendations remain unimplemented. In part this is the fault of certain enquiry panels in not considering the financial implications of their recommendations on service improvements, but it also suggests that politicians are often quick to blame professionals for errors or misjudgements but slow to provide the resources necessary for an effective and efficient service.

It is impossible to give a detailed analysis of each report, but certain key factors are worthy of note. The Auckland report in 1975 concerned the murder of a child by a man already convicted of a previous child murder. It led to government guidance on release of prisoners (see below) and a clause in the Children Act, 1975 enabling care proceedings in cases where an adult with previous convictions for offences against children is or may become a member of the household, even when there has been no offence against those children, although the court would also have to be satisfied that an Order would be in the child's interests. That report also emphasised the importance of hospitals following up missed out-patient appointments rather than simply assuming all is well and closing the file.

The Godfrey report (1975) focused on the role of the probation officer, and Meurs (1975) concerned death from neglect and starvation rather than inflicted injury and stressed the need for worker persistence if parents deny access to the home. Howlett (1976) discussed the vulnerability of siblings in a family where the child 'at risk' had been removed, but the remaining brother left in the home and later killed – if a family needs a scapegoat, removing one will merely shift the focus onto another. Brewer (1977) involved a child returned home by magistrates under a Supervision Order, against the advice of the social worker. Peacock (1978) highlighted the problems of communication across local authority boundaries, with messages lost, delayed or misinterpreted because of different local procedures and practices.

The Chapman report (1979) was not primarily concerned with child injury or gross neglect. This boy died of exposure after running away from home; his parents alleged that they had requested his reception into care which had been refused. However, the report discusses an earlier incident when the boy was seen by a police surgeon and sergeant with weals inflicted by his father using a plastic toy sword. The report criticised the decision not to view this as non-accidental injury, arguing that such injuries could not have been described as acceptable chastisement. Clarke (1979) dealt with a series of confused communications between police, social services and NSPCC about a boy reported by relatives as missing with his mother, and concluded that the police should search for missing children when there are allegations of ill-treatment, no matter who made the allegations.

The Taylor case (1980) involved errors of judgement by the social worker, probation officer and health visitor and is the first case to include drug abuse by a parent. The Brown enquiry (1980) was the third into that case reflecting the politically charged atmosphere surrounding it and highlighting the significant role of local councillors both in providing resources and not supporting their staff. The central role of health authorities was also emphasised. Page (1981) concerned a case of death by hypothermia and made several recommendations about work with non-coping families.

Many now consider these enquiries to be unduly expensive, time-wasting and unhelpful. They damage professional morale for many months and it is an added irony that their recommendations are frequently ignored. Yet given the emotive nature of the subject and the dynamics of local politics, it seems unlikely that these will be the last enquiries on the list.

Government action

In 1970 the Government issued a circular, *Battered Babies*, giving outline guidance on the management of cases. In 1972 a second circular emphasised the need for co-ordination of services through case conferences. The publication of the Colwell report in 1974 was pre-empted by a third circular, *Non-accidental Injury to Children*. This laid the foundation of the current structure of policy and individual case co-ordination. It was purely advisory with no legal force but has had a very significant impact on the pattern of services of statutory agencies, especially social services departments.

The circular advised the establishment of area review committees including senior officer representatives of all statutory and voluntary agencies involved with children and families, with a brief to:

'advise on the formulation of local practice and procedures to be followed in detailed management of cases;

approve written instructions defining the duties of all personnel concerned with any aspect of these cases;

review the work of case conferences in the area;

provide education and training programmes to heighten awareness of the problem;

collect information about the work being done in the area;

collaborate with adjacent area review committees;

advise on the need for enquiries into cases which appear to have gone wrong and from which lessons could be learned;

provide a forum for consultation between all involved in the management of the problem;

draw up procedures for ensuring continuity of care when the family moves to another area;

consider ways of making it known to the general public that health visitors, teachers, social workers, the NSPCC and police may be informed about children thought to be ill-treated.'

The circular also recommended 'a case conference for every case involving suspected non-accidental injury to a child' to meet 'as soon as possible', and advised that there should be 'urgent consideration to setting up an adequate central record of information in each area' (a register). By 1976 all areas had established area review committees (ARC) with case conference and register systems of varying kinds.

Prisoners Convicted of Offences against Children in the Home, issued by the DHSS in 1975, outlined a system for notifying the local authority of possible release on parole of prisoners convicted of offences against children, so that assessment of risk to any children in the home to which they would return can be made and any necessary protective action taken.

Non-accidental Injury to Children: Area Review Committees was issued by the DHSS in 1976 and included an analysis of returns from all ARCs about progress made since the previous circular, together with further guidance. Among other matters it advised that 'all areas which have not yet established a central register should now do so', and separate registers in various agencies should be amalgamated. Details of register operation including data which should be held were given. The importance of case conferences was reiterated and the value of appointing a 'key worker' as a communication channel for all working with the case was stressed. The circular acknowledged that all involved professionally had to be bound by their own professional assessment and statutory duties, but advised that a consensus approach should be attempted, failing which all should be aware of planned unilateral action by one agency so that others could adjust their plans accordingly.

Non-accidental Injury to Children: The Police and Case Conferences was issued by the Home Office and DHSS later in 1976. It advised that the police should attend all case conferences discussing initial management of a child abuse case and gave guidance to the police on disclosure of relevant criminal records to conferences.

Child Abuse: Central Register System was issued in 1980 and consolidated the multidisciplinary approach of early circulars. The major innovation was the extension of the criteria for inclusion within the procedural system to include not only physical injury but also severe and persistent neglect and emotional abuse. Sexual abuse was not to be included, unless associated with physical injury, but discussions on case management were said to be continuing between Home Office and DHSS. Detailed advice on the administration of central registers was also included.

Central register systems

The concept of child abuse registers emanated from the USA. The original reasons for their existence were:

(i) recording suspicion as an aid to future diagnosis (i.e. building up a picture of two or more suspicious incidents which together confirm a diagnosis, but singly do not);

(ii) preventing risks from 'hospital shopping' (i.e. children taken to different hospitals/clinics/agencies on different occasions so as to evade detection and hide the full extent of the problem);

(iii) statistics and research.

An NSPCC publication in 1969 argued for the establishment of registers in Britain as an aid to prevention of repeated injury (a 60 per cent re-injury rate had been found in a random sample of cases).

The 1970 DHSS circular stated 'there is value in the setting up of a registry'. The 1974 circular stated 'a central record of information in each area is essential to good communication between the many disciplines involved in the management of these cases'. The advice was strengthened in 1976: 'all areas which have not yet established a register should now do so.' Registers are local and non-statutory and, unlike most of the US States, there is no legislation requiring reporting. There has been no serious discussion of a national register in Britain. Research by the British Association of Social Workers in 1978 found that most areas had followed DHSS advice, but that many registers had been established in haste with insufficient consideration to the complicated administrative issues involved and the implications of the systems chosen. Comparison between US and British register systems show that they have developed in very different ways.

The main purpose of any register is to facilitate and improve protection of and services to children at risk of abuse and within that, most registers now have five functions:

1 to provide detailed, readily available information about children who are known or suspected to have suffered abuse within criteria agreed by all agencies and professions in the area covered;

2   to provide an aid to the diagnosis of a sequence of re-
    peated injuries or events which might otherwise be seen
    as unrelated and not identified as a pattern of abuse;
3   to aid good communication between and co-ordination of
    agencies and to avoid unnecessary duplication of services
    to the child and his family following an incident of sus-
    pected or confirmed abuse;
4   to provide a basis for regular monitoring of the child and
    family;
5   to provide statistical data about the extent and nature of
    the problem and to enable planning and development of
    services in the area.

Registers have been the focus of considerable controversy
since their inception. US and British research suggests that in
most areas registers are little used, some areas reporting no
enquiries at all to the register (1977 BASW survey). There may
be many reasons for this, including ignorance of the system,
but it would also appear that there is now greater likelihood
of abuse being diagnosed at the first incident and a greater use
of less formal communication networks between agencies. It
would also appear that the incidence of 'hospital shopping' is
much less than early writers feared, although it is probably
still significant in the large conurbations.

The register system embraces not only the register, however, but also case conference procedures, monitoring of case
management, and access to consultation. Professionals in all
disciplines seem to find it difficult to sustain communication
with the many people in other agencies who share an interest
in the many cases known to that individual. There is a
tendency to work in isolation until a crisis occurs, relying on
others to initiate contact if there is a problem. The initial
burst of co-ordinated activity when the case is first identified
can therefore easily evaporate so there is a need for a procedural system to ensure that this does not happen. The
regular monitoring of cases on the register by letter or meeting substantially meets this objective.

In some areas, notably those with NSPCC Units, use of the

register also gives access to professional advice and consultation on case management and procedures. Some registers have been used for research and resource planning, and in some areas the register has become a way of rationing scarce resources; a child on the register is seen as high priority and therefore more needy of other services, e.g. day care. The danger is that other children who do not meet the registration criteria will suffer, even though their problems might be more pressing.

Discussion about registers has become a significant component of the debate on privacy and record keeping. Some have argued that parents and children should have a right of access to the register to check what is recorded and correct errors. The DHSS, area review committees and professional bodies have all been attempting to devise a system which balances the rights of children to protection from violent parents and the need of agencies to record allegations and suspicions of child abuse, against the right of individuals to fair, open and equitable treatment and freedom from unwarrantable intervention. This debate extends beyond registers, however, to all health and social agency records. Whether or not the register existed there would be inter-agency communication and filing systems. Should agencies have the right to keep such records at all? We consider that they are essential to protect children and as a formal record of work undertaken by public agencies, but there must be high standards of confidentiality and parents should be aware of and involved in the recording process.

Guidance from both government and professional bodies has emphasised the importance of co-ordination of policy and case management and there is no doubt that this is important, but some have argued that there has been a preoccupation with formal systems resulting in an excessive bureaucratisation of services to these families, removing all room for professional discretion and innovation. It is certainly easier for administrators to issue guidance on procedures and communication than to tackle problems of inadequate training and knowledge in the field. Improving standards of practice takes time and costs money and effort; procedural guidance is easier to formulate and gives a semblance of action. We hope to show that a formal procedural framework is essential in the management of child abuse cases, but that this can never be a substitute for individual skill and knowledge. In the final analysis, when the parents and child are talking alone with the worker, no amount of procedural guidance will guarantee that the right things are said and done.

Resource implications of public concern

Public and professional concern about child abuse has had a significant impact on policy and expenditure in the health and social services. Considerable professional time has been devoted to area review committees, devising and sustaining procedures, training and individual case management. The number of children in care has also increased significantly, only partly as a result of concern about child abuse, but now seems to have levelled off (1967 69,000 (excluding approved schools), 1974 91,000 (including former approved schools), 1978 94,000 – England only). In evidence to the Commons Select Committee (Appendix 45 Q373), the Association of Directors of Social Services commented 'we find it rather ironic . . . that this informal circular [DHSS LASSL (74)13] has succeeded in achieving a greater diversion of resources to the child abuse area from other areas of work than Statutes that Parliament itself has passed, such as the Chronically Sick and Disabled Persons Act'.

In this field, as in many others, there is a tendency for the public and politicians to call for improved services but a reluctance to approve the necessary expenditure to ensure their implementation. An effective child abuse prevention and treatment service requires qualified and experienced professionals, day care facilities for parents and children (obviously not restricted to abused children only), foster and residential homes, family aide/homemaker services, health services, volunteers (needing expenses), administrative support staff and possibly other services as well. An intensely personal service, such as this, is inevitably expensive but without the resources there is no service.

Alongside public and political concern about the incidence and prevention of child abuse has been a growing debate about the relevance and efficiency of social services departments and social work in particular. The emergence of child abuse as a major public concern has possibly benefited social work, giving it a central, co-ordinating role and an area of expertise it can call its own. However social work is notoriously difficult to evaluate and many have used the findings of the major enquiries to support an attack on social work as a whole: every dead child is claimed as evidence of the irrelevance of social work in general.

This atmosphere has undoubtedly had a damaging effect on social workers and health visitors in particular. There is a commitment to help families, but real anxiety about the personal and professional risks involved, and this is sometimes reflected in decision making: a safety first policy can quickly take root. Some departments have protected themselves by insisting that certain decisions are taken at a very senior level (e.g. a director approves all decisions to return a child home from care). There must be systematic procedures for decision making but such centralisation is ultimately insensitive or inefficient and not to be recommended.

The public have an undeniable right to demand accountability of those employed to exercise authority on its behalf, but this accountability must be realistic. Some adverse press and public response to individual cases has been excessive and the expectations made of social service workers and others quite unrealistic. All health and social service workers have to take risks, such is the nature of human relationships. All that can be asked is that decisions are taken in good faith, based on the fullest possible information which could reasonably be said to be available at the time, and in full consultation with others involved and the supervisor. There will be more deaths by child abuse and no doubt more enquiries.

Politicians, public and press should make their judgements based on these criteria.

Summary

The various enquiries into the deaths of certain abused children have had a major impact on resource allocation, feelings and attitudes in the health and social services. They are expensive and time-consuming and very many of their recommendations have been ignored. Partly in response to these enquiries, but also to public and professional concern, the Government has issued a number of advisory circulars, resulting in the universal establishment of area review committees and the organisation of local procedures, case conferences and registers. Public concern about prevention and treatment of child abuse is meaningless unless translated into resources to provide a service. The evaluation of responsibility for deaths from child abuse should be more realistic. No professional can be held fully responsible for the actions of a client/patient in his absence.

5

Medical Presentation

Introduction

The term child abuse is used in many ways and in its broadest sense can be said to cover a substantial number of children. This chapter is concerned exclusively with the physical manifestations of abuse (injury and neglect), with a brief discussion of sexual abuse. It is important to remember that the child's physical condition is only part of the diagnosis, however, although it may be the reason for drawing attention to him. Of equal concern is the child's emotional and developmental state; very often the injuries are easily treated, but the emotional damage is more difficult to heal.

It is also important to distinguish between the seriousness of the injury and the seriousness of the family problems. The seriousness of the injury often owes more to chance than design, so must never be taken as a sole indicator of prognosis. Before deciding how to respond to the situation, a full family assessment is essential: this is discussed in detail in Part II.

What follows is a discussion of the physical symptoms and problems of diagnosis. Perhaps the most striking feature of child abuse in recent years is the virtual disappearance of the multiply-injured child, described as 'typical' in the early (1960s) literature, and also the apparent decline in the re-injury rate after initial involvement. It would appear that community services and other agencies are being very effective in early diagnosis and prevention of inflicted injury. How to handle a child abuse investigation, when to seek medical advice, how to interview parents and the significance of what emerges are discussed in Part II.

Fractures and brain damage

Injuries affecting the head lead to the most serious long-term consequences, the most serious of all being death. Extrapolation from NSPCC Registers, and research and analysis of the Registrar General's statistics, suggests that roughly one hundred fatalities from child injury occur each year (Creighton, 1980). Most deaths are caused by brain damage.

Head injuries may result from a blow, swinging round or shaking. Diagnosis of skull fractures is usually comparatively straightforward for a radiologist. The fracture itself is usually less significant in terms of the physical prognosis than associated complications, which may also occur after swinging or shaking (without fractures).

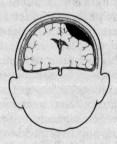

Subdural haematoma

Figure 1

These trauma may result in a collection of blood immediately underneath the skull (subdural haematoma – figure 1) causing increasing pressure on the brain. The effects of this may be drowsiness, vomiting and headaches, leading to irritability, coma and eventually death. The symptoms may emerge some hours after the incident. The increased pressure may be relieved by neurosurgery or removing the blood with a syringe inserted through the open gap between the skull bones in young children (anterior fontanelle). Even when the pressure is relieved it is quite common for permanent disability to follow: e.g. blindness because the back of the eye was damaged by bleeding, weakness down one side of the body (hemiplegia) and mental retardation. The cost of nursing a severely handicapped child in a subnormality hospital in 1977 was estimated at £63 per week (excluding capital and administrative costs), totalling £98,000 over a thirty-year period. The expense would now be higher, indicating the considerable financial cost of failing to prevent such injuries.

Other serious injuries include *fractures of the long bones* (arms and legs). Immobile babies very rarely break their bones and toddlers rarely suffer more than a greenstick fracture (a crack which does not result in a complete break). Non-accidental injury must therefore be seen as a highly probable diagnosis in all fractures in children under one year. One quarter of all fractures in children under two years result from child abuse.

Child abuse fractures are usually caused by twisting and squeezing the limbs, often associated with excessive force when changing a nappy. An X-ray will usually be required to demonstrate the injury. The fractures may be found in the middle of the bone or may occur at the tip, as a result of pulling. In both cases a thin membrane (periosteum) may be sheared off and bleeding may occur between it and the bone, which later hardens and calcifies. It is possible to age the injury by the presence of callus observed on the X-ray (figure 2).

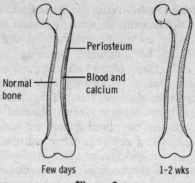

Figure 2

Fractured ribs are particularly difficult to diagnose in a small baby by clinical examination alone: X-rays will always be required. This may be caused by squeezing or a blow. A crying, fractious baby may be suffering from many possible conditions and fractured ribs is rarely an obvious diagnosis. It is clearly impracticable, unethical and even dangerous to routinely X-ray all young children where there is general concern, but if there are other injuries (particularly grip-marks – figure 3), X-rays are advisable.

There has been some recent discussion of the apparent similarity of a rare, inherited bone disease (osteogenesis imperfecta) to child abuse. This condition results in multiple fractures of differing ages and for that reason may be confused with abuse. However it is extremely rare and the bones usually show a characteristic thin appearance. Some have argued that there may be a mild form of the condition, less easily diagnosed, which may be more easily confused with abuse. It is important to remember that the family circumstances form a critical part of the diagnosis.

Internal damage

In a few cases, children may suffer damage to the kidneys, spleen, duodenum, liver or other internal organs as a result of a punch or kick. Such injuries are serious and may lead to death if not treated. They are rare and evidence of assault.

Burns

Burns and scalds are very common accidents in children. About 2 per cent of children who suffer burns are burnt non-accidentally. Around 10 per cent of all abused children suffer burns. A common explanation for a burn or scald is that the child reached up and pulled a kettle or saucepan full of hot liquid over himself. When this happens the child usually sustains burns under the chin and around the armpits. If these areas are clear, a further explanation may need to be sought.

Burns consciously inflicted with an instrument as punishment are very worrying (e.g. sitting a child on a hot radiator for wetting the bed, holding the hand against a hot fire, placing a heated metal object on the skin). These are rare forms of abuse and the unusual outline of the burn itself usually gives a clue to the diagnosis.

Cigarette burns are also significant, especially if there is more than one and of differing ages. Unlike many other types of injury, a cigarette burn is not one of the normal hazards of a child's life, although many children probably sustain very superficial burns by accident if their parents smoke. There is a high rate of smoking in abusing parents. A clear, round, deep burn is most unlikely to have been caused by an accidental brush against a hot cigarette end or falling ash. The child's and adult's reactions are usually too quick to allow a serious burn to develop. Such a burn would probably have been caused by holding a hot object against the skin for an appreciable period.

Burns of the hands or feet of ambulant children, in a glove and stocking distribution, are very suggestive of child abuse, particularly if there is a clear demarcation line. These would be caused by dipping in very hot water. If the child is old enough to walk, he would usually see the steam and know not to climb in, but if he did he would usually jump out very quickly, or fall with shock and cause more serious distribution of injury. Such scalds imply that the child was placed in hot water and probably held there.

Burns to the buttocks and groin area (perineum) are rarely accidental.

The infliction of pain by burning or scalding seems to be associated with parents with very damaged personalities, suggesting a poor long-term prognosis for the safety of the child if he remains in the home. Thus despite the fact that the injuries themselves may not appear medically serious (e.g. cigarette burn), it is essential that there is a full assessment of the family situation before concluding what to do (see Chapter 6).

Non-accidental poisoning

Reports of such cases are sporadic and usually related to individual cases. The most common substances given to children are tranquillisers, and sedatives (e.g. benzodiazepams, barbiturates and tricylics). Excessive intake of water and salt has also been reported. The main symptoms in the children are episodes of coma, drowsiness and unsteadiness, often occurring suddenly without known cause. Saving any vomit or urine taken at the time of the symptoms may assist diagnosis. There is some evidence that the parents in such cases have very disturbed personalities and consciously mislead the doctors about the nature and origin of the condition. There are a few reported cases where parents continued to give the drugs secretly whilst the child was under observation in hospital. This diagnosis should be considered in all cases of unexplained coma and a range of blood analyses should be undertaken. A thorough parental history is essential to the diagnosis, preferably verified from independent sources.

Moderate injuries (cuts and bruises)

The majority of children who are physically abused suffer soft tissue injuries such as bruises and lacerations (about

70 per cent – Creighton, 1980). The severity of the bruising may be less important than the reason for its occurrence.

Bruising of the head and face is the most common presentation particularly in younger children. These are often associated with feeding problems, for example three or four bruises on one side of the face with a further single bruise on the other suggests a grip mark with thumb and fingers, perhaps the result of the adult gripping the baby's face whilst trying to feed him (figure 3).

 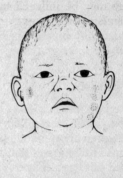

Figure 3

Bite marks and *scratches* are sometimes observed, possibly caused by pets or other children.

Black eyes in a child who is not yet walking are rarely accidental. Two black eyes in a child are only likely to be accidental if there is also a bruise in the middle of the forehead or on the bridge of the nose, which has drained into the tissue surrounding both eyes. Two swollen black eyes are likely to be caused by a hit from something of the appropriate size – a tennis ball or a fist.

Bruises in the middle of the back of young children, usually both sides of the spine, may have significance out of all proportion to their severity. These may occur when the child is picked up and shaken, the bruises being finger-tip grip marks (figure 4). We have already suggested that shaking a child is a socially acceptable form of discipline and that many parents are unaware of its dangers. Sometimes only bruises will result, but if squeezed a little harder, ribs may be broken (figure 5) and if shaken a little harder still, a subdural haematoma (figure 1, p. 66) may develop, causing blindness, hemiplegia, mental retardation and eventually death unless treated (see above). These apparently insignificant bruises on the back should be taken seriously, therefore, although careful investigation is needed before confirming the diagnosis as they may be inflicted by other children in play or be of unsinister origin.

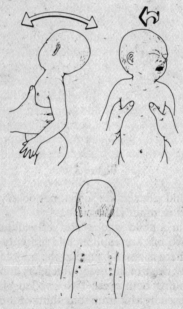

Figure 4

Bruises on the shins are usually accidental and almost universal in toddlers.

Bruises on the trunk are also common, but of more significance if numerous and of different ages.

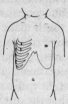

Figure 5

Assessing the ageing of bruises is not easy although the colour changes from purple to brown to green to yellow are familiar to all. As a rule each colour change takes just under a week and so most bruises disappear in three or four weeks, but the rate of change depends to some extent on where they occur (over bone or soft structures) and how deep they are. It is therefore only possible to give a rough estimate.

A torn frenulum (web of skin joining gum and lip) in a young child usually results from something being forcibly pushed into the mouth (spoon, bottle, dummy – figure 6). This may be associated with facial bruising (figure 3). If the result of a punch in the face, other bruising is also evident.

Neglect/failure-to-thrive

Included in the spectrum of child abuse is the grossly neglected child who shows evidence of inadequate feeding, stunted growth, poor hygiene (extensive nappy rash and repeated stomach upsets), inadequate warmth or inadequate supervision: also included are those children who fail to grow normally for no organic reason.

Many children are referred to paediatricians because of concern about suspected inadequate growth. There are many medical reasons for a child to be small: both parents may be small, there may have been intra-uterine growth failure, or there may be a variety of diseases or physical conditions which inhibit growth. It is often possible to reach a decision about the causes of the problem by studying a growth chart (see figure 7), which shows the distribution of heights and weights in the normal child population. As a rough guide, any child falling below the bottom line on the graph (3rd percentile) or who is seen to be crossing the lines should be admitted to hospital for investigation, although a few of these children will be naturally small. If in hospital, with no specific treatment, the child gains weight at more than 50 grams a day it is likely that the quality of his care has been poor. Most children admitted to hospital for medical reasons initially tend to *lose* weight.

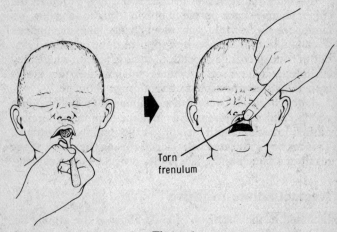

Torn
frenulum

Figure 6

There has been discussion in recent years about whether emotional abuse in a child who nevertheless receives adequate food and physical care, can of itself lead to growth failure. Some argue that 'love' is as essential to physical growth as food, and there appear to be grounds for accepting this, but it remains a matter of dispute.

Many juvenile courts will now accept a growth chart and evidence of rapid weight-gain in hospital as evidence that the child's health and development are being avoidably impaired. If a child is admitted to hospital for an assessment of the possibility of parental neglect, the paediatrician should consider ensuring that the nurses who weigh the child remember to sign the chart by each recording so that they can verify the evidence in court if required to do so. This is an unlikely but a necessary formality.

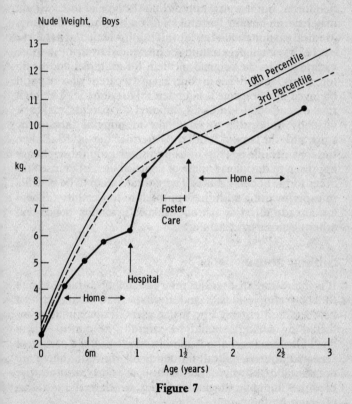

Figure 7

Sexual abuse

In the last few years there has been increased discussion of and concern about sexual abuse of children in the home. Some define this to include not only incest, but also other forms of sexual experience and sexual exploitation. That serious harm is done by sexual abuse of children is generally accepted, and some American studies suggest that the greater the age gap between abuser and abused, the more serious the long-term effects. The abusive act itself has long-term harmful effects, but it would appear that the type of intervention may have an equally harmful effect on the child and family. Medical examination of girls to establish whether or not there has been vaginal penetration is experienced by many as more violating than the original incident for example, and being forced to give evidence in court against a parent who may still be loved and respected, is undeniably traumatic. The high rate of custodial sentences imposed on parents makes it virtually impossible to undertake meaningful therapeutic work with the family. Work by Giaretto in the USA has shown the considerable benefits of using a similar multidisciplinary approach to the management of sexual abuse as that used for other forms of child abuse. There would seem to be benefits in experimenting with that approach in this country. There are already effective liaison schemes involving police and other agencies in certain areas.

Sibling abuse

It is interesting that serious injury of siblings is rare, despite the powerful jealousies and rivalries that occur between brothers and sisters. For that reason, serious injuries inflicted by siblings should be carefully examined. There would be less worry about an isolated event, but a pattern of repeated injuries indicates grounds for concern. There are occasional cases where the parent consciously or otherwise provokes one child to assault another, which we see as a form of abuse by the parent.

Accidental or not?

Some injuries of themselves clearly establish a diagnosis of child abuse – they could only have been caused by an assault;

the majority are less clear-cut. The diagnosis is the more difficult since there are no studies of large numbers of children with ordinary bumps and bruises with which to compare the abnormal. Small-scale studies in Leicestershire and Manchester seem to suggest that most 'non-accidental' injuries are mirrored by 'accidental' ones, again indicating that the diagnosis of child abuse cannot rely on the physical presentation alone.

There are no simple rules to distinguish the two, but certain characteristics of abuse have been noted:

There is a long, unexplained delay between the incident and presentation for treatment (in serious injuries) – most parents bring children with accidents within an hour or two at the most;

The explanation is not consistent with the injuries observed – they could not have happened that way;

There may be injuries of different ages;

There are no witnesses;

Parents are touchy, easily irritated when asked questions, show signs of hostility to, and have unrealistic expectations of, the child (which must be distinguished from normal parental distress and guilt when their loved child injures himself, which may seem like anger);

The parents may hint at other problems.

Increasing understanding of the nature of accidents, as well as similarity between accidental and non-accidental injuries, are creating further diagnostic problems. Accidents often happen at times of stress, provoked by tiredness, anxiety and anger, when people become less careful and do not take usual precautions against risks. Both types of injury are disproportionately represented the lower the social class, as is illness in general. The Court report on the health of children suggested that 'there is extensive evidence that an adverse family and social environment can retard physical, emotional and intellectual growth, lead to more frequent and more serious illness and adversely affect educational achievement and personal behaviour'. The report concludes that 'the boundary between illness and neglect is often ill-defined and what matters is the effectiveness of the collaboration' between agencies involved.

The term 'non-accidental injury' has also confused thinking on diagnosis, since it implies an element of conscious thought on the part of the assailant, in contrast to 'accidents' which are seen as unintended, whereas we know that the vast majority of inflicted injuries are not premeditated, sadistic acts, but sudden outbursts with no considered intent of harming the child. Perhaps the most poignant example involves children who have suffered brain damage as a result of shaking. The parents are often unaware of the dangers of shaking, the act is a momentary loss of control and is usually followed by deep remorse and guilt, yet the damage can be severe and permanent and can lead to serious criminal charges against the parent, although therapeutically these can be among the most hopeful cases. It could be argued that the consequences of the parent's action were accidental – it was never intended, but it is clearly child abuse.

The diagnosis is even more complicated when a child is smacked, hit or pushed and falls on to a hard surface, sustaining cuts, bruises or even concussion. Again, the parent did not intend the injury and the consequences are the result of chance, yet the parent was acting recklessly and should have taken steps to protect the child from injury.

Injuries sustained by children during the course of marital disputes and violence also pose diagnostic problems. Marital discord is a very significant feature in around half the abusing families, sometimes including violence. In some cases the injuries arise out of a marital fight, the child literally walking into the problem. In others, one parent may try to use the child as a protection against the aggressor (consciously or not), who may injure the child whilst trying to hit the spouse. Some children try to intervene to stop parental arguments and are injured as a result. In a few cases the child becomes the symbol of the marital discord and receives the parental aggression. In one case a cohabitee was so angry that his meal had not been prepared that he threw a pan of hot cooking oil over the mother and child. These injuries all come within child abuse, since the parent or caregiver was acting recklessly with no thought for the safety of the child.

Incidents like these may arise when one or both parents are under the influence of drugs or excess alcohol. Alcoholism and problem drinking often have an adverse emotional and social impact on the children, although not necessarily presenting a physical risk. The significance of drinking and its effect on parental behaviour may be missed if those involved only see the parent when sober, but should always be considered when making the family assessment. Drug or alcohol abuse rarely if ever precipitate assault on a child, although one or other may be part of the family problem.

Many accidents in childhood result from negligence, however, some of which could be said to be reckless. Road accidents are a major cause of death in childhood, yet very many drivers speed through built-up areas. Is the parent who fails to fix a secure lock on a gate, so that a child wanders out and is killed on a busy road, any less negligent or culpable than the driver? or the parent who shakes the child whilst ignorant of the dangers? or the one who neglects the child out of ignorance, causing permanent retardation?

Having analysed in retrospect our attitude to many such cases, we have concluded that the major deciding factor is the attitude and response of the parents. There must always be concern if the parent shows no anxiety about what has happened, and coldly blames the child, especially if the child is too young to have been able to anticipate the danger. Most parents express guilt about accidents even when this is misplaced. Repeated accidents of a similar nature, showing evidence of lack of parental oversight or attention to areas of risk in the home, constitute an undeniable form of child abuse (for example the child who repeatedly drinks bleach or household cleaners, suffers repeated burns, is always wandering on to roads or falling down the stairs). In some cases such accidents are clearly 'knowingly not prevented', but in others there may be an unconscious antagonistic motivation leading to failure to protect the child from risk.

Justifiable chastisement?

Perhaps the most contentious area of diagnosis is that related to injuries sustained during punishment. We have already stated our view on corporal punishment (Chapter 1), but this is not universally accepted, and in a recent court case magistrates dismissed a case against a father of causing actual bodily harm to his son who had been beaten by a belt causing bruising to the face; this was held to be acceptable chastisement. It also seems inconsistent for some local authorities to investigate cases of children injured by beating in the home, when teachers and residential care staff in their own establishments are allowed to cane children. There are still those who believe that if you spare the rod you spoil the child, whilst others share the view of Sir Robert Peel that seeking violent retribution is likely to increase violence rather than to curb it. Workers have to make their decisions without the support of a national consensus, and their judgements will inevitably be subjective, and not always supported by the courts.

Summary – making the diagnosis

The majority of children suffering inflicted injury sustain soft tissue injuries, especially bruising to the face. Burns, fractures and internal injuries may also be found. Brain damage resulting from subdural haematoma has the worst physical prognosis, although the outlook for work with the family may be more positive. It will always be necessary to consider the family background in some detail before reaching a conclusion and this will require a team approach involving doctor, social worker and often police, health visitor and others. The assessment should be structured around consideration of:

parental history,
marital history,
vulnerability of the child,
nature of the incident,

lifelines/community supports/social situation.

We consider these factors in more detail in Part II. It is rare for a diagnosis of child abuse to be made on the physical presentation alone.

6

Different Types of Abusing Parents

We have already seen in Chapter 2 that research findings based on studies of large numbers of abusing parents are very useful in defining the population at risk, but add little to the understanding of the specific case, nor do they distinguish clearly between the child abusing population and other problem groups. The non-specific profile which emerges from such studies is that of a young, socially and emotionally deprived person. This can be misleading because it may result in a tendency to fail to recognise the significant minority groups which differ from it, both in cause and response to intervention. Much has also been written on the individual psychopathology of the parents, but although these studies enhance the understanding of the individual parent, many of the features are not confined to people who abuse their children, but are also found in otherwise 'normal' parents. 'Abuse of children is not a disease entity, but a pattern of behaviour and like all such patterns it has a multiplicity of paths by which it is reached' (Scott, 1973a). There is therefore a need to evolve a way of dividing this large, heterogeneous group into smaller groups who not only share common characteristics, but who also have some predictive value in terms of treatment and prognosis.

The suggested typology or categorisation which follows is based on the initial assessment and eventual outcome of cases in Manchester and Nottinghamshire. It is under constant review and modified in the light of experience. It is therefore descriptive and empirical and there may well be alternative and equally valid schemes. However this typology attracts considerable interest when discussed with workers from all disciplines and seems to parallel their experience, suggesting that it is a realistic classification of practical value. It focuses on violence to children, has relevance to neglect and emotional abuse, but does not include sexual abuse.

The typology is based on assessment of the following factors:

The parent   personality and social functioning,
psychiatric status,
presence of stress,
'understandability' of the abuse behaviour,
parental behaviour at the time of abuse and
subsequently,
parental response to intervention,
social circumstances.

The child   nature of the injuries,
general physical and emotional state of the
child and siblings.

Using this information, cases of neglect and inflicted injury can be divided into two broad groups with further subdivisions.

Primary child abuse

The injury is associated with a fundamental distortion of the parent–child relationship of 'understandable' origin. There is little or no evidence of other areas of personality or social problems.

Secondary child abuse

Violence or neglect is associated with either problems in coping with life in general and child rearing in particular, or major personality disorder or mental illness.

The objective of intervention must be to ensure the least detrimental (preferably best possible) outcome for the child; it is not in the long-term interests of child or parents for there to be continuing abuse or re-injury. The initial presumption must be that it is preferable for the child to return to the care of his parents at some stage, but for some this will be impossible. For these children, the best prognosis will involve a satisfactory, long-term substitute placement. In the discussion which follows, the assessment of the prognosis or outcome is based on the possibility of rehabilitation to the family home, and the following distinctions are drawn:

Good prognosis – rapid response to treatment, early improvement in parent-child relationship, no further injuries, child returns home immediately or very soon after the incident, physical and emotional care is good, early termination of involvement.

Variable prognosis – rehabilitation takes longer and may prove impossible: considerable practical help and advice is required, temporary separation may be necessary during future crises, no re-injury but continuing concern about physical and emotional care, long-term involvement.

Poor prognosis – no prospect of rehabilitation of child with the parents; continued disturbance in parent-child relationships, injury of siblings likely, future children are at risk; long-term involvement with child in care and future children, which may be resisted by parents.

We now consider in detail the various sub-categories, but stress that it is not suggested that all families will fall neatly into any one group. The various categories are 'ideal' types, describing commonly observed constellations of factors. The detailed plan of intervention must be specific to each case and constantly re-evaluated.

I Primary abuse

Type 1 – child specific

The parent: The mother is usually responsible. The problem is independent of social class and age. There are only minor personality problems or no significant personality disorder. There is no evidence of problems with social functioning and child rearing in general, other siblings having been success-fully reared. The mothers are frequently over-conscientious and self-critical, with unrealistically high expectations of themselves. Neonatal separation, difficult babies, inability to establish an emotional relationship with the baby, disap-pointment over the baby's sex, excessive fatigue, mild de-pressive illness or anxiety states (especially if the injury oc-curs within six months of the birth), are frequently found, in addition to stress resulting from domestic crises.

The child: Usually under eight months old, well cared for, well nourished and with a good health record. There is no evidence of repeated injury or chronic neglect. They are frequently low birth weight babies who have been in neonatal units.

The incident: Largely 'understandable' occurring at a time of high stress (e.g. financial problems, death of a relative, sud-den redundancy) when coping resources are low. The in-juries are compatible with recent loss of control and the child is presented rapidly for treatment. There is considerable remorse and distress. At least partial admission of responsi-bility occurs soon after. There is appropriate concern, par-ents visit frequently and react with relief to offers of help.

Intervention and prognosis: Good prognosis. The parents usually co-operate and are accessible to a psychotherapeutic approach. They gain insight from discussion of their feelings and past experiences and quickly learn how to cope. It is important to minimise any separation of parents and child that may have resulted from the injury, since previous separation is frequently a major causal factor. Speedy rehabilitation of the child in the family is usually indicated.

Case example: Audrey, aged twenty-three, married to a skilled worker, successfully reared four girls and desperately wanted a boy. The fifth child, a girl, was premature and kept in a neonatal unit for three weeks. She was a difficult, crying baby. At eight weeks she presented with a hypernatraemic coma and bruising of her legs. The mother rapidly admitted that she had been heaping up scoops of milk powder to keep the child quiet, without giving additional fluids (she had done this for her other children) and had been smacking her excessively. She was having difficulty with a jealous sibling and her own parents were getting a divorce. She was very distressed and visited hospital frequently. With treatment she rapidly established a relationship with her baby for the first time, and there were no further problems until exactly the same sequence of events occurred with her sixth daughter.

Type 2 – obsessional

The parent: The parent (usually the mother) has the same characteristics as Type 1, but in addition there are marked obsessional personality traits (see Chapter 15). She frequently has a successful previous life-style and career and is often married to a rather critical and undermining husband. She is usually a perfectionist with high domestic standards, rigid routines, and unrealistic expectations of her own and the child's behaviour. She is often preoccupied with concepts of naughtiness and spoiling. She frequently seeks help before a serious injury occurs, and often exaggerates the degree of abuse that has occurred.

The child: Usually older than the previous group, often a toddler. The child's general physical and emotional state is usually very good. There are no marked behaviour problems; problems are usually more imagined than real.

The incident: The injuries are usually the result of over-disciplining. The parent usually felt provoked or upset by behaviour wrongly perceived as wilful or naughty, often at mealtime or bedtime, and believes that the child was threatening parental authority.

Intervention and prognosis: As above (Type 1), but help is also needed to enable the mother to understand normal infant development and behaviour.

Case example: Brenda, aged twenty-six, was married to a factory manager. She successfully reared a placid and obedient little girl. Her second child, a son, was one month premature and kept in a neonatal unit for three weeks, many miles from the parents' home. She did not establish an emotional relationship with the child, finding him cold and difficult. She attempted to strangle him one night after many weeks of sleeplessness because of his crying and came to the casualty department in a state of considerable distress, saying what she had done. There was faint bruising on his neck. She had recently developed ulcerative colitis and was physically exhausted. She now relates much better to her child, helped by psychotherapy, but still has crises, when she finds him naughty and disobedient, and needs advice.

Type 3 – self-righteous over-discipline
The boundary of this group is incapable of objective definition, given differing attitudes to physical punishment.

The parent: Either parent may be responsible, but the older the child the more likely the father. The parents have no marked personality or relationship problems and have a successful life-style, including regular work. They may be of any social class. The parent is a perfectionist with unrealistic expectations of self and others. Standards of housecraft are high. They seem conscientious and responsible citizens.

The child: Usually of school age, well cared for and developing satisfactorily. He sometimes shows signs of emotional or behavioural disturbance, including possible delinquency, and a vicious circle of either increasing rebellion or continuing loss of confidence and under-achievement in the face of unrealistic parental expectations and excessive punishment. The parents' usual response to problems is physical punishment. The focus may be on one child who is perceived as different, or on all children of similar age.

The incident: Injuries inflicted during punishment, usually involving a cane, belt or other instrument, part of a pattern with previous, unreported injuries. The problem is usually discovered at school and by chance. Parents may agree that there is a problem and accept help with relief, or may persist with self-righteous justification. The child is usually blamed for causing the incident by bad behaviour and may accept the injury as justifiable punishment.

Intervention and prognosis: Variable prognosis, depending on parental willingness to accept help and depth of animosity between parent and child. Family therapy to improve relationships is indicated with older children and activity group work may help to rebuild confidence and redirect 'rebellion'. Fundamental breakdown in relationships indicates admission to care. Individual child psychiatry is often helpful.

Case example: Bernard, aged forty, had a successful marriage and career. He had two adopted children. Since learning of his adoption, the boy developed behaviour problems and became increasingly involved in delinquency, receiving official cautions and fines. His offending continued, with increasing resentment towards parents. He was received into care at parents' request following further theft, and was found to have weal marks of different ages. His father admitted beating him with a garden cane on several occasions, the last including tying him over a chair. He has remained in care.

II Secondary child abuse

Type 4 – social chaos/deprivation

The parent: Either or both parents may be responsible. They have moderately severe personality disorders with evidence of considerable personality and social malfunctioning. They tend to come from severely deprived backgrounds with neurotic and behaviour problems in childhood and adolescence, and frequently delinquency as well. There is often evidence of recurrent mild depressive illness or anxiety states. They are socially isolated and have impaired relationships with their families, short courtships and high levels of marital discord. They are often very young when they marry, and pregnancies tend to follow rapidly. Their life-style is chaotic with a wide range of social and financial problems, and they are often known to social agencies as a 'problem family'. They are unable to cope with the ordinary stresses and strains of life. There are high levels of stress, often self-generated. There is often a lack of awareness of the needs of the child and their behaviour towards him is inconsistent and ambivalent.

The child: Usually shows evidence of neglect and understimulation. His general physical and emotional state improves dramatically in hospital. As the problem is one of child rearing in general, other siblings may be affected and the general level of care is inadequate. The family as a whole will have a poor health record, with many of the siblings attending casualty departments and being frequently admitted for stomach and chest infections.

The incident: The injury results from loss of control. There is unreasonable delay in seeking treatment and varying and inconsistent explanations for the injuries. The injuries are often discovered by others, for example at nursery or school.

Intervention and prognosis: Variable prognosis, depending on parental acknowledgement of the problem and willingness to co-operate with help. Practical help and directive counselling are essential. Older children may benefit from psychiatric or social work help in their own right, for example activity group work.

Case example: Denise married at seventeen, one month after the birth of her first son. She was a factory worker, her husband a miner. One year later she gave birth to twins, the second being detained in hospital for three weeks for a minor operation. Both pregnancies were unplanned. After the second birth, the father had extended sick leave for 'nerves'. The second twin was difficult to feed and spent a further week in hospital. At eight weeks he was admitted with a fractured skull and bleeding on the brain. Parents initially denied responsibility but mother eventually admitted violently shaking the baby after incessant crying. The child was removed into care. Matrimonial and social crises continued and the care of the two remaining children caused frequent concern. The fostered twin is developmentally and physically ahead of the one at home, despite the trauma.

Type 5 – the 'child' parent

The parent: Either parent may be responsible, both usually adolescents with their first child. They have very immature personalities and grossly deprived backgrounds, often having been in care. They 'escape' their unhappy background by forming a relationship with someone usually of the same age and background, pregnancy rapidly follows in an attempt to establish some security. They have high expectations of what the child will do for them and little idea of the realities of child rearing. They both seek romantic love and security in 'marriage' and parenthood and are often isolated and 'at war' with the adult world. They are too young to cope with parenthood and often feel trapped by the baby.

The child: A first baby, well cared for, and in the first few weeks of its life. Classically, the injury is a serious one such as a blood clot on the brain (subdural haematoma) resulting from shaking.

The incident: Sudden loss of control usually triggered by crying, resulting in shaking. Usually the parents have no idea of the consequences of such behaviour.

Intervention and prognosis: Variable prognosis for the present child but may be good for future children. The key factor is the time required for both parents to develop and mature. As this may reasonably require two or more years, it may be better to place the injured baby in care or seek adoption, particularly if he is handicapped or damaged by his injuries. All efforts should then be directed to helping the parents mature and avoid replacement pregnancies until such time as they are ready to be parents again.

Case example: Ella, seventeen years old, was married to a seventeen year old electrician. She had been in foster care as a child, was physically abused herself and later exploited by her parents. She married in order to escape home. She shook her three week old baby causing a subdural haematoma. The child is now mentally subnormal and blind and is permanently fostered. The parents have a warm relationship with the foster mother and frequently visit their son. Three years after the injury they had a baby girl who is now one year old, and there are no anxieties about her care.

Type 6 – multiple handicap

The parent: Either parent may be responsible, but both tend to have the general characteristics of the social chaos group (Type 4) with, in addition, one or more of the following: mental subnormality, chronic schizophrenia, epilepsy, deafness. They often meet in a semi-institutionalised setting. There are usually very severe financial and social problems and often considerable ignorance about coping with child rearing.

The child: Usually a younger child showing signs of neglect, under-nourishment and under-stimulation.

The incident: The injuries result from 'horse-play' because the parents are unaware of how to handle small children, or loss of control in temper.

Intervention and prognosis: Variable to poor prognosis. A practical directive approach is required. The outlook is poor for independent mothering and permanent separation may be the only course, unless there is evidence of considerable bonds of affection, when a very high input of practical help may help the family to survive as a unit.

Case example: Fred, aged twenty-one, was subnormal with a severe personality disorder. His wife, whom he met on a hospital outing, was herself subnormal and severely deaf. She had been in care as a child following her mother's death. Their first baby was discovered at an infant welfare clinic to be covered in 'love bites'. The mother was unable to hear the baby crying and was not prepared to believe that her husband was responsible. The child has been permanently fostered ever since. They have subsequently had a little girl who is clean and well cared for, but has poor speech development, and is generally under-stimulated. They still have considerable marital and financial problems, and require the almost constant attention of a social worker.

Type 7 – deviant

This is a numerically small, but highly significant group as it includes most of the parents who murder their children.

The parent: Either parent may be responsible, although more frequently male and often not the natural father of the child. They bear the hallmarks of either a severe or a sociopathic personality disorder, with a need for immediate gratification, low tolerance of frustration, superficial emotional responses, and a lack of concern for others. They may be plausible and articulate and pursue the case through the courts seeking revocation of the Care Order. They frequently play people off against each other. The men frequently have criminal records for violence, whereas the women may have markedly histrionic behaviour, a difficulty in distinguishing fantasy from reality, and a tendency to self-deception and fantasy. It is a difficult diagnosis to make in women.

The child: There is usually general physical neglect and emotional cruelty. There is often evidence that injuries have been inflicted over a long period. There may be a more positive relationship with the other parent, who nevertheless fails to protect the child (see Type 8) or active collusion between the parents.

The incident: The act of violence is frequently 'non-understandable'. It may be an impulsive, irritable response to a minor event, or it may be the end result of chronic systematic abuse, or even an act of gross sadistic cruelty. There is considerable delay in presenting the child for treatment and adamant and persistent denial of responsibility. The parents' behaviour is often difficult and ambivalent in hospital; they may seek premature discharge of the child and be threatening towards the staff.

Intervention and prognosis: The prognosis is poor. The nature of the personality disorder and the persistent denial of responsibility, make treatment almost impossible. There is almost always a need for prolonged, if not permanent, separation.

The outlook for rehabilitation is bad, but if possible it is important to maintain contact because of risk to other or subsequent children.

Case example 1: Walter was a twenty-six year old man cohabiting with the mother of two children, unemployed, with a criminal record of violence. There was evidence of morbid jealousy and violence towards his common-law wife. He injured his step-daughter and then, three years later, the child of their union was admitted to hospital with a broken arm. Although the child's mother suspected that the father might have been responsible, the police were unable to prosecute for lack of evidence, and the child was returned home only to be readmitted three weeks later with a fractured rib.

The child was placed in foster care. Walter was a plausible, articulate man who applied for revocation of the Care Order every six months, and was extremely critical of both the hospital staff and the foster parents. Eventually, against the advice of the social worker involved, the court returned the child home and considerable anxieties now remain about the child's well-being.

Case example 2: Gladys was twenty-one years old, married to a man in the armed forces. She had an unremarkable background, but had evidence of a severe personality disorder of the histrionic type. She was very socially isolated and had kept a succession of Alsatian dogs, many of which had died in suspicious circumstances. Her child had been taken to the casualty department on a number of occasions with lacerations and burns with improbable explanations, and then at eight months the child was admitted with a blood clot on the brain. The second child was born eight months after this. Initially, the severity of the personality disorder had been underestimated, and the elder child returned home following the birth of the second. The mother became increasingly manipulative and disturbed and told bizarre stories to indicate her distress. Eventually she came to the clinic saying that her dog had died and that she had been attacked by a man with a knife. The GP visited immediately and discovered two severely bruised children who were promptly removed into care. They are now doing well in a foster home whose location is secret because of the mother's threat to remove her children. She frequently writes to the Queen, the newspapers, and her MP, requesting help to regain the care of her children and complaining of the treatment that she has received.

Type 8 – failure-to-protect

The parent: These are almost always women whose failure to protect a child from violent men is significant enough to be a major contributory factor. They tend to establish repeated relationships with such men, who have the characteristics of the deviant group (Type 7). These women often had a violent childhood and aggressive fathers, have low self-esteem and may suffer assaults by their cohabitees. Despite this, they preserve their relationships with such men, at the expense of their children, and even though they may be very frightened of them.

The child: He may be of any age, though usually under five, and not the natural child of the assailant. He may bear the, hallmarks of chronic abuse, or violence. Paradoxically, he often has a good relationship with his mother.

The incident: As for 'deviant' Type 7. The child is often severely injured or killed. The mother may have known of the incident, yet fails to protect the child or seek appropriate help. Sometimes she falsely admits responsibility or 'covers up' for the man.

Intervention and prognosis: The prognosis is variable. There is usually little likelihood of change in the assailant (see above), but the mothers may well be helped to become caring parents themselves. The child is always exposed to risk from future cohabitees unless casework can help the mother build up her self-esteem and learn to avoid potentially violent cohabitees.

Case example: Helen, a twenty-two year old divorcee, lived alone with her three children. All the children had poor health records and there were considerable financial and social problems, but there were obvious bonds of affection between the mother and children. The three-year-old girl was brought to casualty by her mother, very severely bruised following a beating. She was said to have fallen downstairs but later the story was changed, the mother telling the police that she had smacked her. An older daughter had been seen bruised two weeks before, the mother accepting responsibility. It was difficult to believe the explanation because of the severity of the child's physical state. In hospital, the child was obviously terrified of all men. The mother later admitted that her visiting boyfriend had been irritated when the child had interrupted a TV programme and had beaten her up. He was sent to prison, but the mother's next boyfriend also had a criminal record for violence. She has since been helped to avoid such relationships and the children are developing well without further abuse.

Type 9 – mental illness
This is a numerically small group. Mentally ill parents rarely injure their children.

The parent: Usually the mother is suffering from post-natal psychosis. In a very few cases a schizophrenic or severely depressed parent may injure the child. It is unusual for such severe mental illness not to be noticed and treated before the child suffers unless there is considerable social or geographical isolation. Suicide is often attempted at the time of abuse.

The child: Usually a younger child or baby, since older children often take avoiding action. Usually well cared for prior to the development of the parental illness, but may show signs of recent neglect.

The incident: The parent is not only mentally ill but has developed a state of hopeless despair. The parent's perception of the child is profoundly affected by the illness, the parent firmly believing that it would be better for the child to die, or that some injury must be inflicted, for some delusional reason. The injuries may be bizarre and premeditated (e.g. cutting open the child's stomach to release the evil spirits inside), or may result from loss of control or lack of supervision (e.g. the young baby who sustains several fractures resulting from frequent falls downstairs because mother is depressed and asleep).

Treatment and prognosis: The child may die, but if he survives the prognosis is that of the mental illness. This may be very good in cases of post-natal psychosis.

Case example: Sandra, aged twenty-four, was married to an

oil rig worker. She had successfully reared two previous children but the third pregnancy was unplanned and came at a time when the second child was only a year old and her marriage was deteriorating. Six days after the birth of the third child her husband left her, and at ten days she developed a classic depressive psychosis with marked sleep and appetite disturbance, suicidal feelings and delusional ideas of unworthiness. She believed that her two-week-old baby disliked her and knew that she had been unwanted; this was also of delusional intensity. She remembers severely shaking the baby and was found the next day rocking the dead baby in her arms. Post mortem revealed that the child had a subdural haematoma, but was otherwise well nourished and well cared for. She was admitted to a mental hospital and was treated with ECT. She has now fully recovered.

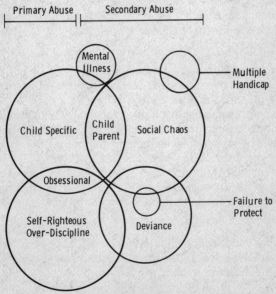

A TYPOLOGY OF ABUSING FAMILIES

Figure 8

Summary

There is a complex variety of parental and paediatric pathology collectively termed child abuse, hence the need for a typology of smaller groups sharing similar characteristics, having predictive value in terms of intervention and prognosis. It is suggested that families with injured children can be divided into primary and secondary abuse with further subgroups. Families will not all fit neatly into a given category and attempts to force such an over-simplistic approach will be misleading and dangerous. The models provide general guidance on assessment and prognosis.

The various groups and their inter-relationship are summarised in figure 8.

7

Fundamental Principles

This chapter describes overall ethical, procedural and emotional issues present in all child abuse work (especially but not exclusively at the initial crisis), an understanding of which is essential if a satisfactory outcome is to be achieved.

Procedures

We have already seen the number and diversity of those professionally involved in child abuse cases and the dangers of misunderstandings and inadequate communication. A major responsibility of area review committees is the formulation of procedural guidelines to overcome these problems. There is potential for good and harm in any investigation and the anxieties of family and professionals are justified, for example the sheer number of people involved can sometimes swamp and overwhelm a family generating additional stress, and thereby increasing risk to the child. (One family was visited by teacher, family doctor, education welfare officer, health visitor, social worker and police all within four hours.) There must be accepted procedures to guard against excessive intervention and to ensure efficient and compassionate investigations.

The preamble to the Manchester City Guidelines summarises our approach:

> Whoever becomes concerned about and therefore to some extent responsible for a child whose well-being is in question needs to know what to do in order:
>
> 1 To get his or her care and physical and emotional condition assessed and treated;
> 2 To prevent further and possibly more serious injury or suffering which is often an immediate threat;
> 3 To make sure that as far as possible his or her intervention does no more harm to family structures and relationships, including those with professional workers, than is necessary to ensure the child's safety and well-being;
> 4 To conform with the law and with professional standards of competence and conduct.
>
> These guidelines are an aid towards achieving these objectives and they are based on the assumption that the exercise of professional autonomy and independence can never be absolute and that the best interests of the child and family are best served within the context of multidisciplinary teamwork, co-operation and commitment to the protection and well-being of the child.

Procedures have now been agreed in all areas, although effectiveness varies. They should be practical, agreeable to all agencies and acceptable to practitioners, sufficiently detailed to give meaningful guidance yet sufficiently concise to be clear and memorable. They should include guidance on whom to consult and refer to, the operation of the central register, who is responsible for investigating (as few agencies as possible), the sequence of events during the investigation and what follows. They can be only basic and procedural, outlining inter- and intra-agency communication and action. Professional assessment, decision and action remain with individual professionals and their agencies. It is essential that they are observed by all. We all experience powerful emotions when facing potentially murderous situations and the last moment to be unsure what to expect of others and do yourself is in the midst of the crisis. Clear procedures and a predictable response from colleagues release energy which is better devoted to forming a relationship with the family and assessing the risks.

Honesty

An open and honest approach with the family and colleagues is essential both to facilitate therapeutic progress and guard personal integrity. Many professionals seem reluctant to discuss their anxieties about treatment of the children with the parents, sometimes due to personal and often irrational fears of parental anger – even violence. Many seem anxious that honesty will destroy their relationship with the parents, preventing future positive contact and exposing the child to future risk. There are also fears of making false accusations. These are all understandable reactions, but if there is suspicion it must be faced openly to be confirmed or refuted. Failure to do so only prolongs uncertainty and sours the relationship, whilst leaving the child at risk. Parents have a right to know what is being said about them so they can have an opportunity to refute what is untrue or learn how to change.

In our experience therapeutic efforts rarely fail because of honesty, whereas many parents complain bitterly that those previously involved were devious, dishonest and unable to help them express their real fears and anxieties. Such comments require cautious interpretation, but our work demonstrates that honesty and openness never destroy a relationship, whereas dishonesty and deceit certainly can and do.

There is often understandable parental resentment about the investigation when suspicion is proved groundless. Many accept that it is better to be alert and make the occasional mistake than do nothing. This attitude will be more likely and residual bitterness will be less if the parents feel they were honestly and fairly treated. There is absolutely no evidence to suggest that professional concern about child abuse is preventing parents from taking children to hospital or seeking advice about genuine accidents or other problems.

Honesty is not only ethically right but also therapeutically essential. Parents must know that those involved are firmly rooted in reality and able to face up to what has happened, however dreadful it may seem, whilst respecting them as individuals and genuinely wanting to help. They will accept occasional weaknesses in their helpers but will soon identify falseness and insincerity and this will inhibit and probably prevent therapeutic progress. An open, honest approach is therefore integral to therapeutic success and should be part of the philosophy of all involved.

This approach should also characterise relationships with professional colleagues but sadly these are often as tense as those with parents. There are many reasons for the existence of such tensions and we discuss these in detail later.

Confidentiality

Confidentiality and civil rights have featured prominently in much recent debate on child abuse. Given that a possible outcome of any investigation is splitting up the family, it is hardly surprising that there are strong feelings. The classic position on confidentiality is that anything said by or about a patient/client to a professional is confidential to those two people, unless it is explicitly agreed otherwise. We have seen that increasing job specialisation and complexity of agency structures can make this unhelpful in some cases. Some argue that a narrow interpretation of confidentiality has resulted in protection being denied to some children, whilst others argue that too much information about too many people is passed around too freely. In our view a full sharing of information forms part of a thorough assessment and is in everybody's interest, but all must guard against gratuitous loose talk. We discuss problems of information sharing and confidentiality elsewhere.

There are two particular problems of confidentiality in a child abuse investigation:

(i) there is more than one patient/client who may have conflicting interests (parent, child, others);

(ii) criminal proceedings could result from professional enquiries directed towards therapy.

Most codes of confidentiality acknowledge that there are times when other principles take precedence, for example the British Medical Association recognises 'a doctor's over-riding responsibility to society' and the British Association of Social Workers' code states

> . . . He will divulge information only with the consent of the client (or informant) except: where there is clear evidence of serious danger to the client, worker or other persons or the community; in other circumstances, judged exceptional, on the basis of professional consideration and consultation.

Almost all child abuse investigations could be said to fit within these exclusions. It is unreasonable for an individual to withhold information about danger to another person – child or adult – thereby exposing him to further danger. However the principles of honesty and fairness dictate that those involved should know about the sharing of information and be somehow involved in the process.

A further dilemma arises when a parent or informant mentions ill-treatment of a child by themselves or another, but requests that this be kept confidential and no action taken. No person should leave a child in danger, yet there are powerful taboos against breaking confidences. We suggest that few parents in this situation are really seeking confidentiality. By talking about the problem, the person is saying that it is worrying, should stop, and that action of some kind is needed. They may fear being identified as the informant and are probably seeking reassurance. By saying 'I have a secret' they are very effectively attracting attention to their problem: we all like to share a secret.

It is unwise for a professional to accept an unconditional confidence. Some subjects are too serious or sensitive and it is best to make this clear with the person before proceeding. Most people accept that professionals have to consult and this rarely prevents further discussion. The alternative is to fall into the 'confidentiality trap', knowing that something has to be done but being constrained by a promise of secrecy. In most child abuse cases, the parent or informant will be relieved to see somebody acting decisively, even taking control of what may have become a nightmare, but feelings will be mixed and there will also be apprehension and perhaps some regret at 'having let the cat out of the bag'.

Some doctors and other workers seem to prefer to ignore or play down such approaches, fearing that discussion with or referral to professional colleagues may harm the patient/client's interest. However inaction can be equally harmful, even lethal. Ignoring this potent cry for help can be a profound disservice to the family.

Authority

The management of a child abuse case inevitably involves the use of authority. The therapist needs to win recognition by the family of his ability to help and therefore acknowledgement of his personal and professional authority. In some cases the personal authority or charisma of the therapist elicits parental co-operation but it may be necessary to evoke legal authority to restrain a parent or protect a child. Many workers are reluctant to enter into an 'enforced relationship' of this kind since the ethos of most helping professions is that people come willingly to seek help. Some cope with this dilemma by dividing families into those who are co-operative and deserve help and those who are difficult and unco-operative and therefore beyond help and deserving of punishment. This is clearly too naïve a view, as we have shown in Chapter 6. The constructive exercise of authority is essential not only to protect the child but also to facilitate therapeutic progress, but there are also risks in the use of power which must be guarded against.

The exercise of power always carries dangers and the legal system is designed to protect people from its excesses. Some have argued that there has been an over-reaction to the problem, with children removed unnecessarily from parents and too heavy-handed a police approach. The emotion of the immediate crisis can easily create an authoritarian response. All involved in a child abuse investigation have to guard against emotional reactions which may cause unnecessary damage to the family.

Some specialists have argued that many parents who abuse their children have such damaged personalities that they cannot tolerate a therapist who seems punitive. They are said to have had such negative experiences of their own parents and other authority figures, that they cannot form a positive relationship with any person they see as being in authority. It is therefore argued that the person taking legal action should not be the one offering understanding, support, counselling and care to the parents. This approach was tested by the NSPCC Battered Child Research Team (Baher, *et al.*) and they found:

> In practice this split between 'good' and 'bad' did not work out as we had hoped for a variety of reasons. We did not find local authority social workers very enthusiastic about playing the 'bad' role, whatever had been agreed theoretically in advance with seniors in their departments. . . . We had not anticipated how often we would be the people most strongly recommending removal of the child. Other workers naturally resented that we should be assigned the 'good' role. . . . We often found the mental and emotional gymnastics necessary a source of strain and guilt, and at times our position was quite untenable.

We consider it both theoretically and practically unsound to suggest that authority and control can be removed from a relationship with a parent like a cancer. One of the problems for many parents is that they tend to split the world and themselves into good and bad and do not see life in an integrated way. A fundamental part of their therapy involves understanding that people are never all good and loving, or bad and hurtful, including their own children and themselves. This learning starts in the experience of the relationship with the social worker or other therapist who demonstrates caring for the family and their problems whilst also taking control of that part of their life which has run out of control. We do not help them to integrate their lives if we collude with their split by the way we organise our involvement.

Far from being an impediment, the use of authority is thus an essential therapeutic tool. At a time when parents often feel they have lost control over their behaviour and emotions, it is a source of reassurance and hope to find that it can be regained. Of course the explicit use of authority will usually generate anger and resentment at first. Coping with this is very stressful for the worker, requiring persistence in the face of rejection and needing considerable professional support. Some tend to deal with this by minimising their own part in the decision and blaming others:

> I know that really you are very caring parents but everybody is worried about child abuse cases these days and THEY tend to over-react, but I shall make sure that it will be all right in the end.

We argue above that parents need and have a right to honesty, and that a less than honest approach, far from helping, is positively harmful. However we accept that there are a very few cases where hostility is so overwhelming and persistent that a change of worker is indicated; this only happened three times in the first 57 cases opened by the NSPCC Manchester Special Unit.

The use of authority in some form is inevitable once there has been violence against a child. The consequences will usually be initial anger and resentment from parents, but working through these tensions offers a therapeutic opportunity to grow towards greater self-control and maturity, provided there is a compassionate and confident therapist. The initial reaction may seem to impede progress for a while, but will rarely present a permanent obstacle to constructive co-operation.

Crisis reactions

There is now a substantial literature on the nature of 'crisis' and ways of helping people cope when faced by such upset. A crisis can be defined as any event which upsets a previous balanced state (a force which disrupts equilibrium). Most people cope adequately with the events and problems of life, but in certain situations some find they do not have the resources to cope. These may be such common life-changing events as death (sudden or not), birth, leaving home, retirement, unexpected events such as natural disasters, chronic ill-health, accidents, or any other event which disrupts the balance of individual personality or relationship patterns. At such times people are very vulnerable to change. Their usual coping and behaviour patterns prove inadequate, they feel distressed and they are searching for something new to restore their equilibrium. Many people resolve the crisis on their own or with the help of relatives and friends, but some will need professional support. There is no guarantee that the solution will be a positive adaptation which will help them in future.

The child abuse investigation will be a time of crisis for family and workers, offering a valuable opportunity for reflection and possible change for the better or worse. However, for the family the crisis may be the intervention of outside agencies, since violence is a part of their normality or equilibrium, whilst the workers see the violence itself as the crisis. In such situations the family may resent the intervention, question its legitimacy and remain out of reach of change. In other cases the worker and family will share an understanding of the reason for the crisis and there will be an openness to change.

For the child, the crisis may well be the outside intervention, rather than the parental assault. Parents and home are known and predictable, if only in their unpredictability, whereas hospitals, medical examinations, doctors and other workers are unknown and appear frightening and threatening. How the child is helped through the crisis will have a powerful influence on how he responds to subsequent offers of help.

Worker feelings and reactions

Most workers will also experience a sense of crisis following discovery of a suspected new child abuse case. We have already acknowledged the stress for workers and suggested that there are often problems in relationships between professional colleagues, which is hardly surprising given the tense atmosphere associated with child abuse. The family is usually in a highly charged emotional state and those working with them are drawn into this to a greater or lesser extent. The pull is especially powerful if the worker knew the family before the incident. Workers and their supervisors need to be aware of both individual reactions and also the dynamics and inevitable strains of multidisciplinary working. We consider group dynamics in Chapter 12 but here focus on individual feelings.

Individual reactions will depend on personality, experience, skill and knowledge of the problem, but violence to children can unleash primitive feelings in everybody, however knowledgeable or experienced, sometimes taking the worker by surprise. The following reactions are common:

Denial that anything is wrong, often presented as: 'all children in that area have those sort of bruises – if we react to this case we shall have all the children on the estate in care'; or 'I have known these people for years and they are really very nice – I don't know what happened but I'm sure they couldn't do anything like that'. Such comments are often valid but do not always fit the facts.

Anger with the family for having let the worker down: 'I gave them all that time and helped them in so many ways yet still they go and do this – well that's all they're getting from me.'

Guilt that more should have been done to help before the incident, or that the worker should have been more skilful or perceptive: 'It's all my fault.'

Fear of personal and professional criticism for not preventing what has happened, and of possible damage to future career prospects (often associated with guilt). Also of getting caught up in procedures over which nobody has control and which may swamp family and worker.

Despair that everything looks so bleak and nothing can be done to help; occasionally justified, but can defeat honest appraisal of alternatives.

Horror that such serious and possibly permanent injuries can be inflicted on a child, inhibiting consideration of what to do next.

Jealousy that somebody else is now involved with a family known for a long time, perhaps associated with *resentment* that somebody else is doing the investigation and formulating an assessment (see Chapter 12).

Omnipotence is perhaps associated with *jealousy*, *resentment* and even *fear*. A belief that 'I know best', 'I have the best relationship with the family', or 'I alone know how to deal with this – leave it all to me'. In practice a multidisciplinary approach is essential, even if one person has most contact with the family.

These are usually initial reactions, although they may persist for days, even weeks. Some cope with the initial crisis by plunging into a whirlwind of unfocused activity, rushing around shouting 'Don't panic!' but doing just that, and not stopping to think what they are doing and why, nor to assess its impact on others (the 'Corporal Jones Syndrome – *Dad's Army*'). Investigatory procedures should control the worst excesses of individual reactions.

As he gets to know the family, the worker becomes increasingly affected by their emotional turmoil. He inevitably becomes absorbed into their conflicts and confusion and may find himself sympathising with a particular member, for example the child, but more usually with one or both parents. The worker needs to be affected by the family emotions, it is a necessary part of the getting to know and assessment process, but it inevitably clouds perception and distorts objectivity, hence the need for consultation/supervision.

The combined anxieties of family and workers often create a strong desire to give and receive reassurance that all is not as bad as it seems, something the parents desperately want to hear but will not believe until the crisis is resolved. For example a doctor may tell a case conference that the injuries must have been inflicted by an adult using considerable force, but feel unable to confront the parents with this, preferring to soften the truth.

This is perhaps more often seen in neglect cases where a doctor may tell colleagues that the child must have been deprived of food and warmth for several days, but when talking with parents this comes over as 'He needs an extra jumper and an orange each day'. This problem often stems from a desire to talk in language the parents understand, and the parents may have a psychological need to minimise the seriousness, but the result is that parents leave feeling that the doctor does not consider the problem all that serious and wondering why everybody else is making such a fuss. The same reticence to face the truth with parents is found in other professions, for example the social worker who is reluctant to mention the possibility of court proceedings.

The need to show compassion and reduce anxiety is human and understandable but false reassurance creates precisely the opposite effect and is a profound disservice to the parents. They will come to trust nobody to tell the truth, and hope of therapeutic progress will be seriously undermined. There must be an honest willingness to face reality alongside the parents, first in an attempt to understand and then to try to help.

PART II

The Initial Crisis

8

The First Interview

Introduction

The following chapters suggest what should happen when a case of suspected child abuse comes to light. The main focus is on cases of children injured by parents or caregivers but much will be relevant to gross neglect and possibly emotional and sexual abuse. For a case to come to professional attention somebody has to voice concern and take the initiative by drawing attention to it; some form of investigation is then inevitable. This may confirm grounds for concern, indicate that it is unfounded or in some cases leave the matter unresolved. Once there is suspicion of inflicted injury we strongly recommend that there be a thorough investigation. This is best for all involved, including the family: better to grasp the nettle early than delay to the detriment of the family and possibly further and more serious injury.

In practice many seem reluctant to pursue their concern and activate the investigatory procedures – perhaps an understandable reaction since we have already seen that our society is suspicious of outside intervention in family affairs. However the loss of control which leads to an assault on a child is invariably symptomatic of an habitual family response to problems and stress which will not change over-night. The response of the professional will depend on his ability to recognise and acknowledge the significance of what he sees and, just as important, to master his feelings, which very often involve a strong urge to deny that there is anything wrong. The family is usually aware of the problem however, and are often seeking a way out. If the distress signal is ignored, the child will face increasing danger. A swift, con-structive response is the only chance for a lasting resolution of the crisis.

Before turning to the contribution of health visitor, doc-tor, police and social worker, we consider certain basic prin-ciples of interviewing. We have already seen that powerful emotional reactions may develop, so very careful attention must be paid to interviewing manner. The worker should be as aware of himself and his own behaviour as of his patient/client and control his own emotions so that they do not distort the discussion.

Keep calm and alert

This is very difficult if there is a feeling of crisis and a need to gather information quickly. The initial interview sets the pace for what follows, so must not be approached in a cavalier fashion. Parents usually resist being hurried or bullied and develop defences which may become entrenched, preventing subsequent discussion of the incident. It is best to use a quiet place for the interview, where discussion will be private and uninterrupted. Talking slowly and quietly, sitting in a re-laxed posture, and breathing deeply impose calm and control on the interviewer and should convey a positive and con-cerned attitude to the parents. All that is said and done is significant and should be noted.

Do not confront

Room layout can be significant. It is best not to sit immedi-ately opposite the parents, nor right beside them unless they are distressed and physical comfort seems appropriate, such as an arm round the shoulder. The least threatening position is at a 45 degree angle. Eye contact is then possible but the parent can also stare into space and put the physical presence of the interviewer to one side if he wishes. Having to maintain constant eye contact can be a great strain for worker and parent.

Most parents are too distressed or frightened to react angrily, but this can happen and a very few react with violence. If met with aggression where there is real fear of violence, it is best to 'retreat and seek reinforcements'. This is really very rare indeed; most parents realise that they will not help themselves by reacting violently. The best response when faced with anger and verbal aggression is to remain calm, sit down, generally avoid making a threat and not to respond similarly. Avoid a shouting match and repeat quietly the reason for your presence.

Maintain a neutral attitude

Therapy begins as soon as the parent and worker meet and start talking; the worker is immediately giving clues about himself and his approach. However he must not start commenting, or giving advice or opinions until he knows what is going on. The initial stance should therefore be empathetic, neutral and non-judgemental, even when met with hostility. It is only later, if the injuries and explanations remain inconsistent, that the parents should be confronted by this. At first their explanations and comments should be accepted without comment.

Listen more than talk

Patient listening and gentle prompting should characterise the early interviews. It is best to use open-ended responses which stimulate a long reply, such as 'Tell me what has been happening', 'Tell me more about that', or 'What happened next?', and then sit back, listen and watch. This allows the parent to decide what is significant to him. If the flow dries up, repeating the last words can help, such as 'Then you couldn't stand any more?', or something sympathetic but non-collusive such as 'Yes, that must have been awful, but then what happened?'. Closed questions such as 'Do you have trouble getting him to sleep?' or leading statements such as 'You must have trouble with his meals', are best avoided because they distort but may be needed at the end of the interview to fill gaps and clarify detail.

Avoid selective information gathering

As much information as possible should be gathered as quickly as possible before contact with the family begins to influence the worker's understanding and perception. Information must be organised in a structured way to ensure things are not lost or overlooked and to avoid the dangers of seeking information to confirm earlier impressions. The formulation of an assessment should be left until as much information as possible is available. This is sometimes impossible because urgent decisions have to be taken, but these are rarely irreversible and thus leave options open.

Interviewing children

It is almost inevitable that somebody other than the parents will talk with the child about what has happened, even if only casually whilst driving in the car or during the medical examination. It may also be necessary to ask the child about the origin of the injuries as part of the formal process of investigation, although what is said must be treated with caution, whatever the age of the child or young person. Many workers are reluctant to question children and young people, thinking it unreasonable and unethical, not least because the child cannot be expected to understand the consequences of what he is doing. There may also be a reluctance to provoke a potential conflict of evidence between the child and his parent, with unforeseeable consequences for future family relationships.

Very great care is needed in the interpretation of remarks made by children under five years old. Young children are very suggestible and it is possible to lead them to say what the questioner wants to hear, which may bear little resemblance to the truth. The words used may also carry a different meaning for the child, for example 'My Daddy hits me' may mean that the father inflicted the injuries, but is equally likely to refer to normal chastisement which did not cause the injury in question. Fear and guilt are frequently present in the child and may inhibit him from talking at all or may lead to a total denial that the parent was involved; the child's previous experience may have led him to believe that he was beaten because he was 'bad' and thus that the injuries are his own fault. Questions about family life are often more revealing than direct questions about the injury, for example 'Who's the favourite in your house?' or 'You are a pretty girl – what does your Dad/Mum think?' In general, little weight should be given to the comments of younger children. Of more significance is their overall physical condition and behaviour, especially when with the parent.

What is said becomes more reliable the older the child or adolescent is, although there have been a number of cases of young people in conflict with their parents making false allegations as part of their struggle against them. Most children are confused and frightened when the incident is discovered. They wish to protect the parent and avoid more trouble and some will blame themselves for what has happened. It is usually best to see the child or young person with somebody he knows and trusts, often a schoolteacher, who can help him to talk honestly and interpret what is said in the light of previous knowledge of him.

It is important to remember that the child and parent may continue to live together after the investigation and thus have to come to terms with what has happened within the context of their continuing intimate relationship. Many parents and children are left feeling confused and uncertain, especially about the extent of legitimate parental authority over their children. Some children exploit this 'vacuum', for example by threatening to report the parent if there is an argument. This problem may be particularly evident where the abusive incident involved parental over-reaction to continuing mis-behaviour by the child. In such circumstances it is important that the total situation is discussed with the child, which may include acknowledging his contribution to the parent's reaction. The worker must walk the fine line between criticising parental behaviour and destroying parental authority.

When deciding what to do after an incident of child abuse, it is essential that somebody, usually the social worker, spends time with the child in an attempt to understand his perspective of his situation and seek his views about what should happen next. What is said about the incident itself may be of limited value and carries little, if any, legal signifi-cance; in the vast majority of cases it would be unthinkable to call the child as a witness against the parent. Nevertheless the child's reaction, whatever it may be, will be significant in the formulation of the family assessment and in planning what to do next. The child has a right to be consulted about his future.

9

Health Visitors, Doctors
and Police

Health visitors

Health visitors have general concern for the health and development of all children and have a statutory duty to visit every home within days of the birth. They also run well-baby clinics and undertake routine home visiting so are well placed to identify families where there are parenting problems and are very likely to be the first to suspect child abuse in a young child. In most areas, health visitors are advised to refer such children to the social services department for full investigation, but before doing so they need to establish that there are reasonable grounds for concern. This may involve their going with the child and parent to see a doctor. Much of what follows will therefore be relevant to health visitors, including the chapter on the social work investigation. It is important that local procedures are followed, however, and that referral is made to an investigating agency as soon as reasonable concern has been established.

Medical assessment

In all cases of suspected child abuse a medical assessment is essential regardless of the severity of the injuries. Medical treatment is obviously the first priority in cases of serious injury, something parents usually seek themselves. Assessment is equally important in cases of minor injury, however, because:

(i)   there may be evidence of previously undiagnosed injuries;

(ii) there may be more serious injuries which require specialist diagnosis; and

(iii) the outcome of the case is unpredictable and a qualified medical opinion may later be necessary for legal purposes.

It is usually best to take the child to an experienced paediatrician who has access to X-ray facilities and hospital beds, but local practice varies and any doctor can give a professionally and legally acceptable opinion. In all cases the doctor should be advised of the suspicion before seeing the child and that a written diagnosis may be required for use in legal proceedings. Some doctors prefer not to become involved in such matters and there will be serious difficulties later if the examining doctor was not informed in advance and is not prepared to divulge his honest opinion to the case conference, and court if required.

During the initial examination the doctor should usually accept parental explanation of the injuries and if possible avoid a confrontation. In all cases of serious, multiple or repeated injury the child should be admitted to hospital for treatment and to allow further investigation whilst safe from further risk. (Investigation inevitably increases tension and anxiety for the parents and could contribute to a further assault if the child were at home.) If the parents refuse consent, a Place of Safety Order should be sought, usually by the social worker (see Chapter 13). In cases of minor injury, admission to hospital or removal from home by other means should be considered but may not be indicated.

The doctor has the ultimate responsibility for informing the parents of the medical diagnosis when this has been clarified. The explanation should be detailed, including X-rays, for example, and honest. It must be phrased in language the parents understand and will probably need repeating several times. Only the doctor can give an authoritative opinion, and how this is presented to the parents is crucial to the effectiveness of subsequent work with the family. Doctors often find this discussion painful for themselves as well as the parents and so tend to minimise the seriousness of the diagnosis. This may help the doctor but is of no help to the parents. It is preferable for the social worker to be present during this discussion so that he is fully aware of what the parents have been told and can build on this.

Police investigation

The police have three main objectives:

the prevention and detection of crime,
the protection of life and property,
the apprehension of offenders.

The approach to these and the balance drawn between them varies from force to force, and it is not for us to outline in detail the way an officer should fulfil his responsibilities. However it is clear that police concern can be broader than the bare facts of a particular offence and the prosecution of the offender. A judgement is possible about what action is best to balance these objectives in a given case.

Child abuse is criminal behaviour and thus police investigation is usually inevitable, but it is not possible to generalise about prosecuting parents. Some cases are so grave and the treatment of the child so shocking that it would be difficult to argue against prosecution of the parents. Children have the right to protection under the law and the police and social workers a duty to ensure that they are protected. Nevertheless few would argue that all parents who abuse their children ought to be prosecuted. Individual judgements have to be made in each case, based on a number of factors including seriousness of the offence, therapeutic potential, parental attitude, needs of the child, and consistency with local practice.

There is no legal obligation to report child abuse cases to the police (except in the case of death) but there is a moral responsibility for doctors and social workers to do so. Any reluctance is usually based on the opinion that either police investigation or prosecution may not be in the best interests of the child. In some cases it is never possible to establish exactly what happened and who abused the child. An investigation which does not lead to a formal outcome (prosecution or caution) may jeopardise care proceedings and also result in parents' refusing intervention. If under police questioning parents deny harming their child it is often difficult for them to admit to others that they need help. Notification can also destroy the relationship between the parents and the person they assume told the police. Many police officers, particularly the less experienced, find child abuse emotionally disturbing and react with harshness and insensitivity which damages prospects for future therapeutic work.

On the other hand, police investigation can produce vital information, and skilled interrogation sometimes results in an admission of considerable value for subsequent work with the family. We also know cases where the reluctance of social workers to ask direct questions has reinforced parental guilt, leaving them desperate to talk with someone who can accept what they have done. In one such case, sympathetic questioning by a police officer produced a full account of what had happened. When the mother was asked why she had not told the social worker she replied 'I have been trying to tell him, but he kept saying "Don't worry, it's not your fault he fell down the stairs" – he believed my lies and then I couldn't tell him the truth'.

In recent years there has been a welcome improvement in relationships between police and other professional groups. An officer usually attends case conferences and police decisions about whether or not to pursue investigations and prosecute are made in the light of the opinions of those at the case conference. We have been impressed by the willingness of the police to co-operate in a multidisciplinary team and exercise discretion.

Recent experience has shown the value of constructive working relationships between police and others. There are mutual responsibilities and if the police take a narrow view of their role, simply pursuing the offending parent to court without consideration of the wider issues, then they will place co-operation in jeopardy. Fortunately that attitude is now rarely expressed and the present commonsense approach to decision making works reasonably well.

Summary

A full medical examination is always recommended in a suspected child abuse case and police involvement is usually inevitable. Both need sensitive handling. Both doctors and police may be unfamiliar with a process of diagnosis and decision-making involving each other and people from other agencies, but co-operation is essential in the interest of the future safety and welfare of the child.

10

The Social Worker

The social worker has a central role in any child abuse investigation by virtue of his statutory duties, professional responsibilities and commitment to future work with the family after the initial phase is over. His prime concern must be the safety and future welfare of the child, but this cannot be disentangled from concern for the parents and brothers and sisters. The competence with which this initial phase of contact with the family is handled crucially affects subsequent social work with them, so must be thorough, considered and compassionate.

Request for action

A social worker from the local authority or NSPCC is usually asked to investigate suspicions of child abuse by referral from parents, relatives, the public or other agencies. The referral is best made as soon as possible after the initial concern is expressed. This often precedes medical diagnosis and so the social worker should take the child to a doctor (see Chapter 9), usually accompanied by one or both parents. In an increasing number of cases parents themselves request help – an encouraging trend. The Darryn Clarke enquiry highlighted the importance of responding urgently to all allegations, even if at first they seem malicious or unjustified.

It is better to interview the informant before seeing the child if possible, although this will depend on the nature and urgency of the referral. It is worth taking a written statement which clarifies the nature of the allegation for all concerned and also discourages frivolous complaints. This applies to professional as well as to public referrals; it is not unknown for a professional to allege grave concern but then deny the full force of his orginal allegation at a later stage. The House of Lords has ruled that the identity of an informant in a child abuse case may be confidential, but a witness statement can be used in court and informants should be advised of their responsibility to the child and as a citizen to present relevant evidence. Should there be any discrepancy between the allegation and the findings of the investigation, the informant should be interviewed to ensure that no matter has been inadvertently overlooked.

In all cases the child should be examined and the parents interviewed as a matter of urgency, and at the most within twenty-four hours of the referral. It is perhaps here that pressure feels most intense. If child abuse is suspected, somebody must decide whether it is safe for the child to remain at home and what is in the best interests of the child and family, usually on the basis of only limited information about family background and attitudes.

Separation may exacerbate the root cause of the problem or generate feelings which will inhibit later work with the family towards resolution of the crisis, but the return home may precipitate further abuse. The decision is usually made by a social worker in consultation with others in the network who know the family and have some responsibility for the child. The siblings must also be considered. If there is any doubt about family attitudes and behaviour, it is best to seek removal to hospital or into care pending further investigations, and this may include siblings. It is always possible to allow a return home immediately it seems safe.

Long, in-depth interviews are a tempting hazard at this

stage because there is a lot to discuss and much anxiety. These can be exhausting and too demanding for all involved and thus counter-productive. Frequent, brief interviews are usually better. In many cases the parents will need almost daily contact during the first week or two, because:

(i) there will be a lot happening and the parents will have questions to ask and need to be kept fully informed;

(ii) anxieties and stresses felt by the parents need to be voiced, and infrequent contact simply increases stress and may precipitate impulsive behaviour (such as attempting premature discharge of the child from hospital);

(iii) comprehensive information must be gathered in a short time on which to base an assessment and plan future work with the family; and

(iv) priority must be given to building a relationship with the parents and this can only grow from contact and practical demonstrations of concern.

We now outline the social work approach we use. The initial process may involve several interviews, although it is best to cover the explanation and history taking in the first two or three.

Explaining what is happening

We first explain to the parents who we are, what powers we have, what is happening and why we wish to talk with them. This will probably need careful and repeated explanation as anxiety and confusion often inhibit understanding at this stage. The possible involvement of the police must be made explicit. The social worker may be the first to discuss the concern with the parents or he may follow questioning by doctor, police, health visitor or teacher. Whatever has happened, the parents will feel anxious and confused and these feelings may be masked with hostility and aggression, or passivity and withdrawal. It is important that our approach be sympathetic, even when faced with hostility, but also direct and honest, as we have stressed already. Having clarified these matters we usually find that it is possible to put them to one side and talk openly with the parents about the problems they face.

Showing concern for the parents

These opening remarks usually generate expressions of anxiety and often protestations of innocence. After a short time we acknowledge their distress or anger, and express concern for their immediate problems, saying that we shall return to talk about the child later. It is perhaps more important to express concern for the parent than the child at this stage, so we firmly shift the focus of the interview into a discussion of what has been happening *since* the event which led to their child being referred for professional help. This allows all sorts of anxieties and fears to be voiced and discussed.

The social worker should not dominate the interview during this phase but listen and watch. He should go out of his way to make practical offers of help and explicit caring gestures such as providing a cup of tea or food, a lift home from hospital or financial assistance. These will provide important clues to the parent about the kind of person he is; again actions speak louder than words. We find that in most cases this approach reduces parental anxiety to manageable proportions.

Parents are often puzzled by our approach. One mother said: 'You have been here nearly an hour and I'm still waiting for you to lay the law down like all the other social workers, but you haven't done so and I can't understand why.' This mother's confusion at not having her negative expectations met provided a very good opportunity to explain our general approach and led to considerable feelings of reassurance, enabling her to move on to sharing the task of resolving her problems.

Finding out what happened

Having established some mutual understanding and demonstrated our caring concern, the foundation is laid for a discussion of the circumstances of the injury. If the police are to be involved, they usually prefer to be first to discuss these matters with the parents. Again, it is necessary to follow local practice, but the needs of the parents and child are urgent. History-taking is fundamental to social work intervention and must not be delayed.

We explain to the parents that in order to discover how best they can be helped it is necessary to know what has happened. If they are being asked to repeat what they have already said to others, it is important to acknowledge the pain which this may cause, but also to explain that the social worker must make enquiries to decide what to do. Some social workers seem reluctant to expose parents to such questions, especially when the police have already interviewed them, but we stress that it is unavoidable. Discussion of the incident forms the basis of future understanding and therapeutic progress and if avoided at this stage, the emotional significance for parent and worker may be difficult to recapture.

This aspect of the interview is necessarily formal and detailed. The parents are told that we are taking notes and shall be making a report for agency records which may be used in legal proceedings. Parents usually understand the necessity for this and again honesty prevents later misunderstandings and suspicion.

The parents are then invited to explain in their own words what happened. It is best not to interrupt with questions, except when extreme reticence makes some facilitating question necessary: 'What happened next?' is usually sufficient. We like to talk with each parent separately at some stage in case there is something which cannot be said when together; this is not infrequent and cannot be predicted, so individual interviews are essential. They also help to develop some understanding of their different perspectives and ensure that both are given equal consideration. We also spend time with the child, but how we mention the incident will depend on his age and outlook.

It is usually best to go to the alleged scene of the incident to test the consistency of the explanation. If a child is said to have fallen from a settee or high chair, or turned on a scalding tap, we measure heights and distances, ease of turning the tap, quality of floor covering. If neighbours or relatives have witnessed events, they should be seen and statements taken if appropriate, as with other informants (see above); the parents should be told of this unless confidentiality has been requested by the informant.

We are seeking answers to the following questions: What was done? By whom? To whom? How? When? Where? Why? Who saw it happen? A shared understanding of the answers is fundamental to future social work with the family. However there are many cases where these questions are never fully resolved. In general, the more time has elapsed the less likely it is that the parent will tell all. Some genuinely fail to remember the detail of what happened; the memory is so painful that it is suppressed. Others are too frightened to talk; whilst a few choose to lie or deceive. Certainty is helpful, but it is not essential to therapeutic progress. What is important is that there is a shared recognition that the parents have in some way ill-treated their child and there is a problem which needs resolution. We discuss the implications of parental attitude, and in particular denial of the obvious facts, in Chapter 11.

Some will protest that this approach sounds too authoritarian, as if we are policemen. We have no doubt that this is a necessary and therapeutic approach to the parents' problems at this stage in our work with them. Social workers have statutory duties including a legal duty to investigate allegations of maltreatment and to initiate juvenile court action if children need protection. In this limited respect social workers have very similar functions to the police and should be just as meticulous in their enquiries and recording as any police officer. The child, the parents and the public have a right to expect that social workers will be thorough and competent. Social workers differ from policemen by virtue of their continuing responsibility for and commitment to providing help to the family after the initial investigatory phase is completed, and this must affect the tone of our questions.

Detailed discussion of the circumstances of the injury

inevitably poses the question of whether the account is consistent with the medical findings. More parents now seem able to acknowledge loss of control and problems with children and this makes a better context for seeking resolution of the crisis, but in a significant minority, especially most cases involving serious injury, the explanation will be incompatible with the injuries. It is necessary to be frank with parents about this and seek clarification. It may be necessary to say that the explanation has left doubts which must be explored with the doctor before we can say what conclusion has been reached. There may be several discussions with the parents, perhaps jointly with the doctor, attempting to establish a shared understanding of what happened, but there is little point in the social worker becoming obsessed with this issue above all else, as we argue in Chapter 11.

Finding out about the family

Having made progress in our 'forensic' enquiries, we acknowledge with the parents that something serious has happened (it is important not to minimise the significance of the incident), and that we now have to look to the future and would like to explore ways of helping with their problems. It may still be unclear what action will follow so it is important not to hold out false reassurance (see Chapter 7). It is helpful to stress the need to balance the interests of the child with those of the parents.

We have already seen that an act of child abuse is a common symptom of many different family problems. We therefore need to know whether the incident was an atypical reaction under unique circumstances or part of a chronic pattern of behaviour. Recent events have to be placed in the context of the family history. Most people like talking about themselves, so it is usually not difficult to go through the family history of each family member in turn so that by the end a complete picture emerges, if possible confirmed from other sources. Parents often find it easier to start with their early life and then, as the story unfolds, they relax and are able to be forthcoming about recent events and problems. The following information should be sought:

Personal history of each parent:

> *Own parents* – age, health, occupation, current relationships and memory of them as parents;
> *infancy* – milestones, medical problems, separations;
> *childhood/adolescence* – education, significant events, behaviour, contact with social agencies/care/police, relationships with peers;
> *adulthood* – age of leaving school/home, work experiences;
> *current home circumstances and finances;*
> *marriage* (present and previous) – age, duration, number, courtship, current relationships, problems if any;
> *medical history* – physical/psychiatric, in family or self, treatment, current problems;
> *significant relatives;*
> *criminal record.*

History of each child:

> planned/wanted, pregnancy and birth experiences, separations, milestones, medical problems, education, referral to social agencies, behaviour, relationship with peers, perception by parent.

Personality of each parent:

> social contacts, leisure activities, use of alcohol, tobacco or other drugs, religious/political beliefs, usual mood and recent changes (subjective description and observation), appearance, movement, social skills competence, obsessional traits, psychiatric symptoms.

This information is usually gathered over several interviews with family members together and individually. It is also helpful to talk with other professionals who know the family. We tell parents of our intention to have these consultations which are essential if we are to compile a thorough family profile which is the basis for assessment of future risk, if any, to the child.

II

Evaluating the Data

Having investigated the case, decisions must be made about the future of the child and family, preferably agreed with them, but sometimes imposed on them. Some decisions have to be taken hurriedly, based on the informed intuition of the worker with only a minimum of background information and consultation, such as whether to seek a Place of Safety Order, admit the child to hospital, or hold the suspect in custody overnight. The legal process allows slightly more time before longer-term decisions have to be taken and therapeutic decisions evolve even more slowly.

We have already seen that child abuse is not a unitary phenomenon with a single cause and unique characteristics, but rather a common symptom of many different family problems, with no empirically validated basis for decision making. Research and experience are informative, but our lack of knowledge warns against dogmatism and stereotyping family problems and needs. Furthermore, the available information in most cases is usually incomplete and unverified, derived from discussions with family members under great stress who are inevitably suspicious of the motives and intentions of the enquirer. We know from experience that initial impressions and assessments often change radically, for better or worse, as we get to know a family; increasing trust often brings alarming revelations. The risks in making wrong judgements are obvious, yet decisions have to be made.

General principles of assessment

Actions speak louder than words
It is easy to concentrate on what people are saying but very often behaviour is more revealing. Any discrepancy between words and actions is always very significant, although hurried interpretation is dangerous as there may be several possible explanations. For example, a mother may express great affection for her baby but leave him alone in a different room all the time. Her words and actions are not consistent, but there are many possible explanations, such as:

(i)   she may lack knowledge and experience of the needs of children;

(ii)   she may be clinically depressed;

(iii)   she may have only limited intelligence;

(iv)   she may have feelings of rejection but cannot bring herself to express them;

(v)   she may be consciously trying to mislead about her true feelings;

(vi)   she may be under pressure from others, possibly the father, to ignore the baby.

It is always essential to pose the question: does the behaviour confirm what is being said?

The observer affects the observation
Parents especially will be very conscious of being watched and assessed, realising that much is at stake. The observer can never assume that he is watching a 'normal situation' and he must make allowances for his presence. Demonstrating an understanding of the problems and frustrations of child rearing, together with the general approach described in earlier chapters, should minimise this tension but it will always

remain. Some workers seem so anxious to make allowances
for this effect that they interpret all abnormal parenting as a
consequence of their own presence – a dangerous assumption. Others feel uneasy in their role of observer and cope
with this by false reassurance. The worker must never allow
himself to become a family friend but must remember his
duty to observe, assess and reach conclusions.

The observed are assessing the observer
We have already said that the therapeutic relationship begins
as soon as the worker becomes involved. The parents will be
desperately searching for clues about the worker's attitudes,
personality and whether he will be able to help. Everything
that the worker says and does is therefore laying the foundation for future work with the family.

**Fact, opinion, comment, rumour and interpretation must
be distinguished**
The worker will be told some things which are clearly factual,
although memory is unreliable and even agency records can
be inaccurate or incomplete, so it is difficult to verify all facts
beyond doubt. Some comments will be interpretation of facts
or events, either as general remarks or professional opinion,
the factual basis for which must be independently verified.
Innuendo, gossip and rumour are often revealing but notoriously unreliable. This sounds obvious but in everyday talk
professional and lay people do not always make the distinction – for example, 'The child was unkempt' is a statement of
opinion not fact, unless supported by observational detail.

Cultural and religious factors affect the assessment
In a multi-racial society, cultural background and religious
beliefs which control or influence behaviour might affect the
final assessment. For example, ritual scarring of an African
child or ritual circumcision take on a different and less pathological significance than similar behaviour without external
sanction. Likewise, the expectations of baby care in some
Asian communities, which keeps them indoors and deprives

them of sunlight thus exposing them to risk of rickets, is a source of concern. The behaviour may be more understandable in the cultural context, but this does not indicate whether the behaviour should be treated as child abuse in this society or whether a different standard should be adopted. In general it seems unacceptable to operate a double standard, but the cultural assessment will influence the pattern of intervention.

The structure of the analysis

Good decisions require:

 (i) a predetermined framework to ensure that nothing is overlooked and all cases are treated consistently;
 (ii) the fullest possible information;
 (iii) worker awareness of feelings and reactions which may cloud objectivity.

Some years ago Kempe suggested that a child abuse assessment should focus on five factors, to which we have added a sixth:

parents' personality
marriage
child's vulnerability
social circumstances
precipitating incident
resources available.

We have found this framework helpful and the rest of this chapter is structured around it.

It is extremely important to remember that a child abuse assessment is not a simple matter of completing a checklist and adding up the total of positives and negatives. We list below a number of relevant factors, but the significance of each has to be weighed in every case; it may be that a long list of negatives is of less importance than one over-riding positive.

Parental history and personality

Facts

A detailed individual and family (longitudinal) history is essential. It is worrying how often this is not prepared because of lack of confidence in seeking information, or lack of awareness of what to look for and its significance. In a case of child abuse the history must be as detailed as possible and the social worker has the prime responsibility for its compilation, drawing on his own investigations, consultations and discussion at the case conference. The conference must identify gaps which need to be explored.

We itemised the areas of enquiry in Chapter 10, and in Chapter 6 outlined a suggested typology of child abuse which included analysis of the relevance of events in parental backgrounds. In summary, features which may be worrying include:

> violent childhood (experienced or observed),
> inadequate/inconsistent parenting,
> significant periods in hospital/substitute care,
> persistent truancy/under-achievement at school,
> lack of close adolescent friendships,
> left home when very young,
> poor relationships with extended family,
> poor employment record (frequent moves/unemployed),
> no close friendships,
> brief cohabitations/marital relationships,
> disabling physical/mental illness (not necessarily severe),
> psychiatric delusions, especially if family members involved,
> histrionic personality disorder,
> psychopathic personality disorder,
> record of criminal violence, especially if involving family,
> marked mood swings including violent tempers,
> persistent migraines,
> mental subnormality,
> obsessional personality traits,
> alcohol or drug abuse.

The opposite or absence of these factors can be seen as hopeful.

Attitudes

Assessment of the parents' attitude to life and memory of childhood is important, seen in both words and behaviour. Recollection of objectively unusual or disturbing childhood events as normal is worrying, for example unthinking acceptance of the appropriateness of regular, violent beatings as punishments for minor misdemeanours, or routine acceptance of violence as an inevitable or acceptable part of life. Memory of an unhappy childhood may be significant. Complete or significant lack of childhood memories often indicates a disjointed and unhappy experience. Angry feelings about their own parents, especially if apparently excessive, are worrying.

Perhaps the most significant overall feature is self-esteem. Lack of self-confidence, feelings of worthlessness and a belief that nobody could possibly see them in a positive way are all worrying. Assessment of self-esteem is perhaps best made by reference to the parents' response to the worker. A bland, fatalistic, compliant response suggests inner unhappiness and hints at an inability to seize control of their own life and destiny, which indicates a poor prognosis for positive change. If available, the use of psychological tests can be of considerable value in making these assessments.

Relationships

The worker should create opportunities to observe the nature of the parents' relationships with others, especially other family members. It is hopeful if there are some relatively long standing, stable relationships with an ability to sustain them despite disagreements. The worker is best able to assess the nature of his own relationship with the parents and this is an important aspect of the assessment. The experienced worker will know that people have different effects on him, influenced by both the worker's personality and the other person.

If there are problems in the parent/worker relationship it is important to decide if this is due to the worker's personality or the circumstances of the family; if the former, more positive relationships with other workers will be observed, although this difference may also be due to differences in the role of the other workers. If it seems that the problem lies with the worker, then if possible there should be a change. It is essential to have supervisory guidance in making that judgement.

Parental relationships with authority figures should be assessed to see if there are established ways of coping with police intervention, rent or power bill demands or other authority figures. Habitual use of aggressive behaviour is worrying. Regular forgetfulness suggests an indecisive, fatalistic approach with little self-confidence on which to base a therapeutic approach.

Denial and projection

A central concern must be the extent to which the parents are defended against reality, or, put loosely, living in a 'fantasy world'. If the parent is seriously out of touch with reality, it is evidence of profound problems: the more out of touch the less amenable to change.

People with the most serious or disturbing problems protect themselves from the awful reality of their situation in many ways. A common defence is simply denying what is true ('denial') and blaming others for everything ('projection'). Sometimes such behaviour is conscious and deceitful and this would indicate that it will be virtually impossible to work positively with the parents. Equally worrying, but possibly more hopeful, are those cases where denial is unrecognised, subconscious or unconscious. The most obvious area of denial is about the abusive incident itself, for example refusing to believe that the child has injuries or is neglected, despite patient explanations. This may be accompanied by statements that the doctors are making it all up. We return to this aspect later. The crucial assessment is the extent of denial and whether it intrudes into other aspects of life; and if so, how the parents manage to sustain their 'fantasy world'.

Denial is often accompanied by projection; blaming others for actions, motive or intent which are not supported by facts. Experience suggests that there is often an element of truth behind projection: 'I'm not paranoid, they really are out to get me.' Nevertheless the striking feature of projection is its illogical or irrational quality sustained in the face of contrary evidence.

For some, projection becomes a defence against the fear of rejection. They assume that everybody must think they are as worthless as they feel and so fail to seek help with problems: 'I'm so bad, why would anybody want to help me?' The pain of rejection and ill-treatment by their own parents has taught them never to trust those in authority, they therefore protect themselves from the pain of another rejection by what is, in effect, a pre-emptive strike. The approach is made in an aggressive and assertive way which usually produces the response they fear, confirming them in their attitude. There is a perpetual, vicious circle of implied motives, illicited responses and self-justification. It is essential to explore the extent to which this is an established pattern of responses or simply a reaction to the child abuse investigation. The clue is usually found in the extent to which such feelings are modified from interview to interview. An ability to change and come closer to reality is hopeful, but if denial and projection persist and are clearly well-established, the prognosis for effective therapy and change is very poor.

'Marital' relationship

An NSPCC study of 592 cases of child abuse found only half the children living with both natural parents, which confirms our impression of families with unstable marriages and atypical structures, and a higher than average proportion of one-parent families. This section must therefore embrace not only formal marriages but also *de facto* marriages, cohabitations and consideration of previous relationships.

Stability
The length of the relationship is obviously important. If the parents have successfully coped together with previous life crises, the outlook is more positive than where there have been a succession of cohabitations of short duration suggesting an inability to form lasting, close relationships of a mutually supportive nature. The presence of a step-parent, especially step-father, statistically increases the risk of abuse.

Escape
One or both parents may have entered the relationship as an escape from previous, unhappy relationships, usually with their own parents or former spouse. This is particularly true of those who are too young to cope. The typical pattern here is for the parent to have an unhappy childhood with feelings of being unloved. There is a fantasy that marriage and a baby bring love, including a sense of belonging and being needed which has never before been experienced. Reality turns out to be very different from this romantic dream. The baby is messy and demanding and seems to give no love, whilst the partner typically has similar problems and so is unable to give care and support. The dream turns sour and resentment mounts, with feelings of being imprisoned in a hated relationship. The blame is then projected on to the baby. The more escapism, denial and projection are evident, the greater the risk to the child.

Complementarity
It is important to assess the amount of mutual support and concern in the relationship. Expressions of love and concern seem rare. More common is a pattern of collusion based either on fear of one by the other or a desperate clinging together in the face of a shared sense of guilt and shame. A lack of mutual trust and respect, a pattern of recrimination and disparagement, and an inability to support each other through the crisis suggests risk to the child. Evidence of mutual understanding and an ability to compensate for each other's weaknesses suggests a more positive outlook.

Sex

Where relationships are generally poor it is usual to find inadequate and dissatisfying sexual relationships. Mothers very often express feelings of being used. They fear pregnancy but yet give little attention to contraception. There is an overwhelming sense of powerlessness and futility. Some may drift or be forced into prostitution by men they see as powerful and protective, even if violent to them. The sexual attitudes of the men we find more difficult to describe, possibly revealing a gap in our work but perhaps also suggesting that many fathers are not sexually active, even impotent. The presence of a consistent, caring and mutually satisfying sexual relationship is a positive feature.

Many workers find discussion of sexual matters an area of difficulty, perhaps more for themselves than the parents, and thus the subject is avoided. Important insights can be gained by exploring this area, however, and it will sometimes have a bearing on the assault on the child. The ability of parents to plan their families is of particular significance, as it gives insight into their general approach to life. Sexual relationships are often a major area of concern for parents and we do them a disservice by ignoring it.

Conflict

It is important to assess how the parents handle conflict and disagreement in their relationship. An ability to resolve differences by discussion and without resort to violence is clearly positive. In some cases one parent is under the dominance of the other, living in fear and unable to protect herself or the children. This would suggest that the child would be at risk at home since the weaker parent would be unlikely to seek help if the child were injured by the stronger. In a few cases there is evidence of the father ill-treating the mother who abuses the child. The use of violence within the marriage is always a worrying feature, especially if it extends into other areas of life as well. It suggests an impulsive and uncontrolled or a bullying response to stress.

It is important to note whether conflict subsides whilst the child is away from the home. In some cases parents are unable to cope simultaneously with the demands of marriage and baby, but in the absence of the child there is an impression of marital harmony and stability which quickly disappears when the child returns home. It is essential to evaluate the relationship prior to the incident and not base the assessment purely on what is observed in the absence of the child.

The extent and persistence of 'marital' disharmony has a direct bearing on the parents' capacity to relate positively to their children and for this reason frequently becomes the major focus of work with the family.

Vulnerability of the child and his siblings

The vulnerability of the child will be affected by objective factors (such as neo-natal separation and ill-health) and subjective perceptions held by the parents. The parents' understanding of how children develop and their needs must be explored; genuine ignorance is common and must not be mistaken for deeper problems. Standards of parentcraft as such are important, but more significant are parents' attitudes to and behaviour with the child; parentcraft skills can be taught, attitudes are more difficult to change. The child's own view of the situation will need to be assessed and taken into account.

Birth
Information about birth is highly accessible and of enormous significance whatever the age of the child; recent research by Kempe in the USA suggests that observation of parents at the time of birth provided 76 per cent correct predictions of successful and unsuccessful parenting. Most parents remember the birth event with great clarity and affection but it is striking how often abusing parents have no sense of pride in the achievement of parenthood and in some cases persistent feelings of repugnance and distaste about all that happened. Such unresolved reactions suggest disturbance in the parent–

child relationship. Inability to remember the birth at all is very worrying.

Certain objective factors occur more often than chance in abusing families:

neo-natal illness in mother and/or baby,
difficult pregnancy or birth,
prematurity,
low birth weight,
neo-natal separation (in special care units or for other reasons),
rapid succession of pregnancies.

We stress that these are not individually causative factors but characteristics frequently found and seeming to contribute to parents' problems with their child.

Other factors which suggest concern include:

profound disappointment about the sex of the child;
death of a close relative or friend at a significant point in the pregnancy;
serious consideration of abortion which was refused or rejected;
unwanted pregnancy with no subsequent change of attitude;
other major crises which profoundly affected the parents during pregnancy and with which the child becomes associated.

The role of the father during the pregnancy, the birth itself and afterwards is significant. It is worrying if he offered no help, understanding or support to the mother, and absence from the birth itself is more disturbing now that paternal presence is commonplace. Transient parental feelings of resentment at the demands of the baby are probably very common following the birth, especially in fathers, and they are not significant, but in some cases feelings of jealousy are evident which, if unresolved, indicate concern. It is also worrying if the birth profoundly and persistently disrupts the marriage.

Bonding

This term sums up the process of initial relationship building between parents and baby. It now seems clear that the initial days, even hours, are the optimal time for attachment between child and parents. The closer the contact, the more likely things will go well. Most can recover from disruption of this process, but in a few cases failure of bonding contributes to rejection.

Bonding failure often seems to be associated with separation of mother and baby at or soon after birth because of ill-health or some other problem in mother and/or baby. Most recover from this initial disruption without apparent long-term ill-effects and only a small proportion subsequently become involved in child abuse, but the risk is statistically very much greater that such children will be injured by a parent. The emerging understanding of this problem, which has been very recent, has led to very significant changes in the operation of maternity wards and special care baby units. Most hospitals now have a policy that mother and baby must not be separated unless absolutely necessary, but if it has to happen, the mother is brought to the unit as soon as possible to see her baby, however sore or ill they both are. She is encouraged to touch and feel him and, if possible, to feed him as well. The father is encouraged to visit at any time and brothers, sisters and grandparents are also welcome. Whenever possible, the mother's own breast milk is fed to the baby, so that she is helped to play a central part in ensuring the baby's survival. The mother is given a photograph of her baby to place beside her own bed as a constant reminder.

If the mother is ready for discharge before the baby, she is usually able to choose whether to go home or remain with him. If she goes home and subsequent visiting is infrequent, a home visit will usually be made, often by a social worker, in order to encourage visiting and to provide help to facilitate this if needed.

A bad memory of the pregnancy and especially of the birth, or some external event around that time which affects how the parent sees the child, can also affect bonding. The death of a close relative or similar upset at this time should be noted and its significance for the parents observed.

Discussions of bonding have tended to focus on the mother–child relationship but there is evidence that paternal bonding is also significant, particularly with 'marginal' fathers who are known to have problems. If there is concern about expected poor mothering and a decision to introduce intensive support services in the home, it is very important not to exclude and isolate the father, thereby feeding his jealousy and possibly disrupting bonding. In one case involving subnormal parents, where there was concern about the mother's likely lack of competence, individual ante-natal parentcraft classes were arranged for her, followed by intensive support after birth. A family aide helped with care of the baby before and after discharge, providing a consistent link between hospital and home, and there were regular home visits by social worker, midwife and later health visitor. A part-time place in a day nursery for mother and baby together was arranged. After only a few weeks at home, the baby presented at hospital with several fractures inflicted by the father over a period. Building the relationship between father and baby is just as important as the mother–child bond.

Physical health
The child's health record since birth will help assess the standard of parental care and the extent of health pressures, for example frequent stomach complaints in a baby may indicate poor hygiene. Frequent visits to clinic, doctor or hospital with apparently minor problems may indicate parental anxiety and insecurity and possibly a cry for help which was ignored or misinterpreted. The health record also gives some insight into the demands made by the child on the parents; children with frequent minor health problems ('sickly children') may be slightly more at risk of abuse than healthy or severely disabled children. Hospital admissions, even for genuine illness, and other separations may undermine the parent–child relationship and may contribute to behaviour problems in the child himself. Frequent visits to

casualty may indicate a lack of parental concern and oversight, but this must be interpreted with caution.

Parental perception

There should be numerous moments during early contact when parents and children can be seen together; observing a parent feeding or changing a baby, bathing a child, getting him ready for bed or riding together in the back of a car all give insight into the quality of the relationship and how the parent sees the child. In one case a doctor noted:'Mother held her on the edge of her knee, her infant looking as if it were sat in a chair, maximum distance was achieved between mother and child, even in the most intimate position of contact.' On another occasion a father was in a room for fifteen minutes with his crying child and his lack of any sign of concern or attempt to reassure spoke volumes about his lack of understanding and inability to respond in a normal caring way.

A worker in such a situation may experience a dilemma: should he intervene to comfort the child if the parent does not? Intervention would demonstrate concern for a distressed child and appropriate ways of meeting his needs, but it might undermine the parent's self-confidence even further and build resentment against the 'powerful intruder'. In our view, if the parent is failing to meet the child's needs, the worker must not be seen to ignore this. He should gently encourage the parent to do something, failing which he should act himself.

Talking with parents about their daily routine, or lack of it, offers an opportunity to discuss how they feel about their child, to examine the quality of their response to normal child care events and understanding of child rearing, and to assess their tolerance thresholds. This is particularly helpful with parents who have acknowledged abuse of their child. It identifies specific situations when stress develops and enables discussion of different parental responses.

A sense of irritation, annoyance or anger in the face of normal behaviour is worrying. Irrational feelings that the baby or toddler is consciously setting out to annoy them and work them up, ascribing motive and responsibility to the young child, demonstrate a serious distortion of their perception. These feelings may be accompanied by disappointment with the child's response to them. One mother of a two-year-old said: 'Why the hell should I love her – she never shows me any affection; never so much as says thank you.'

A self-righteous and dogmatic approach to physical punishment, especially of young children, is worrying. Some parents justify the use of vicious threats and excessive beatings by saying: 'You've got to toughen them up – it doesn't do to be too soft,' this from a father who punished his three-year-old son by standing him against a wall and throwing a hard plastic ball just above his head. The child was petrified and dared not move. Not only were this father's expectations unrealistic given the boy's age, but his behaviour was totally inappropriate. When talking with such parents it is often easy to accept and even approve of their sense of parental responsibility whilst forgetting the nature of the injuries inflicted and the grossly inappropriate behaviour used to put their ideas into practice.

The parent who is unable to tolerate normal childhood behaviour, such as crying, soiling, messy eating and inquisitiveness, or who believes the child is deliberately getting at him, or who uses excessive physical punishment because the child fails to meet the parent's unrealistic expectations, is clearly under considerable stress and will pose a risk to the child, unless there is clear evidence of an ability and willingness to modify behaviour.

Scapegoat role

Some therapists have commented on the apparent tendency of some children to attract violence by their own behaviour, as if they knew that the whole family will suffer more if they do not play this role to the full. They may have learnt that they only receive concern and attention after being hurt and thus seek violence for the care which follows. Such children frequently act in the same way at school, in hospital or in care. Their caregivers soon find themselves experiencing exactly the same violent feelings as the parents, although their feelings are – or should be – controlled and do not lead to violence. This is not very well understood, but if present will be significant.

Some families can only maintain cohesion by rejecting one family member; a scapegoat is essential for everybody. If a child is removed from the family, it is important to watch for the emergence of an alternative scapegoat, who may become equally at risk.

Siblings
The dynamics of child abuse sometimes involve only one child but more often other children in the household will also be at risk and their needs must not be overlooked. In some cases, removal of one child will simply shift the focus to another, whilst in others siblings may already have been abused without detection. In some families children are at risk during a certain age, but if this is successfully passed the risk declines. All children in the family must be given equal consideration in the assessment and, if all are at risk, their removal must be considered.

Summary
The overall aim of this part of the assessment is to judge the extent to which parental attitudes to and care of the children in the family differ from the wide range of normal. The greater the difference, usually the more difficult it will be to help and the more likely the need for the child to be removed from the family.

Social circumstances

Abusing families are frequently beset by pressing social problems such as debt, unemployment, threat of eviction, poor housing and social isolation. The need for action is urgent and the worker can easily demonstrate his caring concern through practical assistance to resolve the more immediate crises. It is often difficult to assess the extent to which multiple social problems are the result of low socio-economic status or of a fundamental inability to cope with life. Understanding of the parental background should throw light on this. The main significance lies in the extent to which multiple social problems are chronic and persistent or acute and transitory.

Chaos

A repetitive cycle involving crisis, intervention by some social agency, resolution of the immediate problem, relapse and further intervention, indicates an unwillingness or inability to learn from experience. Such parents frequently have immature personalities and feel powerless and unable to plan their affairs. Behaviour is impulsive, for example buying expensive presents when there is no food in the house. The outlook for children in such families is generally poor, although with practical assistance and support they may be helped despite their parents' problems. The outlook is more positive where inability to cope is due to parental youth and inexperience; support, guidance and the passage of time can produce lasting improvement.

Obsessional behaviour

In contrast to the previous group, some parents demonstrate an excessively high standard of home care and parentcraft. There will be no evidence of social problems and the parents may have successful careers and social relationships. Problems develop because they have difficulty accepting the child's disruption of their routine and order.

Isolation and lifelines

It is always instructive to ask parents whom they turn to when in trouble. Isolation from family and absence of friends usually suggest inability to form reciprocal, supportive and trusting relationships and thus an inability to seek out and take up informal means of support, meaning that stress remains within the family. Assessment of the extent of social contact with friends and neighbours is therefore important.

Police records may give evidence of domestic disputes or neighbourhood arguments. In general this assessment must be based on discussion with parents and observation, since it is clearly unethical to tour the neighbourhood talking about the family.

In many cases it will become evident that the only lifelines are from those professionally involved – the social worker or health visitor, for example. Where there is evidence of repeated, impulsive behaviour involving the child, these lifelines are clearly insufficient to protect the child until there is evidence of growth in self-control and an ability to seek and use help in anticipation of times of stress.

Precipitating incident

We have already discussed the importance of conducting a thorough forensic enquiry into the cause of the injuries, and the problems associated with this. We emphasise again that the approach should not be that of an interrogation with a persistent and insistent demand for 'The Truth'. It is helpful to establish the facts, but of equal importance is an assessment of the extent to which the parents are able to face up to what has happened and demonstrate an ability and willingness to prevent repetition.

The injuries
The injury is significant for what it reveals of the abusive act, but its severity does not necessarily parallel severity of family problems or pathology. Chance plays a large part, for example one child thrown on to a bed may bounce and laugh whilst another may hit the wall, fall on to the floor and sustain fractures. A child with a fractured skull may be safer at home than one with minor bruising. The significance can only be assessed by reference to surrounding factors and it is therefore unreasonable to place all responsibility for diagnosis and assessment on the doctor. The decision must be multifactorial and inter-professional.

Premeditated, sadistic and bizarre injuries always indicate

a poor chance of returning the child to parental care, for example cigarette burns, burns after placing a child on a hot surface, dipping in scalding water, lacerations with a knife, attempted circumcision and pin pricks. All are even more worrying if repeated on several occasions and if the child was tied or forcibly restrained.

Injuries inflicted using instruments are always disturbing. If premeditated, for example a child being tied over a table and beaten with a stick, the assessment is the same as described above. If the parent seized a random object in temper and used it to injure the child there is continuing risk unless the parent develops more self-control. Instrumental injuries in young children are rare and would usually indicate need for a Place of Safety Order.

Attempted smothering, drowning or poisoning are also rare and must be regarded as serious. All forms of abuse described so far tend to indicate the need for removal of the child with a poor chance of return to parental care.

The presence of long-standing forms of abuse, such as gross neglect, incest or persistent emotional abuse, increase the degree of concern about any inflicted injury. In general, severe and persistent neglect is more worrying than repeated minor injuries because it implies lack of basic care over a considerable time, but the presence of both injuries and physical neglect indicates a serious degree of risk and a poor prognosis for change in the family.

Fractures and head injuries usually require medical treatment and all children should be admitted to hospital pending full investigations. Familiarity with the parents tends to blunt the seriousness of what happened, so those involved must never forget the considerable loss of control required to cause these injuries, even if only momentary. The overall assessment will sometimes indicate that rehabilitation is possible, but careful timing of return home is necessary (see Chapter 18).

Increasing awareness of the problem has resulted in an apparent decline in the number of fractures, head injuries and deaths, but an increase in the number of children seen with bruises and other moderate injuries. These are often difficult to diagnose as abuse and are commonly known as 'grey area cases'. It seems reasonable to suppose that earlier diagnosis explains this trend. The assessment in a case of moderate injury is always complex. It is necessary to decide whether the abuse is evidence of a family with a serious degree of pathology indicating a poor chance of return home, or alternatively a comparatively mild abnormality of parenting which can be modified by therapeutic intervention. Again, this assessment cannot be made on a consideration of the injuries alone.

Parental attitude

Following most accidents, however trivial, most parents show exaggerated concern, guilt, regret and usually self-blame. If the abusing parent reacts in this way it is a hopeful sign, but often some or all of the following are present, creating a distinctive profile:

> delay in seeking help,
> absence of guilt or remorse,
> unsatisfactory explanation for the injuries,
> self-righteous justification of parental behaviour,
> blaming the child,
> denial that there is anything wrong,
> projection of blame on to others.

In one case the father said 'It serves the bugger right – he should keep still when I'm getting him ready,' after his two year old fell from his arms into a bath of scalding water. In a sense that injury was accidental, but the father's reaction was grossly abnormal and signalled clear danger to the child.

Evidence of denial or projection (see 'Parental relationships', p. 138) in this context should cause concern. It is common for parents initially to blame siblings, pets, baby-sitters or even passers-by, and some persist in denying that there are grounds for any concern. Refusal to accept responsibility for the abuse is not in itself indicative of a poor prognosis; it is the quality of the denial and the extent to which it intrudes into other aspects of life which are significant. Denial can sometimes be masked by an outward compliance or obsequiousness which acknowledges the need for intervention and expresses superficial openness, but is accompanied by resistance to any real self-examination. Over time it becomes clear that there is no willingness or ability to change attitudes or behaviour.

Such cases pose profound problems for decision makers since they inevitably question the original diagnosis. Very often all that is left at the end of the investigation is the doctor's unease about the injuries and a shared concern that all does not seem well, but insufficient evidence to take further action and no grounds for continuing social work with the family. Legal proceedings to protect the child may still be possible in some such cases, but this is unusual and requires expert legal advice.

Stress factors
It is important to assess whether the incident was the culmination of a build-up of stress resulting in an acute crisis, for example ill-health, death of a close relative, sudden redundancy, unexpected bill, family row, or whether it is a part of a pattern of chronic and recurring crises, this being more worrying.

Resources available

Planning work with a family involves balancing their needs and problems with the forms of help available. In most places the options are comparatively few, usually the time and expertise of the social worker and possibly health visitor and perhaps a day nursery or school. Family centres and sophisticated treatment units are unlikely to be available. The resource assessment must be realistic, for example if a 24-hour phone line is considered essential, it is not sufficient to rely on the home number of the social worker who will not always be at home. If daily visiting by social worker and health visitor is necessary over a long period, given other work demands, this is clearly unrealistic.

Excessive intervention also brings its own risks and stresses for family and workers, and rarely works out as hoped. The number of people visiting the family should be kept to a minimum and multiple referrals for different types of help at the same time should not be attempted.

If consideration is being given to the child remaining in care, there must be a realistic assessment of whether this experience will really improve on home. The 'rescue' philosophy can cause much pain, especially for older children, removing them from known and comparatively secure surroundings to a strange environment with the likelihood of numerous changes in substitute caregivers. It is easy to idealise care in contrast to the poor home background of the child, but it is the reality of care which must be remembered. (See Chapter 17.)

The assessment must not be based on enthusiastic and optimistic hopes expressed in the heat of a case conference, but rather an honest and realistic evaluation of sustainable, long-term possibilities.

Formulation and decision

Having reviewed the case, it should be possible to write a brief summary indicating why the incident happened. It is then worth writing a problem list covering all aspects of the case. In the second column indicate whether they are internal (to do with personality and family dynamics) or external and coincidental. In the third, state whether the problem is transitory or recurrent. Next indicate what is needed to overcome the problem and the likely time-scale. Finally indicate whether change seems realistic.

This must be balanced against positive features in the family: previous satisfactory care of the child, potentially remediable problems, an abusive incident that is understandable in its context (as opposed to bizarre or sadistic), parental acceptance of problems and a willingness to seek and use help, all indicate a reasonable chance that work with the family will be possible and that the child will be able to return home (see Chapter 18). The converse would indicate the need for work with the family before return home and consideration of permanent alternative care. Most cases fall between these extremes and decision makers must use their knowledge and skill to weigh the risks.

12

The Initial Case Conference

The initial case conference usually provides the focus for the burst of activity which follows discovery of a new case of child abuse. Much of what has been described in the previous chapters will have been completed, but major decisions will be held in abeyance pending the full review of the case at the conference. This chapter discusses the reasons for holding conferences and how they should be conducted, as well as criticisms and problems associated with them. Much of the discussion will be relevant not only to the initial conference but also subsequent case reviews and inter-agency collaboration in general.

The initial case conference has particular significance because there is a recent event on which to focus, urgent decisions have to be made, and a variety of people involved. Some initial conferences are held to review general concern about the care of children in a family with no specific precipitating event and these are often more difficult to structure and outcome is inevitably less decisive. A third type of case conference or review is that held by law on children in care or on statutory Orders, and finally there are the many case reviews, ranging from formal to very casual, within and between agencies.

The rationale for holding case conferences

> A case conference is recommended for every case involving suspected non-accidental injury to a child. In this way unilateral action will be minimised and all those who can provide information about the child and his family, have statutory responsibility for the safety of the child, or are responsible for providing services, will be brought together to reach a collective decision. (DHSS circular LASSL (74)13).

This recommendation forms the basis of most current practice. We have already seen in Chapter 3 the large number of individuals and agencies potentially involved in a given case, and in Chapter 4 that inadequate communication between individuals and agencies may have contributed to certain tragic deaths. Unco-ordinated intervention will be very stressful to families – many different people visiting in quick succession with different purposes and approaches – and it will also be unproductive for the workers involved. These overt reasons therefore seem self-evident, but others have also been suggested.

The risks involved in managing child abuse cases are obvious and have been mentioned already. Some have argued that such life-and-death decisions should not be left to one person but shared for greater efficiency and to relieve individual stress. It is also said that some use case conferences as a means of self-protection, going through a ritual to ensure that if things go wrong later no individual blame can be apportioned, rather than as a positive case management exercise. Neither of these is a sufficient justification for a case conference, although both have an element of truth.

Some police and social workers see the conference as a means of gathering evidence to be used in subsequent court hearings. This may be very disturbing to others present, who may be unaware of this, believing the conference to be a forum for planning therapeutic intervention. There will be resentment and reluctance to participate in the future if it only emerges at the close of the conference that participants will be called to give evidence; although if court action is necessary to protect a child, all involved in that judgement should feel an obligation to ensure that it can be implemented, including giving legal evidence if necessary. The conference can be a valuable forum for reviewing evidence and the need for legal action, provided all are aware of this purpose.

The case conference formalises the decision-making process, giving it added status and significance in relation to other case decisions, and thereby ensuring that it receives considered attention and thus that the eventual decisions are better. The negative aspect of this is that formality may constrain some of those involved, but given the risks, complexity of the judgements and public concern about such cases, it seems right that there should be such a formal process.

The reasons for case conferences can therefore be summarised as:

sharing information,
co-ordinating intervention,
planning action and defining responsibilities,
searching for legal evidence,
relieving individual stress,
self/agency protection,
formalising the decision making process.

Criticisms of case conferences

Some criticisms of conferences are concerned with the need to improve their functioning, whilst a few advance more fundamental arguments against the need for conferences. Most of the latter refer not only to conferences but also other inter-professional communications, such as concern about breaches of confidentiality, erosion of individual professional freedom and erosion of the civil liberties and right to privacy of the family.

Concern about ill-treatment of children over the last hundred years has increased the right and power of the State to intervene in family life and all the evidence suggests that the public generally support this trend, provided there are safeguards. Whenever the State intrudes into personal and family life there is a potential erosion of individual freedom and this threat is compounded when the State and professions are working in harmony. However such intervention can save life and enhance the freedom of the child to live and grow; this is its sole justification. We discussed issues of confidentiality and multidisciplinary working in earlier chapters and so shall not repeat the arguments here, except to say that a narrow interpretation of confidentiality and dogmatic adherence to professional individualism do not seem in the best interests of the abused child.

Procedural criticism of conferences include:

too many on trivial cases,
time wasting,
inconvenient time,
inconvenient place,
too many absentees,
poorly structured/inefficient,
undermine individual and agency accountability,
witch hunts to apportion blame rather than future planning.

Since these can be overcome in well run conferences, they are discussed below when considering conference structure and effectiveness.

Problems of multidisciplinary working

Professional differences

The objectives, purpose and ethos of each profession are subtly different, reflected in and often upheld by training. It was thought that the clash of 'frames of references' might create communication problems, but experience, and research by Hallett and Stevenson, suggest that the problem is overcome in many cases. The differing emphases cannot be ignored, however, for example the police tend to operate on a justice model assuming individual responsibility for crimes, whereas psychiatrists or social workers often adopt a more deterministic approach, looking for background causes, not to find excuses but to seek out reasons as a basis for future intervention. A doctor may feel exclusively concerned about the threat to an abused child's life and not feel disposed to enter a debate about possible long-term rehabilitation. Experience suggests that such problems are more likely where individuals adopt a narrow approach to their professional brief, rather than a general concern for the child in the family and the need for prevention of further abuse.

Professional differences are also seen in language or jargon used. Jargon is often a useful and essential shorthand but its use excludes the uninitiated. It is best never to assume that those from other professions understand jargon. Attempt to explain everything in an understandable way, even if this takes longer.

Agency structures
The differing organisational structures of the various agencies create problems of communication and decision. Some are extremely hierarchical, with important decisions always being taken by senior officers, such as the police and some social services departments, others delegate considerable decision-making powers, whilst consultants and family doctors are accountable to nobody for their professional decisions. In a conference this may mean that some individuals can confirm decisions immediately, whilst others have to report up and back.

Agency policy also affects conference discussions and may over-ride the inclinations of the field worker.

Power relationships
The different agencies have different degrees of responsibility for the action required after an incident of abuse. Teachers have very little power or immediate responsibility for decisions although their response to the abused child in the classroom may be crucial for his recovery and development. Doctors have significant responsibilities for physical health

and thus have potential power over placement of the child, but no direct responsibility for legal action to protect him. The police have to decide whether or not to prosecute and may choose to ignore the opinions of others; the social services department/NSPCC have the power to initiate care proceedings, as do the police. The social services department has the exclusive responsibility to decide placement of a child in care.

Power is also invested in individuals by others because they are perceived as knowledgeable or authoritative, thus the opinion of a consultant paediatrician often carries more weight than that of a health visitor, regardless of comparative experience of or knowledge about the problem.

In many areas there seems to be a tendency for a polarisation between the social services on one hand and all other agencies on the other, perhaps with the police uneasily between. There is resentment that social services have taken no action in certain referred cases, whilst action in others is seen as excessive. There are also occasional feelings that some conferences are used by social services, and sometimes other agencies, to manoeuvre or force others into action which is considered inappropriate. It is quite common to hear comments that social services try to dominate conferences and dictate what is decided without consideration of the views of others. The prevalence of such feelings suggests that the cause is at least partly structural. Referring agencies are often generalist whereas social services are problem-focused and thus each case has to be assessed to see if it attracts sufficient priority. There will be inevitable disagreements, but these will be made worse if there is no explanation by social workers of the reasoning behind their decision. Social services also have statutory powers in relation to child abuse and must make an independent decision about action required.

Teams and networks

A group of people working closely together and in regular contact usually develop tried and trusted patterns of communication, but in most child abuse case conferences the members do not form a coherent team but rather a community-based network whose common link is the abused child. Some members will know each other well from previous conferences and other work, whilst others will probably be complete strangers, yet this group has to develop sufficient cohesion and mutual trust to share sensitive information and agree future action. The sense of crisis associated with the incident adds a further inhibiting dimension. It is perhaps a credit to all involved that, despite these handicaps, most conferences do manage to agree on far-reaching conclusions in such a short time.

Individual differences/worker feelings

Whatever the effect of the matters discussed so far, the response of the individual worker will determine the effectiveness of the conference and quality of inter-professional communication. Agency managers can create the context for good or bad relationships but the worker must put the policy into effect. In many areas, high turnover of staff makes it difficult to develop lasting relationships and understandings, particularly in hospitals where junior doctors rotate every six months.

Individual knowledge about child abuse in general, and local agency structure and procedures in particular, is also important, and if lacking undermines the effectiveness of the conference.

Individual reaction to child abuse and the specific case also have a powerful impact. Worker feelings have already been considered in Chapter 7 and it is obvious that such powerful emotions may influence the discussion, for example feelings of guilt may prompt withholding important information. Jealousy of others involved can also have a damaging impact.

Group dynamics

There have been virtually no studies of case conference processes, although studies of professional teams have been published. There is a considerable literature on small group theory, rarely applied to case conferences, for example evidence of considerable pressure towards uniformity in small groups and of course no guarantee that the consensus will be the best outcome; it is rare to find conferences in open disagreement. Some studies also suggest that the larger the group, the more acceptable are individual differences and the less likely a consensus. Some studies suggest that those with high status participate more and have more influence on the outcome, whilst low status people have less commitment but must implement decisions. It seems that where there is an absence of clear leadership the group will degenerate into cliques and factions, with general dissatisfaction and no clear outcome. Such findings have to be interpreted with caution but are of obvious relevance.

The conference may come to mirror the family conflicts and tensions, individual members identifying with certain family members. This may be conscious, for example a probation officer supporting his client's perspective in the face of family and conference rejection, but as often it develops unnoticed, a reflection of the force of family feelings. This effect is perhaps most marked when the abusing parent is isolated in the family; the conference might absorb the overt family rejection or rally to the defence of the outcast. Problems may arise if plans evolve out of these unconscious dynamics.

Conferences can become preoccupied with supporting colleagues, distorting discussion about future work with the family, and losing objectivity and direction. It is also possible for an individual member to become the focus of collective anger and it may be that the reaction against the police is sometimes a projection of collective anger about the need to make difficult decisions and act authoritatively.

Some of these dynamics develop because of the nature of child abuse and its effect on us all. Others arise because conference members are anxious about the conference itself and uncertain about what is happening. Both can be overcome to a large extent by a skilful chairman and clear agenda.

When to hold the conference

The general advice is that the first conference should be held as soon as possible, but clearly some time will have elapsed and certain urgent decisions will have been made, such as medical treatment, and whether to arrest the abuser and seek a Place of Safety Order. Some see value in a very early conference, certainly within three days, to make an initial assessment and decide what further action is necessary, with the next meeting three or four weeks later to finalise plans. Others see this as unnecessary duplication and prefer a single conference after the initial investigation is complete, preferably within a week. Whatever the local policy, the conference should be held before any agency is committed to irrevocable action.

The DHSS advise that a conference should be held in every case of suspected child abuse and this seems to be most local practice. Some argue that a conference is only necessary in serious cases. This is a dangerous argument. Part of the rationale for holding a meeting is that nobody is in full possession of the facts in advance and it is comparatively common for discussion to reveal unexpected information. The seriousness of the case cannot be assessed before all the information is known and it is not sufficient to rely on inter-personal contact to gather this. A conference is therefore advisable in every case of child abuse.

Who should attend the conference

A case conference should normally include:
  a) persons having statutory responsibilities for the continuing care of the child;
  b) persons concerned with the provision of services likely to be relevant to the case;
  c) persons with information regarding the child and his family (. . . previous and present contact . . .).

Others may also be invited as appropriate (e.g. police, housing official, legal adviser) (DHSS LASSL (74)13).

In practice the conference should comprise seven or eight members, except in unusual circumstances. The social services and family doctor should always be invited, together with the consultant and police (if involved), and health visitor if the child is under five or if she is otherwise involved in the family. The school is important if the child attends, as are other individuals/agencies closely involved in the family. Resource controllers may be helpful, for example residental care admissions, fostering or day care officers.

Significant absences inevitably cause problems and detract from the quality of decision-making. Those most conspicuous by their absence are family doctors, as is reported from all areas. Sometimes the health visitor represents the doctor's opinion, but this is unsatisfactory unless she has access to his records and they work closely as a team, since the purpose of the conference is not only to contribute but also to learn and share in future plans. Something known to the doctor may seem insignificant to him until it is seen in a new context. It is regrettable that the physical health record of many families is often unavailable to conferences, despite its crucial significance. Some argue that family doctors fail to attend because of inconvenient times or venues, others because they are too busy to give over an hour to a conference, others that they are not interested and do not want to become involved, and others that the conflict of loyalty to parent and child is too stressful. Some health authorities now make a sessional payment for attendance and it will be interesting to see if this changes the pattern.

Class teachers are perhaps another significant absent group, the school usually being represented by the head teacher. This may mean that the conference is deprived of the detailed observations of the teacher, who is probably the person who knows the child best after the parents. This may be overcome if there is good liaison between head teacher and his staff.

Whoever arranges the conference must assess the relative importance of those invited. If it is impossible for all to be present, the conference must be held when the crucial people can attend, and others asked for a written report.

Venue of the conference

The venue should be the most convenient for all concerned. Territory can significantly affect the discussion, some feeling less at ease and thus less able to contribute outside their normal surroundings. If one person is essential, it may be necessary to hold the meeting where he can attend. In some places the choice of venue affects who chairs the meeting. It is probably best to have a consistent policy on chairmanship not dictated by venue.

Preparation for the conference

Conference members must come to the conference prepared. It is impossible to summarise a complicated family history and a long period of contact without some notes; reference to ill-ordered, bulky files is inefficient and time-consuming. It is helpful if the social worker can prepare a one-side hand-out detailing family structure and a brief outline of the recent crisis, including dates and times. The presentation of voluminous background reports is not recommended and may be positively dangerous. People rarely have time to read and digest written material in a meeting, so the report is given little weight in contrast to spoken contributions, which may be less significant. The writer may also assume that he need not repeat the written material, which is thus ignored.

The conference agenda

We have already suggested that good decision-making requires:

  (i)   a predetermined framework,
 (ii)   the fullest possible information,
(iii)   worker awareness of factors which cloud objectivity,

and in the chapter on data evaluation we outlined a structure for gathering the information which has proved helpful. That structure is equally useful as the basis for the conference agenda.

It is helpful if the agenda or structure of discussion is known to all in advance, and the best way to ensure this is for there to be a more or less uniform agenda throughout a given area. Those attending can then prepare appropriately. Regardless of this, the chairman should outline the order of discussion at the beginning; this prevents inappropriate interjections from people anxious to ensure that their contribution is not missed but uncertain of the right time to speak. Such conferences frequently degenerate into a sequence of individual statements of concern, each bearing little relationship to the one before, and the whole impossible to summarise and evaluate.

The conference should open with introductions of those present (name, job, agency, reason for being there). The chairman should then state why the conference has been called (name of child(ren) and brief description of the injuries or reasons for concern), outline the decisions to be made and explain the agenda. The details of the family structure follow next, including absent members, children who have died, all members of the household, and extended family or friends who are significant. Dates of birth of children and parents are important; it is surprising how often records disagree and this can be especially important when assessing child development.

The conference should next turn to the precipitating incident (i.e. the crisis which led to the conference). This is best discussed first, because it will be fresh in everybody's mind and experience shows that if left until later, anxiety about the incident will disrupt consideration of other matters. It would probably be more logical to start with family history and progress towards the recent incident, but this does not seem to work well, whereas dispensing first with the incident does seem to enable conference members to be more considered and objective about family background.

Contributions are best taken in chronological order of

involvement, starting with whoever was involved first and following through in sequence. This may mean one person presenting his contribution in stages (e.g. referral from school to social services to doctor, further social work involvement, residential social worker, police, further social work). Taking the contributions in sequence highlights any inconsistency or changes in explanations and gives a good impression of parental reactions to those not involved.

The conference should next consider the family history, dynamics and circumstances, following the outline suggested in the previous chapter (i.e. each parent in turn, then the marriage, subject child, siblings, social situation and lifelines). Some conferences take participant contributions in order rather than having a subject focus. This is confusing, does not facilitate orderly gathering of information, and makes evaluation very difficult. A family member focus is strongly recommended. It may be helpful to conclude with a list of problems and positives, perhaps on a blackboard, which then leads into evaluation of the significance of what has been said.

The chairman should summarise this discussion and lead into consideration of decisions. These include whether there has been abuse and if so, prosecution, care proceedings or other child protective legal action, registration, services to be provided and plans for future co-ordination. If abuse is confirmed, a key worker should be nominated.

The whole conference should last one and a half hours at most.

Chairmanship of conferences

The ability of the chairman is perhaps the single most important factor in the success or failure of the conference. The task is complex and requires training. It is best if the number of potential chairman in an area is kept to a minimum to ensure consistency and the development of skill.

Decision-making

The DHSS suggested that the conference should reach a collective decision (see above), but later recognised that the decision 'cannot be binding on representatives of bodies with statutory powers and duties'. Hallett argues that conferences are a unique form of delegated inter-agency decision-making, yet ultimately no agency or individual can abrogate statutory powers or professional duties. It therefore seems helpful to view the conference as a consultative forum, not taking decisions but making recommendations to its constituent parts. Consensus is the preferred outcome, but each member has an individual responsibility to decide that within his professional sphere. Nobody should be able to argue later that he disagreed with the decision but acquiesced in the majority view.

Any agency deciding at the conference or later not to adhere to conference recommendations must inform the others so that they can adjust their action, and if necessary, call a review conference.

Subsequent co-ordination

It seems that most areas now have some procedure for co-ordinating immediate action but maintaining this over months or years of a case is difficult. Some areas have routine case reviews, but these are often poorly attended, if the family seems to make progress or no further incidents occur. Some registers have periodic monitoring of those involved by issuing standard forms. Ultimately the success of inter-agency co-ordination of long-term work with a family will depend on the commitment of the field workers involved and the support for this approach of their supervisors.

It is generally recommended that a key worker should be agreed at the initial conference who will co-ordinate the work of the network and ensure that communication occurs and necessary action is taken. This role usually falls to a social worker and impressions suggest that further thought must

be given to the precise role and significance of the key
worker.

Recording

It is essential that there is an accurate record of the conference discussion indicating why the decisions were reached.
Recording a lengthy meeting is a skilled task and must be
performed by somebody who knows the significance of what
is said and therefore what can be omitted. A verbatim report
serves little purpose. The report should summarise discussion under each of the headings already outlined. Some argue
that appropriately trained secretarial staff can perform this
task, but in our view it should be a professional person not
directly involved with the case, possibly the senior social
worker supervising the field worker involved.

Pre-requisites for effective case conferences

The following should be present to ensure a successful meeting:

  shared commitment to the value and purpose of the meet-
    ing,
  theoretical and ethical agreement between those present,
  knowledge of the problem in general,
  agency co-operation, not coercion,
  convenient time and venue,
  not too large,
  no key absences,
  adequate preparation,
  good chairmanship,
  shared agenda,
  absence of jargon,
  appreciation of worker feelings and group dynamics,
  understanding of agency decision-making structures,
  focus on future planning (not recriminations/witch hunt),
  decision and action-focused discussion,

clear and agreed allocation of responsibility for implementation of recommendations,
adequate recording.

Given this seemingly formidable list, it is reassuring to find that its achievement is possible and that conferences in many areas are making an effective contribution to a sensitive and efficient response to the needs of abused children.

13

The Law and Court Proceedings

Court proceedings are an inevitable part of child abuse work, although not of every case. They provoke anxiety in both parents and workers, especially those whose work does not normally involve court appearances. This chapter discusses the process of preparing and presenting a case in court and gives guidance to social workers about preparing themselves and the parents for the hearing. Chapter 14 provides a summary of relevant legislation. Matrimonial and wardship proceedings are not discussed in detail, although they are increasingly used in child abuse cases.

Many fear that a court case will destroy any hope of a positive, therapeutic relationship with the parents. This is avoidable provided there is careful preparation and the social worker has established a relationship with the family in the manner already described. In deciding what to do, the future safety and welfare of the child must be the prime consideration.

Prosecution of parents

Prosecution of the person who inflicted the injury is more likely the more serious the injury. Men are more likely to be prosecuted than women, regardless of the severity of the injury and other factors. Serious cases go to the Crown Court, and if there is a not guilty plea may take months to complete. In such cases it is sometimes necessary to defer the care proceedings concerning the child pending the finding of the adult court, but this is not legally necessary and the case should go ahead if there is sufficient evidence. The criminal courts have been requested to expedite child abuse prosecutions so that the future of the child is not left in balance in the interim.

The burden of proof in a criminal case is that the matter has been proved 'beyond reasonable doubt', which is a more stringent test than civil proceedings (including care proceedings – see below). Thus it may be that a parent is found not guilty but there is still sufficient evidence to justify care proceedings. It is not always necessary to have proof of who inflicted the abuse for the juvenile court case to be successful.

Prosecution rates vary significantly in different places – probably from 5–10 per cent of parents – but we have little doubt that in most cases the consequences of prosecution are very damaging for the family, regardless of the outcome. We seriously doubt the deterrent effect of punishment on parents who have such poor control over their feelings, and prosecution often compounds the child's problems. Press reporting of the case, often in graphic detail, exposes the child to publicity from which he is protected in the juvenile court; perhaps there is a case for extending this anonymity to prosecution of parents. There are also problems for the child living with the stigma of having a parent with a criminal record of child abuse.

A conviction rarely leads to imprisonment, but this is unpredictable. Parents in prison rarely receive treatment or help, are often ostracised by other inmates and, along with sexual offenders, are highly vulnerable to hostility, including attacks by other prisoners. One father spent the whole of his sentence under Rule 43, completely isolated in his cell for his own safety, with no association with other prisoners. It is hardly surprising that such parents return to the community embittered and hostile to potential sources of help.

We are concerned about this lack of treatment facilities for prisoners. It should be a matter of public concern that parents convicted of serious offences against their children can be imprisoned for years without rehabilitation which might reduce the risk of re-offending. This is particularly disturbing given that most will be released after a comparatively short time and return to a family with children, usually embittered and unwilling to accept help: 'I've done my time, now get off my back.' This problem should receive urgent attention. Fortunately most convicted parents are not imprisoned but remain in the community, a far better context in which to try to help them. If a Probation Order is made, the social worker and probation officer will need to work closely together and define their respective roles.

When to initiate juvenile court proceedings

'It shall be the duty of every local authority to . . . promote the welfare of children by diminishing the need to receive children into or keep them in care . . . or to bring them before a juvenile court' (1980, s1). It is therefore the presumption of the law that, if possible, a voluntary approach to helping families will be adopted. However if this seems impossible or there is any significant doubt, the local authority has a duty to bring the matter to court, provided that one of the statutory conditions appears to be satisfied (1969, s1(2)). If there is grave concern about the welfare of a child but insufficient evidence for care proceedings in the juvenile court, the local authority has a duty to consider alternative proceedings, such as wardship (1969b, s7). Any person can apply to a magistrate for a Place of Safety Order, but care proceedings can be initiated only by social services departments, the NSPCC or the police.

Each case of inflicted injury is unique and an individual assessment must be made, but the following factors usually indicate the need for proceedings:

parental history of inflicting child abuse;
bizarre and sadistic injuries indicating premeditation;

physical injuries combined with severe neglect;

extensive or severe injuries indicating marked loss of control;

repeated injuries indicating strong negative attitude to the child;

self-righteous parents enforcing a harsh, oppressive régime;

low parental tolerance to stress plus high external pressures;

socially chaotic home situation with little prospect of change.

Not all such cases will go to court and of those which do, some children will remain in long-term care, others return home in due course, and some return immediately under a Supervision Order. A few cases are found 'not proved', or the magistrates make a different Order from that recommended. Such cases are always difficult to work with, as discussed below, so careful review of the evidence and the likely outcome is essential before the decision is made to go to court.

The court hearing highlights the authority and controlling dimension of child abuse work which many workers find difficult to come to terms with. Most professions assume a client/patient–worker relationship based on consent rather than compulsion; they are helpers rather than controllers. The therapeutic necessity of integrating help and authority, care and control has been argued above and is reiterated here. In certain cases a Court Order is vital to the management of the case in the child's interest.

Preparing the case

The need for proceedings will have emerged from the case assessment described above, so should be based on all the information reasonably to hand. The application to the court must usually be made within days of the incident, but the first hearing is often an interim one, leaving a month or more to complete preparations, during which time it is possible to withdraw the application if it no longer seems appropriate.

The social worker has to ensure that three groups of people are prepared for the hearing:

Himself and his advocate ('The Applicant'),
Witnesses (including professional colleagues),
The family (Parents and also child if old enough).

The applicant
The presentation of the social worker's case is usually made by a solicitor or social worker with special court experience (Courts Officer). The NSPCC always briefs a solicitor and this is increasingly local authority practice. These cases are becoming increasingly complex. Legal Aid has enabled more solicitors to appear on behalf of the child (sometimes briefed by the parents on the child's behalf). There is also evidence of a higher rate of appeals to the Crown Court. The local authority has no right of appeal from care proceedings, but only the child (or somebody acting on his behalf, usually the parents), so the application must be right first time, and it is essential that the application is presented by a lawyer with experience of child care law. It is a matter of some concern that many authorities give child care cases to newly qualified and inexperienced lawyers for the issue at stake is the future welfare and liberty of a child until his eighteenth birthday. Every case demands the most serious consideration.

Although a lawyer should present the case, the social worker must share the preparation. He knows the significant witnesses and the important facts and opinions which have led to the application and which must be presented to the court. He may take witness statements himself or this may be done by somebody else. The social worker should feel a shared responsibility for the presentation of the case and instruct his advocate accordingly.

The witnesses
Decisions to take care proceedings in child abuse cases usually emerge from case conference deliberations and reflect the

shared assessment of those present. Having contributed to the outcome, all have a responsibility to give evidence, if required, and to support the application not only in discussion but also by ensuring that their work with the family does not undermine the agreed approach. Use of the law is essential to the management of some child abuse cases and it is regrettable that some seem anxious to express concern about a child and urge the need for action but are then reluctant to provide essential evidence. This reluctance is often associated with confidentiality or fears that future relationships with the family, in particular the parents, will be impaired. Difficulties may indeed follow a court hearing, although these can usually be overcome in time, but the safety and future welfare of the child is surely paramount and should over-ride issues of confidentiality.

The reluctance to give evidence may also stem from ignorance about the nature of juvenile court proceedings and the legal process. Social workers are usually trained and experienced in such matters but other witnesses may not be and will need guidance and support. It is in the social worker's interest to build and maintain the co-operation and commitment of his witnesses and this is an important aspect of the preparation for the hearing. A pre-hearing meeting to discuss the reason for the application and the contribution of each witness is helpful; this often happens at the conference itself. If this is impossible, each witness should be seen independently. They will need advice on the rules of evidence, the order of questions from the lawyer and the nature of cross-examination. It is helpful to anticipate 'difficult' questions, which may arise if the application is opposed, and prepare a suitable reply.

In some cases reluctance to give evidence arises from hesitancy about justifying a professional opinion in a legal setting. There may be misunderstanding about the admissability of evidence and opinion, or perhaps a rash statement was made in the heat of the crisis which on cold reflection does not seem supported by the evidence. It is to avoid such problems that it was recommended above that the social worker should make explicit the possibility of legal proceedings at the outset, carefully test interpretations of and opinions about the evidence and, if possible, take a brief written statement at the time of referral.

Health visitors have particular concern about court appearances and the Health Visitors' Association has advised that evidence should only be given under subpoena (a witness summons issued by the court requiring attendance). This is to emphasise to the parents, and parents in general, that health visitors only give evidence under compulsion, rather than of free will. This is felt necessary to maintain public confidence. However it seems inconsistent for a health visitor to contribute to a recommendation for legal action, but then argue that formal evidence is given unwilllingly.

The anxiety of some professional witnesses would be eased if the Chairman of the Bench routinely opened with a statement explaining the public and professional duty to give evidence. It would be even more helpful if the hearing was inquisitorial rather than adversarial, as suggested below. In practice, social services departments do their best to avoid calling professional witnesses.

It is even more unusual for non-professional witnesses, such as neighbours, to be called. However this may be essential, in which case even more careful preparation will be required.

The family

The social worker has a professional duty to make explicit his legal powers and duties, advise the parents and child of their legal rights (including the advisability of seeking legal representation and rights of appeal) and to explain legal procedures and what will happen in court. It is usually necessary to go over these matters several times to ensure they are fully understood.

Legal representation of the parents is extremely confused. At the time of writing the only parties to the proceedings are the applicant and the child. The parents have no legal status in the hearing although in practice they are given an opportunity to have their say. In the past the parents have usually sought representation on behalf of their child and the solicitor has, in effect, presented their case. Increasing social and legal recognition of the independent rights of the child has led more solicitors to take the child's needs seriously and not automatically speak for the parents, a very difficult ethical balance to maintain. In some cases the local authority or court itself appoints a solicitor to represent the child, who has the difficult task of forming a view when his client may be too young to brief him.

Since the parents are not formally party to the proceedings, they are not entitled to Legal Aid, so many are not legally represented. Many parents bitterly resent this anomaly and rightly believe that it puts them at a considerable disadvantage. Pressure is building for a change in Legal Aid regulations or the law itself, the only reason for the delay, according to the Government, being the public expense. This is a monstrous injustice which must be righted.

Most parents find legal proceedings traumatic and confusing. They understandably fail to appreciate the subtle distinction between adult criminal proceedings and civil care proceedings. The parents usually feel that their parenting and therefore they themselves are on trial, an entirely realistic perception in practice. The formality of the procedure and language used will usually be alien to them and they often feel isolated and powerless.

This may be compounded by the highly ambiguous 'messages' given by the social worker, who asks them to believe he wants to help but then turns 'prosecutor'. The social worker will also feel this conflict if he failed to make explicit his legal duties and introduced himself on a 'false prospectus'. One parent said 'I began to trust you and then this happened'. To overcome this problem, some have argued that the worker responsible for providing help should not also initiate legal action; the 'good' and 'bad' roles should be split so as not to damage the therapeutic relationship. It has been suggested above that this dichotomy is unhelpful and that the integration of the two roles in a single worker is in the long-term therapeutic interest of the parents.

The social worker should have the fullest possible discussion with the parents in advance of the hearing, in keeping with the overall principles of honesty and openness, including a description of the layout of the courtroom, a consideration of who will be present and why, and a review of the possible outcomes. The parents must be advised of their right to ask questions and present their views.

There is a dilemma in deciding how much to discuss in advance. Some argue for a full review of the evidence, whilst others feel this may jeopardise their case if the parents convey this to their solicitor. There is little doubt that a detailed preliminary discussion is essential if there is to be any hope of a positive, therapeutic relationship with the family. The social worker's evidence may be hurtful to the parents, expressed in terms not usually used with them. Preparation does not necessarily lessen the pain, but it usually reduces the sense of shock. Detailed discussion of the evidence also offers a unique opportunity for honest discussion of family problems with the parents.

Evidence should be balanced and fair, avoiding exaggeration and overstatement, leaving the facts to speak for themselves. Opinion should include reference to positive features in the family as well as failings and weaknesses. The credibility of evidence is enhanced by presenting a balanced picture, demonstrating genuine concern for the future of the child and welfare of the family. Some social workers fear that presenting positive attributes of the parents will jeopardise the case, but this does not seem to happen. Most magistrates seem impressed by a witness with sufficient confidence to acknowledge strengths as well as weaknesses and parents are more likely to accept the outcome if a balanced impression is given.

Part of any honest discussion with parents must include consideration of what will happen after the hearing. The outcome cannot be predicted because the decision is made by the magistrates and the full force of the evidence in support of and opposed to the application will not be known until the hearing. It is therefore unwise to give premature undertakings, for example about return of the child under a Care Order. As suggested in an earlier chapter, false reassurance serves no purpose and may be damaging in the long-term.

The juvenile court hearing

The juvenile court hearing will be less formal than the adult criminal court, but there are still rules of procedure and evidence with which all have to comply. The hearing is in private before two or three magistrates (who will have been through some specific juvenile court training). Also present, as well as the parents, will be the magistrates' clerk (almost always a qualified lawyer who advises the magistrates on points of law, ensures that proper procedure is followed, and watches over the interests of any unrepresented party), the applicant's advocate, legal representatives of the child and parents (if any), possibly a probation officer and/or social services department representative and the usher. The child must be present if of an age to understand, but need not sit through the evidence.

The rules of evidence in the juvenile court are similar to those of criminal proceedings, in particular that hearsay is inadmissable. Witnesses can give expert opinion, if qualified to do so. The rules of evidence are in practice more flexible than they might at first seem and legal advice should be sought when preparing what to say. A witness must not be in court before giving his evidence but may remain to hear subsequent witnesses.

The magistrates have to decide the case on the basis of the evidence presented, according to the 'balance of probability' (more probable than not), a less stringent test than 'beyond reasonable doubt' used in criminal proceedings. This important distinction is not always fully understood by witnesses.

The credibility of the evidence given by the social worker will be significantly influenced by how he presents himself and his case in court. He should have gone through the case with his advocate, like the other witnesses, and have prepared a response to possible 'difficult' questions. It is not simply a matter of getting the facts right and telling the truth, but also of knowing what is significant and why, and of conveying this to the magistrates. Style of dress, general attitude to the court and self-confidence may all influence the outcome. The social worker will not always be giving the evidence about the incident, but if he is doing so, he should clearly indicate what was done, by whom, to whom, when and where, who saw it and, perhaps most important in this context, why it happened.

Magistrates often seem to give much more weight to the opinion of a doctor than a social worker, presumably reflecting their relative status in the view of the court. In one recent case a doctor was asked whether he thought the parents were likely to repeat the injury. The doctor gave his opinion, despite never having met the abusing father, whilst the social worker who had undertaken a full family assessment and was recommending a Care Order, was never asked for an opinion. In explaining the decision to return the child home, the chairman stated that the medical opinion had been taken into account. The decision may have been right, but the relative status of the two witnesses seemed to be more significant than their respective knowledge of the situation. This lack of relative status in court is sometimes the result of social workers' diffidence about expressing an opinion. An experienced social worker is an expert witness and should not be reticent about expressing a view, provided it is based on evidence and reached after careful deliberation. It may be helpful for him to start his evidence by briefly stating his qualifications and experience of similar cases.

The hearing is invariably painful for the parents and they may be very angry with the social worker afterwards, however carefully they have been prepared. This is an understandable reaction to a tension-ridden situation and should not be taken as an indication of a permanent attitude. Occasionally parents break down in tears in court and if nobody else shows a willingness to comfort them, the social worker may wish to seek a brief adjournment to talk with the parents. Some parents are unable to contain their anger and frustration and lose control in the courtroom or storm out in a rage. The chairman then has to decide whether to continue in their absence. Such reactions are surprisingly rare, most parents being awed by the surroundings and controlling their feelings until afterwards, when they are often directed against the social worker.

Proceedings in other courts

An increasing number of child abuse cases are now being heard in matrimonial or wardship proceedings before a judge. The judge is not bound by statutory conditions, but has the general responsibility for deciding what is in the child's best interest. The rules of procedure and evidence are therefore very different. The increasing awareness of wardship means that social workers cannot decide to take no action if there is cause for concern, but it seems that there is insufficient evidence for juvenile court proceedings, as used to be the pattern. Failure to consider wardship in that situation would be negligent.

After the hearing

Every parent reacts differently to the making of a Care or Supervision Order. The most difficult to manage is persistent denial that the child was abused and repeated demands for the child's return home. Rehabilitation becomes the central repetitive theme, excluding consideration of all else. There is no basis for therapeutic understanding and progress towards accepting problems and change. The parents sometimes apply for revocation or variation of the Order and, if successful, interpret this as a complete vindication, and their resistance to intervention is further strengthened. The social worker's dilemma is often that there is some doubt about what happened. Sometimes a change of social worker has proved beneficial, but more usually the parents remain inaccessible.

In other cases, anger and anxiety are quickly followed by

relief and acknowledgement of the need for an Order. In some cases this reveals developing insight into their problems and a good chance of eventual return of the child. In others there is a passive compliance linked to a pervading sense of powerlessness indicating lack of energy and motivation for change, making progress very difficult.

The magistrates have to reach their own decision on the evidence presented within the confines of the law. If they decide that the case has not been proved, however great their concern, they may not make an Order. They also have to make an independent assessment of what to do if the case is proved and occasionally they do not follow the social worker's recommendation, as is right and proper.

Work with families where the case has been found not proved is very difficult. They usually see the outcome as a vindication of their case and may refuse further co-operation. This may also apply if a Supervision Order is made instead of the recommended Care Order. The social worker is left holding considerable anxiety about the child but, in effect, is undermined by the court decision. It takes considerable determination and persistence to persevere with such a case. If concern remains and the situation deteriorates, it is possible to go back to court to seek the substitution of a Care Order.

Discussion of future plans with parents, following the making of an Order, is very difficult, especially when the child is in care and the parents are asking about eventual rehabilitation. Nobody can predict the future, although past behaviour and current attitudes give clues about the likely outcome. The parents usually want to know what they have to do to ensure the child's return. Change is usually needed in parental attitudes and behaviour to the child, but it is very difficult to put this into words they will understand; if they knew what had to change they would be half way to solving the problem. Even if they understand and accept the need for change, the likely timespan is impossible to predict. If there is reluctance to acknowledge problems or complete denial, it is possible that time will bring change. In deciding what approach to take, the social worker will need to refer to issues discussed in Chapters 11 and 18.

If the outcome is uncertain it is difficult to know how to plan and especially how much contact to promote between parent and child. How long should a child be left in limbo whilst the social worker pursues ill-defined and illusive goals? This point is discussed further in Part III.

Is the juvenile court a suitable forum for decision?

There is increasing debate about the nature of care proceedings and the procedure of the juvenile court. The present system is an adversarial approach, with the parties calling witnesses and making statements, leaving the magistrates, in effect, to decide in favour of one or the other. This encourages a polarisation of attitudes and militates against a balanced and comprehensive review of the family situation.

There seem powerful arguments for substituting a less formal, inquisitorial system in which the parties may call evidence, but the magistrates also have the right to do so and act as seekers after truth rather than adjudicators between opposing factions. The magistrates should be able to summon expert witnesses and take the initiative in calling people who know the family but who may not have been called by the parties. It would also be helpful if the magistrates could insist on a psychiatric examination of the parents.

The inquisitorial system would also be more suited to the currently developing pattern of three or more lawyers, representing the child, parents and applicant. The increasing use of solicitors to represent the child's independent interests, many of whom seek independent social work reports, and also of court appointed guardians *ad litem* to fulfil a similar function, go some way to meeting these points. There has been great interest in the Scottish juvenile panels and there is an undoubted need for a wide-ranging debate about the future of the English and Welsh juvenile court system.

14

Child Care Legislation

This chapter outlines the main legal provisions relating to abused children in England and Wales. There are different laws for Scotland and Northern Ireland, although they are broadly similar in their provisions. The law relating to children is complex, so what follows must be seen only as a general guide. Legal advice must be sought before taking action in specific cases.

'Voluntary supervision'

Statute
: Child Care Act, 1980 (Section 1) (previously Children and Young Persons Act, 1963).

Grounds
: The local authority has a duty to promote the welfare of children by attempting to prevent their coming into care by the provision of advice, guidance and assistance in kind and (in exceptional circumstances) cash.

Decision
: The local authority cannot refuse to exercise this duty in a given case if there is a demonstratable need for intervention. The

parents can refuse to co-operate, for example by refusing access to the social worker.

Duration   For as long as necessary until the child is eighteen, and thereafter provided that the client's problem is covered by other legislation (e.g. the Mental Health Act).

Appeal   Since intervention is not based on a Statutory Order, there are no statutory rights of appeal on either side. If the parents refuse co-operation to 'voluntary' intervention, the authority has a duty to consider whether to seek a Place of Safety Order, initiate care proceedings or take other legal action. The client(s) may seek referral of a grievance to the local government ombudsman if there appears to be evidence of maladministration, but not professional assessment. There are also discussions about introducing departmental appeals procedures for social services clients.

Reception into care

Statute   Child Care Act, 1980 (Section 2) (previously Children Act, 1948 (Section 1)).

Grounds   a) the child has no parent or guardian,
b) the child has been and remains abandoned,
c) the parents or guardian are prevented from providing for his proper accommodation, maintenance and upbringing (for whatever reason).
In such circumstances the authority must receive the child into care, provided that this is thought to be in the best interests of the child. The child must be under seventeen.

Decision   The parents may request reception into

care, or it may be suggested to them, or it may be necessary for the authority to act in the absence of parental agreement (e.g. if the child is abandoned). The child himself may request reception into care.

Duration   Once in care, the authority has a duty to promote the child's welfare throughout his childhood. The parents may request the child's return at any time, but the authority has a duty to assess whether this will be in his best interest. The authority may retain the child in Care, following the parental request, for such reasonable time as is necessary to make enquiries and, if agreed, appropriate transition arrangements. After six months in care, the authority may demand up to twenty-eight days' notice before the child is returned. If return home does not seem to be in the child's best interest, the authority must consider seeking a Statutory Order to retain the child in care (e.g. assumption of parental rights, wardship). If there are no grounds for an Order or an application is refused, the child must be returned to parental care.

The care status ceases on the child attaining his eighteenth birthday.

Appeal   See above (Voluntary Supervision). There is no parental appeal against the refusal of an authority to receive a child into care. The authority has no rights of appeal, but may oppose parental wishes by applying for a Statutory Order.

Comment   This provision is commonly known as voluntary care, because there is no formal court process or Statutory Order. However it will now be clear that this does not mean that the authority has to accept the demands or requests of the parents, regardless of the consequences for the child in care. This should be made explicit to parents before the child is received into care if possible, otherwise they may be misled about the full implications of their decision.

The local authority may 'receive' but not 'take' children into care under this section. If the parent and/or the child refuses consent, alternative legal action must be considered.

Assumption of parental rights

Statute   Child Care Act, 1980 (Section 3) (previously Children Act, 1948 (Section 2))

Grounds   The child must already be in care under Section 1 of the 1980 Act (even if only for a few hours) and at least one of the following must be found true:

a) both parents are dead and there is no guardian or custodian;

b) (i) the child is abandoned;
   (ii) the parent suffers from some permanent disability rendering him incapable of caring for the child;
   (iii) the parent has a mental disorder (permanent or not) rendering him unfit to have care of the child;
   (iv) the parent is unfit to care for the child because of his habits or mode of life;
   (v) the parent has consistently failed to discharge the obligations of a parent without reasonable cause, so as to be unfit to care for the child;

c) an order is in force relating to one parent of the child or an adult who is (or is likely to become) a member of the household comprising the child and the other parent;

d) the child has been in care for the whole of the previous three years.

Decision   Local authority social services committee passes a resolution assuming parental rights. The parent may indicate prior agreement.

Duration   Until the eighteenth birthday, or any earlier date when the authority rescinds or a juvenile court sets aside the resolution.

Appeal   If the parent does not give agreement to the passing of the resolution, notice must be served on him and there is then opportunity to object to the Order by writing to the authority, in which case the resolution lapses unless the authority brings the matter before a juvenile court within fourteen days. The court must decide whether the resolution was properly passed. There is a right of appeal to the High Court.

Termination   a) The social services committee may rescind the resolution on its own initiative or following application by a parent.

b) At any time the parent may apply to a juvenile court for the resolution to be set aside, at which time it must be shown that the situation has changed since the passing of the resolution or since the previous application to the court. All parties have a right of appeal to the High Court.

Comment   It must be noted that a resolution under this section can never lapse but continues until rescinded or set aside. Thus a child who has been in care, subject to this section, and returns home continues to be in care and parental rights remain with the authority until positive steps are taken. It is therefore possible to return a child 'home-on-trial' under this section, and at a later date remove him from the home against parental wishes, although they have recourse to the courts. It is significant that, although the local authority and the courts have a general duty to act in the best interests of the child, an order can only be made if there are statutory grounds, all of which relate to parental circumstances. In practice the grounds are very restricted and the use of wardship to secure a child in care is increasing.

Place of Safety Order

Statute   Children and Young Persons Act, 1933 (Section 40); Children and Young Persons Act, 1969 (Section 28)

Grounds   Any person may apply to a magistrate for an order to detain a child and take him to a place of safety. The applicant has to show that he has reasonable cause to believe that one of the following primary conditions is true:

a) his proper development is being avoidably prevented or neglected, or his health is being avoidably impaired or neglected, or he is being ill-treated;

b) it is probable that the above would be satisfied since this was proved in relation to another child of the household;

bb) having regard to the fact that a person convicted of a first Schedule offence is or may become a member of the same household as the child (i.e. somebody convicted of violence to

or ill-treatment of a child);
c) he is exposed to moral danger;
d) he is beyond the control of his parent or guardian;
e) he is of compulsory school age and not receiving efficient full-time education.

Decision   A magistrate on application from any person but usually a local authority or NSPCC social worker.

Duration   Up to twenty-eight days at the magistrate's discretion.

Appeal   No formal right of appeal by any party. The matter can be reviewed by application for a writ of Habeas Corpus or by judicial review of the procedure.

Police powers   Any constable may detain a child if he has reasonable cause to believe that any one of conditions a) – d) above is satisfied, without application to a magistrate. As soon as practicable a senior officer must investigate the matter and on his own authority may detain a child for up to eight days. The child or his parent or guardian may apply to a magistrate for his release, whereupon the Order either lapses or the magistrate makes an Interim Order (see below). The 1933 Act also empowers a magistrate, on application from any person, to issue a warrant authorising a constable to search for and remove a child who is thought to have been ill-treated, assaulted or neglected, including the right to force entry to find the child and the right to require medical examination.

Termination   The Order lapses at the end of the stated period unless application is made, usually to a juvenile court, for a further Order, usually in care proceedings (see below).

The child may be returned home at any time, but remains subject to the Order until it lapses. If it is decided to take no further action, it is good practice to inform the magistrate of the outcome of the case.

Comment   A place of safety is defined as virtually any place willing to receive the child (e.g. hospital, community home, relative, foster home). The child is not technically in local authority care and parental rights remain with the parents, although most children are cared for by the local authority. It is not necessary to prove the grounds for concern at this stage, merely to show that the applicant has reasonable grounds for believing them. Evidence may include hearsay and rumour if this has direct bearing, and the applicant need not have actually seen the child, although this is usually preferable. There is current debate about the appropriate duration of the Order, with some arguing that the matter should be brought before a full juvenile court as soon as possible (i.e. within a few days) since the parents and child are not usually represented before the original magistrate and should have a right to challenge the Order at the earliest possible time. In practice, cases heard within days of the Order are inevitably brief, witnesses are not available, and most lawyers will be unable to proceed at such short notice. The magistrates usually hear an outline of the evidence and allow only brief comment from parents before making an Interim Order (see below) pending a full hearing at a later date. Parents usually find this procedure painful and they resent their sense of powerlessness. If a twenty-eight

day Order is made, it is often possible to
complete the hearing within that time. An
Order under this section does not
necessarily result in care proceedings: this
is at the discretion of the local authority,
NSPCC or police. In some cases alternative
legal action is taken and in others none is
required. A short Order usually results in a
juvenile court hearing, although in a few
cases more time would have prevented this
necessity. There are powerful arguments
for always granting twenty-eight day Orders and if necessary the legislation should
be amended accordingly.

Interim Care Order

Statute   Children and Young Persons Act, 1969
(Section 2(10), 20(2), 22, 28(6))

Grounds   As for Place of Safety Order (above), but
also

   f) the child is guilty of an offence (excluding homicide).

The court must also be satisfied of a secondary condition, that he is in need of care or
control which he is unlikely to receive unless an Order is made.

Applicant   Local authority, NSPCC or police through
care proceedings (see below).

Decision   Juvenile court (or individual magistrate –
rare).

Duration   No longer than twenty-eight days, but may
be renewed.

Appeal   High court.

Comment   An Interim Care Order may be sought in
care proceedings without recourse to emergency removal of the child, or may follow
the granting of a Place of Safety Order. It

transfers parental rights to the local authority and has the full status of a Care Order, apart from the time limit. Courts differ over the amount of evidence required before making an Order, some hearing an outline of evidence, others demanding that the grounds be proved. Situations when an Order may be appropriate include cases where the evidence is not yet complete, a witness cannot be present, an adult prosecution is pending which takes precedence, one of the parties is not legally represented and wishes to be so, the court has insufficient time to hear the case. There is no limit on the number of successive Interim Orders and in some cases they extend over a year, usually because adult prosecution in a higher court is pending. It is recognised that this is not in the best interest of the child and courts have been advised to facilitate a speedy conclusion to the case.

Care Order

Statute	Children and Young Persons Act, 1969 (Section 1(3)).
Grounds	As Interim Care Order, above.
Applicant	Local authority, NSPCC or police.
Decision	Juvenile court.
Duration	Until eighteenth birthday (nineteenth if made when child over sixteen), or until otherwise discharged by the court on application from the local authority, child or parent acting on his behalf. Such application may be made at any time.
Appeal	The child (or parent acting on his behalf), but not the applicant, may appeal to the Crown Court.

Termination	By the juvenile court on application from the child, parent acting on his behalf or the local authority. The court may substitute a Supervision Order (see below), make no further Order or refuse to vary the Care Order.
Comment	Once in care, the local authority has absolute right to decide where to place the child, what access to allow the parents, and how to care for the child. The child may be placed with the parents, but the authority retains parental rights until the Order is discharged by the court, and so may remove the child at any time without the need for a Place of Safety Order; this situation is commonly known as 'home-on-trial'.

Supervision Order

Statute	Children and Young Persons Act, 1969 (Section 1(3)).
Grounds	As Interim Care Order (above).
Applicant	Local authority, NSPCC or police.
Decision	Juvenile court.
Duration	Up to three years or eighteenth birthday, whichever is earlier.
Appeal	As Care Order (see above).
Termination	By the juvenile court on application from the child, parent acting on his behalf, or local authority. A Care Order may be substituted, in which case it is not necessary to prove again the primary condition, but it is necessary to prove the secondary condition that the child is in need of care and control which he is unlikely to receive unless an Order is made (see Interim Care Order, above).
Comment	Supervision Orders can also be made in

criminal proceedings (s7), matrimonial, divorce, wardship and guardianship proceedings. These all differ and legal advice is necessary in individual cases. Except for criminal proceedings, these Orders may last longer than three years. The Section 1(3) Order discussed above does not give the supervisor right of access to the house, nor the right to remove the child from the house without consent. In an emergency, a Place of Safety Order is required to protect a child by removal. The Children Act, 1975 enables the court to make a condition requiring regular medical examination, but it seems that this gives the supervisor no powers to ensure that this is complied with (e.g. no power to remove the child to a medical practitioner) and thus the condition appears to be of limited value.

Wardship proceedings

Statute	Inherent power of the Family Division of the High Court. Family Law Reform Act, 1969 (Section 7).
Grounds	That an Order is in the best interests of the child.
Applicant	Any person who can demonstrate an interest in the child may apply to the court for the child to be made a ward of court. The court may take the initiative without need for application. A local authority may apply.
Decision	High Court.
Duration	Until sixteenth birthday (except in rare cases).
Appeal	Court of Appeal, Civil Division. (The child himself cannot apply.)

Termination

The High Court may vary the Order as it thinks fit in the best interest of the child, and application for variation may be made by any party at any time (not the child).

Comment

The use of wardship is increasing rapidly in the field of child care, and especially in child abuse. The only grounds to be demonstrated are that an Order would be in the child's interest and thus there is no requirement to prove the specific grounds outlined in the Children and Young Persons Act 1969, for example. It is generally accepted that Wardship proceedings should not be used when there are reasonable grounds for initiating care proceedings, but where there is concern and insufficient grounds, wardship is possible. A social worker would be negligent if he had concern about a child but insufficient grounds for care proceedings and did not consider wardship proceedings. Wardship is an expensive, often protracted and cumbersome process and some argue that the same protection to children could be afforded by amending the Children and Young Persons Act 1969 to include an additional ground for proceedings, namely that the child is demonstrably in need of care or control which he would not receive in the absence of an Order (i.e. in effect the second leg, or something similar, would be sufficient grounds on their own). This would give magistrates the same scope as the wardship judge, whilst making the procedure less costly and more accessible for all concerned. It would seem to have the disadvantage of increasing the risk of being removed into care by lessening the strength of the test to be applied. Orders under wardship proceedings may include removal into care of the local authority, supervision by the authority, placement with specified adults and other conditions as the court thinks fit in the interest of the child. Such Orders usually give less discretion to local authorities than the Children and Young Persons Act 1969 Orders, since all changes which materially affect the welfare of the child have to be reported to the court for guidance.

Matrimonial laws

Statutes   Matrimonial Proceedings (Magistrates' Courts) Act, 1960
Guardianship of Minors Act, 1971
Guardianship Act, 1973
Matrimonial Causes Act, 1973.

The laws as they affect children who are involved in the divorce or separation of their parents are complex and too detailed for discussion here. When considering divorce or legal separation, the court must consider the needs and future welfare of the children. The courts have wide powers to commit or retain a child in care, to make a Supervision Order or some other Order. Once children have come within the scope of this legislation the courts retain an interest in their future welfare and may receive applications to make or vary Orders from any person with an interest in the child, including the local authority. Thus if there is concern about confirmed, suspected or risk of child abuse and the child's parents are legally divorced or separated, it may be preferable for the local authority to bring this to the attention of the relevant matrimonial court, rather than initiate care proceedings.

PART III

Continuing Work with the Family

15

The Helping Process

Introduction

Our aim in this chapter is to describe a way of helping families with their problems which they seem to find helpful and which we find can result in some progress towards a greater sense of fulfilment for them. However we must stress again that child abuse is not a unitary phenomenon, but a symptom of many very different family and individual problems and, as suggested in previous chapters, the appropriate treatment/intervention should vary according to the nature of that problem. There is no single form of treatment for child abuse; work with abusing families potentially embraces any or all forms of treatment practised by many different professions. There are nevertheless certain fundamental principles (see Chapter 7) and common knowledge about human behaviour which should underlie all attempts to help families in distress.

Whichever approach is chosen, and this will depend on the unique circumstances of the family and the available skill and resources of the therapists, it will always be necessary to balance the individual needs of family members, and in particular the parents on the one hand and the child on the other. It is never acceptable to sacrifice the interests of the child for the therapeutic benefit of the parents.

We concentrate specifically on the needs of the abused child in Chapter 17.

It will also be necessary to remember the multidisciplinary dimension. After the burst of activity and co-ordination at the time of the initial crisis, it is easy for this to be lost. Workers concentrate on their particular role and other work, and tend to drift apart. Routine three or six monthly review conferences do not necessarily overcome this because evidence suggests that commitment wanes if there is nothing specific to discuss, and so attendance falls. The multidisciplinary team should meet at least once a year, there should be regular contact by 'phone or informal meeting and additional review conferences when issues arise.

Treatment approaches

All theories about the treatment of individuals who have personal or social problems acknowledge the contribution of past experience. However the conceptual frameworks which theorists construct to explain the origin of behaviour differ significantly, and from these differences arise different methods of changing behaviour. What follows is a very basic review of a number of different approaches.

Psychotherapy

All psychotherapeutic methods have their origins in psychoanalytic theory of human personality development, but there are many variations which differ significantly in perspective and orientation (from traditional psychoanalysis to forms of social casework). They all share a sickness model derived from a medical approach. Treatment is within the context of a relationship between therapist and patient/client, aiming to produce trust, attachment, identification, insight into the deeper cause of the problem and motivation for change. Thus child abuse is viewed as a symptom of personality disorder in the parent and the success of the treatment will be seen in identification with the therapist, improved impulse control and social functioning, enhanced self-esteem, and the maintenance of mutually satisfying relationships with others.

Behaviour therapy
This model derives from learning theory, which asserts that behaviour is a function of past experience and learnt responses. Undesirable behaviour itself is the nub of the matter, rather than some underlying personality problem or disorder. The treatment mode is therefore re-educative, focusing on specific behaviours which need to be modified. Treatment techniques are highly specific and can only follow a thorough assessment of individual/family functioning. They have the virtue of being based on what is observable and therefore change can be seen and measured. Success with one task may enhance general self-confidence and capacity for self-criticism and learning. In child abuse, the problem will be seen as inappropriate behavioural responses of the parent to the child in certain situations, which will be modified by exercises and gradual progress.

Family therapy
This approach is based on study of the family as a social system. It is argued that problems arise from the way people relate to each other rather than from the behaviour of one 'sick' individual. Behaviour and interaction become the focus for intervention. Family interaction is assessed and demonstrated during sessions involving all family members together. More helpful ways of relating are shown using such techniques as role play, sculpting, role reversal, communication exercises and discussion. The approach requires very active intervention and the full co-operation of the whole family. Such an approach would tend to see child abuse as an inappropriate way of coping with tensions in family relationships in general.

Group work
Working with groups of parents or children can take many forms, from groups of highly articulate people talking about

their common problems and gaining insight into and mastery over their feelings and social behaviour, to groups of verbally inaccessible people who can engage in activities and shared tasks through which social isolation is reduced and social behaviour and social skills are enhanced. Some groups operate on a psychoanalytic model, others behaviourist and others with no explicit theoretical base, but aiming to reduce isolation and encourage friendship. In all forms, the role of the therapist is acknowledged to be only part of the therapy, the group members themselves acting in effect as 'mutual therapists'.

This can be a very valuable approach in work with abusing parents. Bringing parents together reduces their sense of isolation. They are often reassured to meet other parents with similar problems, particularly those who are able to talk about progress with their difficulties. Sharing in activities provides opportunities for the acquisition of practical and social skills. Formal discussion needs sensitive handling and in our experience cannot be sustained for long. Specific task groups seem more productive and much learning flows from natural conversation. Children obviously benefit from group experiences in playgroup or nursery, and we suggest in Chapter 17 that group work may be a very valuable approach to work with adolescents who have been abused.

Task-centred casework

There have been a number of publications recently advocating a reality-based approach to problem solving. Most require explicit agreement between therapist and client about problems and objectives, which forms a 'contract' including specific tasks to be completed between sessions. Most have a time-limit and there is evidence that as the sessions draw to an end, the client becomes increasingly motivated to change ('the goal gradient'). This approach can be usefully incorporated within a more long-term strategy in child abuse cases, but the short-term nature of the 'pure' approach makes it inappropriate as the sole model in most abuse cases.

Advocacy/practical help

This approach sees the client as relatively powerless in his situation and the therapist acts on his behalf, for example in negotiations for financial benefits, over debt problems and also the provision of practical help. The hope is that the parent will learn from the approach of the therapist and gradually assume a more independent role.

Touch and relaxation

Some have found that personality inhibitions can be relaxed by use of therapies using touch and massage. This forms an important part of the approach of The Triangle family centre in Amsterdam. Through physical relaxation, touching exercises and even meditation, families are helped to develop more self-awareness and control over their impulses.

Unitary approach/patch systems

This model of social service delivery sees the social worker as not only therapist but also community facilitator and co-ordinator. His role is to seek out and if necessary create groups and activities in the community to which he can refer people with problems. This may involve him in supporting a tenants' association, bringing volunteers together to visit house-bound people and working with other agencies (e.g. schools and police) to alleviate common problems. He may personally visit and act as therapist for some clients, but the aim is to encourage self-help and support from others in the community. Such an approach would help the social worker trying to reduce the social isolation of an abusing family, although skilled intervention would probably be required as well.

Whilst theorists tend to argue persuasively for their own approach, most workers are eclectic in their approach, drawing on those aspects of the various theories which they find helpful. There is some evidence that knowledge about and skills in using the various models are not as developed as would be hoped and there is a need for training and encouragement for workers to become more discriminating in the approaches they adopt. There is also some evidence that the method or theory applied has less effect on outcome than the confidence and determination of the worker/therapist.

None of these approaches can be undertaken without careful assessment of the social functioning of each individual within the family and of all their social roles. Continuing re-assessment and evaluation are essential. All require the co-operation of the family and considerable expenditure of time by the worker. It is also essential to have regular consultation with a supervisor or consultant, to retain objectivity and test perceptions.

Many workers find that by far the most difficult task they face is engaging the parents' co-operation and commitment to change. Very little has been written on this subject, despite its crucial significance for social work and other professions. One approach is to see resistance as a consequence of denial or projection (see Chapter 11), which result from 'immaturity'. We now consider this problem, within the context of developmental psychology, a grounding in which is essential for all working in the field of family problems, regardless of their treatment approach.

Reaching the 'immature' parent

Not all abusing parents have serious personality disorders or grossly immature personalities, but some do and this section focuses especially on this group. These parents are impetuous, angry, sad and easily frustrated, with poor self-control. Their capacity to give and receive love from other adults and especially from children is seriously impaired. Many are 'stuck' in their own childhood; they have never matured because of the damaging emotional environment in which they were reared, but have developed negative personality characteristics which inhibit all their relationships.

If this interpretation of their psychological state is correct, it follows that one of the major tasks of therapy is to promote emotional growth, maturity and an ability to cope with life, especially relationships with others. Such maturation is usually very slow and thus may not meet the immediate needs of the child.

In Chapter 1 we discussed the various stages of child development, concluding with a summary of Erikson's 'eight stages of man'. It is helpful to think of treatment for this group in terms based on this approach. It is not the only theoretical model and may not turn out to be the best, but it reflects our understanding of the problem at the moment. Erikson suggests that development consists of a series of crucial growth points which form natural stages in growing up. At each stage positive or negative personality characteristics may predominate. We now consider these growth points in the context of our work with parents.

Most babies learn 'basic trust' through their relationship with a predictable, caring parent. This is fundamental to all subsequent relationships. If the infant finds that trust is misplaced, met by coldness, rejection or even cruelty, a sense of inner danger, threat or fear will permeate future relationships unless there is a subsequent healing experience. A sense of security in mutual dependency is equally important for the future. The ability to form mutually satisfying relationships, especially with spouse and child, is significantly influenced by the experience of childhood. The therapeutic relationship with parents whose own childhood was damaged is based on this 'good parent' model, helping them come to terms with their own childhood experience in order to improve the relationship with their own children.

Forming and nurturing this 'parent-like' relationship is stressful and time-consuming for the worker. Parents who abuse their children are not always easy to like and often make the worker feel unwanted and rejected because of their massive denial of their problems and inability to acknowledge help. As we discuss in Chapters 11 and 17, many will have learnt that all motives are suspect and those closest to them are as likely to be cruel as kind. There is no reason why the parents should welcome or trust the worker at first and they have every right to be suspicious.

Refusal or inability to acknowledge the problem is common and may persist long after the parents have accepted and benefited from help. The worker may feel it something of a paradox to be helping somebody with a problem the existence of which is denied, and this will be particularly stressful for those who believe that the client's expressed wishes must always be taken at face value and respected. One young mother seriously injured her four-month-old baby, but could never admit doing so. Eighteen months after intervention her second child was born and she was able to provide good care for her. The nearest she could go to acknowledging the original problems was when she said: 'It's funny, you know, but I don't get angry with Timothy like I used to do with Karen.'

In the initial stages parents will typically react with aggression and hostility or alternatively appear very co-operative and submissive. Both reactions mask feelings of fear and desperation and should not be taken at face value; they are the result of life-long experience of adults in positions of power or authority. There may also be considerable ambivalence to the worker, one day very welcoming and the next angry and rejecting, reflecting their desperate search for love and acceptance but also their deep-rooted fear of rejection. We have already discussed the significance of denial for case management in Chapter 11.

The worker's response to this must be as a 'good parent'. He has to prove to the parents that they can safely place trust in their relationship with him, and that he believes they are really worth helping. This message is most powerfully conveyed not in what is said, although that is important, but in what is done. The worker has to demonstrate that his concern is genuine – he really does want to help this parent in particular. This can often begin by helping sort out the many financial and practical problems which beset many abusing parents, although it is important that they are encouraged to use their existing sources of advice or support, if any. Tangible assistance such as a lift to clinic, writing to the housing department, sorting out the budget, getting a pram or cot, some bedding or badly needed clothing will show that the worker does care.

The parents' response will often be 'I don't know why you bother – it's only your job – you're paid to do this so you can't really care'. This can be hurtful and the worker may feel angry and dispirited, especially if he has put himself to considerable inconvenience, but they are an inevitable part of the testing out of the worker to see what he is really like. Lack of sincerity or commitment will be sensed and will undermine any effort to help. Very often such statements are really questions seeking reassurance. In one case, a visit on Saturday morning to replace two broken window panes led the mother to say 'I wish I could care as much for Mandy as you seem to care about me'. Growth had begun.

Patient and attentive listening, and recalling with them what they said in a previous conversation, help parents to develop a sense of worth and self-esteem. It also provides a good model of behaviour for them to copy.

In our experience, those working with abusing parents cannot be remote and aloof. We emphasise informality and give a lot of ourselves in the relationship. It is useful to find areas of common interest, to share experiences, acknowledge each other's fallibility and thereby to reassure them that they are relating to a real person. In talking about our own successes and failures, the parent can begin to learn that everybody has good and bad parts to their personality and that life is a struggle between them, but that it is not necessary for the bad always to win. It is especially important to praise anything done even marginally well and to search out and encourage anything they are interested in.

A good parent is always available to the child or makes arrangements for somebody else known to the child to be there instead. The worker has to emulate that model. Round-the-clock availability is essential in child abuse cases, even though parents rarely make contact out of hours. It is nevertheless important and necessary for them to know whom they can ring when there is a crying baby, family row, overwhelming loneliness or depression, or anything else needing urgent attention. Many will have looked to the child to satisfy such feelings in the past, with disastrous results, and must now be helped to turn to the worker instead, albeit temporarily – just long enough to enable them to develop greater self-control and more informal support networks.

This approach poses a number of problems, not least that the worker cannot realistically be expected to be always available. His time is not unlimited and there are others with equal needs. He also needs relaxation so cannot be on call the whole time. Workers need not feel anxious or guilty about this. The good parent makes alternative arrangements if he cannot be available to his child and we do the same. Out-of-hours rotas can be made more personal by introducing the parents to those who may respond to their call. They should be encouraged to relate to the whole team, not just to one worker. This is more difficult where there are small duty teams serving large populations, but the effort should be made, for example by taking the parents to see where the out-of-hours team works. These families will not be helped by a rigid, nine-to-five service which does not respect their 'right' to crises at other times.

The good parent offers unconditional love ('Whatever you do and however angry I am, I still love you'), but also defines acceptable behaviour. The worker also has to balance these in his relationship with the parents. The use of authority can be positive and constructive (see Chapter 7), giving the parents a sense of security. It is sometimes mistakenly seen as only punitive; personal and professional authority should be a source of strength to the family, not a threat. Abusing parents are usually aware that their behaviour was unacceptable and expect to be judged, accused and punished. They need to learn that acknowledging the wrong-doing is not eternally damning, but that the worker is optimistic that things can get better.

The desire to be seen and felt as a helping person must not undermine the reason for being involved. There must be an honest, mutual understanding that the prime concern is protection of the child and that if necessary, the worker will act authoritatively (e.g. by removing a child from the home). Ambivalence will therefore be at the heart of the relationship. This has to be met with frankness. The worker can never be seen to condone maltreatment of the child or other anti-social behaviour, but, whilst still caring for them, help parents to struggle to develop self-control. Helping them to express their anger in words rather than action is a beginning. Parents often express relief in being able to share their feelings in this way. For the worker, there is always the fear that the anger will run out of control and the violent thoughts become reality. If the child is with the parents there is always the question of his physical safety. It is often at such times that parents need basic advice and education on coping with life, and especially with their children, whilst the worker needs access to somebody with whom he can share and test out his perception of what is happening and the risks, if any.

This approach to work with families is demanding and exhausting for parent and worker alike. Parents begin to rely heavily on the practical and emotional help given and many workers fear that they will encourage more dependency than is good for them or the parents. Over-dependency can become difficult to manage, but in most cases emotional proximity is resisted because of the parents' lack of familiarity with close relationships and their fear of rejection. Their impaired capacity to invest basic trust in others prevents over-dependency.

After some time (months or years) a desire to be like the worker often emerges, sometimes verbally expressed ('What do you need to do to be a social worker?'), sometimes seen in behaviour (e.g. growing a beard like the worker's). Beginning to identify with an adult and wishing to please that person is an important step forward in the progression from dependency to identification to autonomy. At this stage it is even more important to encourage use of other sources of help and advice, not necessarily responding so quickly, and encouraging the parents to work through their own problems.

At some stage it is usually necessary to attempt to help the parents understand the origin of the problems which generate such powerful feelings of anger and depression. They usually wish to explore three main relationships – their own parents, their marriage, and their children. Many of these unresolved feelings have been acted out in the past in their relationships with their children and others. We have found that although parents can be helped to adapt to the needs of their children, their capacity to do so is limited unless they have begun to understand something of their feelings.

When they have learnt to trust the worker the parents usually begin to talk of extremely sensitive and painful aspects of their childhood, including memories of physical or sexual abuse, rejection or withholding of affection. They demonstrate no deep attachment to anybody in their life and no real understanding of giving and receiving love. Their feelings often express a sense of loss and yearning for what might have been, perhaps for the first time, and this usually proves painful for parent and worker alike. One of the most difficult tasks is helping them to come to terms with their disappointment and even anger with their own parents.

It is never possible to make up for the happy childhood which they have missed, but their feelings can be allowed to surface and be expressed, an important step towards bringing them under control. Sometimes the worker will be idealised as the parent who never was, whilst the real parent is rejected as all bad. This is rarely true and the worker must help the parents towards an integrated view of themselves and their parents. This is particularly sensitive and demanding for the worker and can trigger strong feelings. He has to be able to face the depressed, anxious and needy parts of his own personality and his ambivalence about his own parents if he is going to be able to help others face theirs. This is when trusting support and consultation are essential.

There is often a need for marital counselling as well, frequently hampered by the reluctance or refusal of one parent to participate, usually the father. In some cases all that can be offered is help to survive the emotional upheavals, but in others real progress towards a more satisfying marriage can be made. Considerable damage to children is done in an environment of persistent marital conflict and this is a major contra-indicator for the return home of the child.

Further progress will be seen when parents show an increasing ability to manage their own affairs and decreased reliance on the worker. They should be able to talk about their own parents, children and others in a more balanced way, indicating a greater capacity to sustain relationships on a realistic basis. They will seem less harsh and punishing to others. There is always a danger of premature closure of the case when practical problems seem to have passed, and the parents are coping better with life and making minimal demands. We argue in Chapter 19 that closure or disengagement is the ultimate goal in all cases, but the worker must work through the progression to autonomy, rather than desert the parents in mid-stream, thus compounding all their previous life experiences of abandonment.

'Therapeutic separation'

In a few cases it will be decided that the child should never return to the care of the parents, either because the pace of change in parental behaviour will be too slow for the child's needs or because there is no likelihood of change (see Chapter 6). The focus of work will be finding and sustaining a good placement for the child. In the former group it is equally important to encourage parental maturation whilst trying to avert a 'substitute' pregnancy until they are able to provide adequate care; whilst in the latter there may be a need for involvement to ensure that other children are not at risk. In both there is a need for continuing contact which may be difficult to sustain in the face of parental resentment and the absence of the child. It is especially important not to ignore the developmental needs of the former group, if only for the sake of subsequent children.

If such a decision is made, the likely response to a future pregnancy must be considered. If removal at birth of a subsequent child is a possibility, the parent should be warned.

This is a contentious issue, but parents will have a legitimate grievance if they were not warned and their baby is removed from them.

Dividing up the problem

Whichever therapeutic approach is chosen, the worker will be faced with a multiplicity of problems, some more easily tackled than others. It is important for both worker and family that an attempt is made to divide these into manageable segments. Both need tangible goals to aim for which are within reasonable reach. Success is most likely where parent and worker agree on the problem and what needs to be done. This is often referred to as a 'contract' and it may be helpful to write it down, giving a copy to the parent for future reference. This gives a criterion by which to measure progress. The task-centred model has much to offer here, although a strict application of the model is impossible since the worker cannot end the relationship if the parent breaks the contract, because of the continuing concern for the safety of the child.

Behaviour modification is one approach to dividing up or partialising the problem. This requires an analysis with the parents of behaviours which pose problems and agreement on a plan to overcome them in incremental stages. One mother had great difficulty showing any affection to her five-year-old daughter. She could not tolerate any physical contact and rejected her daughter's attempts to show her affection. The girl became increasingly disruptive, soiling, stealing and aggressive to her siblings. Over a period of months the mother was helped to read to her for a short time each night, then to kiss her goodnight and then give her a cuddle on her lap. Physical and emotional contact was gradually increased until she finally reached the point of enjoying her child for her own sake. The progression was not easy and she needed considerable support and encouragement, especially during a phase when the girl constantly demanded attention as she tested out the genuineness of her mother's new behaviour.

Some hesitate to use this approach in child abuse cases because they fear that the struggle to complete the task will result in parental frustration, loss of control and further abuse. Others report that this approach can have valuable results leading to modified behaviour, enhanced parental self-esteem and changed attitudes. It is clearly important that the parents have regular support and access to a telephone lifeline. It may be best to undertake initial tasks in the presence of the worker, rather than at home when help is not so accessible.

The histrionic parent

People with a histrionic personality indulge in dramatic, attention-seeking behaviour and exaggerated, panic-stricken reactions to stress. They are often impulsive and intolerant of stress, use alarming, superlative-ridden language, and demand instant attention. Typical examples include the parent who 'phones saying 'If you don't take him into care immediately I'll strangle him,' or 'If you don't do something I will kill myself,' yet within half an hour they are quite calm as if nothing had happened. Or there is the parent who says 'I threw her across the room,' or 'I beat her black and blue,' but on examination the child is smiling with not a mark.

Such exaggeration sometimes arises out of a need to convince people that things really are bad, a more moderate approach having been tried and failed; resource limitations push more people into this sort of cry for help. Sometimes it is due to upbringing and life-style. Whatever the cause, it is necessary to 'listen' to the behaviour as well as to the words. The parent needs to be shown that histrionics are not necessary. Repeatedly diluting the hyperbole will often work over time (e.g. 'I threw him across the room' – 'You mean you *felt* like throwing him across the room and smacked him?' – 'Yes'). Regular, frequent and predictable appointments will often reduce the number of crises and calls, and save time in the long run.

It is best to remain calm and avoid being drawn into the

escalating panic. Other workers should be informed of this approach and advised not to respond over-swiftly to demands, or threats of suicide or child abuse. Deeply ingrained personality traits and habits take time to change, but persistence, consistency and modelling on a calm, supportive, honest and consistent worker form a large part of the 'unlearning' process.

The obsessional parent

Obsessional people are excessively attached to routine and order, and only able to cope when things are predictable and planned. They find chaos and mess extremely distressing, are usually very neat and tidy with inflexible attitudes, high moral codes and high, often unrealistic expectations of themselves and others, in particular their children. They quickly feel guilty if they feel they are falling below their high standards and are very vulnerable not only to stress, but also to situations which are inherently messy and unpredictable (e.g. toddlers eating chocolate pudding). Under stress they tend to develop a depressive illness with obsessional features (e.g. unpleasant, intrusive thoughts, a compulsive need to check everything), or may become vacillating, indecisive and self-doubting, unable to sustain their normal routine.

Whilst efficient at work, many such mothers find their first pregnancy and initial months after the birth very anxiety provoking. Change itself is stressful and adaptation takes longer than with more flexible people. They tend to become preoccupied with concepts of spoiling, training and discipline at an early age, and may seek help with infants perceived as having feeding or behaviour problems (see Chapter 16).

Fathers with such personalities may be a source of stress to their wives with young children because they expect that the usual routine and high domestic standards will be maintained and have unrealistic expectations of their wife's coping ability. They may have later problems in relationships with their teenage children, finding their increasing independence and defiance difficult to tolerate, and reacting with excessive strictness and authoritarian discipline.

These parents frequently respond to advice and guidance from a professional they respect and may then be able to see the child's behaviour in the context of normal development, exhausting and trying as it may nevertheless be. Helping them to understand the full range of normal parental feelings may make them feel less guilty and inadequate.

Tranquillisers, sedatives and sleeping tablets

Many people are helped by the judicious use of tranquillisers like Valium and Librium, in conjunction with counselling and support, particularly if there are distressing physical symptoms (e.g. butterflies in the stomach, aching muscles, headaches, palpitations, tension). However, others do not respond and may even feel worse. This is particularly likely if there are also feelings of irritability or aggression. If a parent of a young child complains of tension and anxiety, but also irritability and fear of losing control, minor tranquillisers may remove the last bit of control and make aggressive behaviour more likely, leaving him feeling worse. This seems more likely if the prescription is given without opportunity for discussion of underlying problems and referral to appropriate helping agencies.

The same reaction is found with alcohol. Alcoholism is not commonly associated with child abuse, but frequent drinking is. Even a small amount, drunk in the circumstances described above, may disinhibit the parent long before he is drunk.

Sleeping tablets pose a similar problem. Most of those commonly prescribed (e.g. Mogadon) are minor tranquillisers from the same drug group as those mentioned above. If a parent takes one and is then woken in the night, he may be in a drowsy and disinhibited state and therefore more likely to lose control.

If the parent's symptoms are severe and disabling enough

to warrant treatment in their own right, particularly if the parent is also depressed, alternative drug therapies do exist. Antidepressants (e.g. imipramine and amitriptyline) and drugs like oxypertine and the phenothiazines seem not to have the same properties of disinhibition.

Re-injury

It is almost inevitable that at some time a child at home will suffer an injury. A judgement is then required about whether it has been inflicted and if so whether the child is safe to remain at home. The worker is better able to make these judgements than earlier, when information was limited, and thus it seems that minor inflicted re-injury does not produce the same anxiety and activity, at least in those cases where it is not part of a pattern and the parents are prepared to talk, and want to avoid a re-occurrence.

It is more difficult when it is not clear whether the injury has been inflicted or is accidental, especially as the parents will naturally be anxious and defensive. In some cases there is a sequence of minor injuries, some explained as accidental and others unexplained. This may represent a pattern of repeated abuse, or alternatively an unusual number of trivial accidents which may result from a high level of stress in the family, a failure to protect the child, or an 'accident prone' child.

Deciding how to respond is difficult. Most procedural guidelines recommend that all children with suspicious injuries should be referred for medical examination and enquiries made to determine the cause. This involves a major confrontation with the parents, which is likely to reinforce their negative feelings about those trying to help. However failure to obtain a medical opinion may expose the child to unacceptable risk and the worker to criticism if further and more serious injuries occur. Lack of a medical opinion may mean that insufficient evidence is available if protective action becomes necessary. All injuries and explanations should be recorded in detail. Medical examination is not always necessary, much depending on the level of suspicion and overall assessment of the parent/child relationship. If injuries are associated with resistance to help, stress within the family relationships or persistent failure to relate in a caring and loving way to the child, a poor prognosis is indicated and an urgent review of the treatment plan is indicated. Repeated injuries to children not yet walking suggest grave concern. Accidental bruises on young babies are rare, so if a baby is regularly bruised, serious consideration must be given to the need for removal from the home.

Paradoxically it is often the well managed cases, where there is regular family contact by a worker prepared to look closely at what is happening, where injuries are most likely to be observed. As one mother put it: 'You see too much – how do you know this sort of thing doesn't happen in a lot of families,' and another commented: 'When she got bruised in the nursery you were prepared to believe the staff, so why not believe me?' Being under constant scrutiny is a real burden for parents. In some cases sharing the dilemma helps to preserve the relationship. With more vulnerable parents, repeated confrontation further inhibits the development of basic trust and in a few cases will lead to a breakdown in the relationship. A change of worker may then be needed, representing a considerable setback for the family.

In cases of repeated injury of uncertain diagnosis we are handicapped by a lack of knowledge of what is usual in similar families within the community who do not come to notice. Accident studies usually draw on casualty attenders, who may not be typical of all children with histories of repeated minor injury. A study of children who suffer accidental minor, soft tissue injury, matched for social class and circumstances with abused children and under the same observation, would be helpful.

Re-injury represents a crisis for the worker, whose judgement and reactions may be influenced by emotional attachment to the family and feelings of guilt arising from a misplaced sense of responsibility and failure. Supervisors must be aware of this. It is important not to consider the injury in isolation, but to review the whole case, including sharing information with others involved. It may be necessary to re-convene the case conference.

Review and supervision

There should be a thorough review of every child abuse case at least every three months and it is preferable for both parents to be involved in this. Constant evaluation of goals and progress, both with parents and professional colleagues, is essential. It is very easy to drift into inconsequential visiting with no clear understanding by anyone of what is being attempted. It seems that the social worker often has an objective which has not been shared with the family, who remain mystified by his continued involvement. Nothing positive can come of this and it may do actual harm. We discuss this further in Chapter 18. Whatever the social worker's style or theoretical base, he must be able to formulate in simple terms the purpose for continued involvement and his short- and long-term objectives.

Throughout this chapter, as elsewhere, the vital importance of regular supervision/consultation has been stressed. This should help the social worker retain some objectivity, despite his close involvement with the family, and also to be alert to his own feelings and reactions. There is considerable evidence from all disciplines of workers struggling to contain feelings of anger and denial, and also focusing on one part of the family to the detriment or exclusion of another. This work is physically and emotionally demanding and the worker must be able to operate in an enabling environment, with skilled support and supervision/consultation, preferably in an understanding and mutually supportive team.

Supervision of staff should therefore be more than a ritual checking-up or authoritarian oversight, although managers have responsibilities to ensure that work is done to a satisfactory standard. The supervisor should take the initiative in exploring aspects of each case and above all must not wait for the worker to seek help. It is of paramount importance that there is a regular and consistent pattern of sessions. Indeed the supervisor should demonstrate in the organisation of his work how his staff should relate to the families they supervise.

Summary

The method of intervention chosen to help the family will depend on assessment of their personalities and situation, the worker's skills and available resources. Psychotherapy, behaviour modification, family therapy, groupwork, task focused approaches, advocacy, touch therapies and community work all have their place. A long-term dependency model derived from psychodynamic theory seems to help the most damaged personalities. This takes time. In some cases permanent separation of parent and child will be indicated. Care should be taken over the type of drugs prescribed to relieve tension and anxiety. Re-injury is a major crisis for family and worker and indicates a need for a thorough review of the case. Whatever method is chosen, the worker and parents should partialise the problems, set attainable goals and constantly review progress. The worker must have access to regular, supportive supervision and consultation.

16

Common Parenting Problems

This chapter discusses problems in caring for young children, a few of which all abusing parents will have, but which are also common in a wide range of families. They may play a fundamental and central role in the abuse or may just be associated with it.

Most young children spend much of their time in the care of the mother, and the chapter reflects this reality, but fathers may also experience these problems and need help. Advice and discussion will sometimes help parents change their approach, but very often an experiential method is more effective, involving watching and copying how somebody else tackles the problem. In a few cases the problems of parent and/or child will be such that referral to a specialist will be necessary. In whatever context the problems occur, helping the parents to see them in a new light and as potentially manageable will improve the quality of parenting and self-esteem.

The crying baby

Difficulty in coping with the crying baby is a problem that most abusing parents have in common. Feelings of anger, irritation, frustration and even violence that are evoked by a crying baby, particularly if the crying is persistent and not easily placated, may well be the central, or even presenting problem in the child specific group (see Chapter 6). There are few mothers left unmoved by a crying baby and most first-time mothers will experience the same quality, if not the quantity of feelings on occasion. It is of great advantage in helping parents with such a problem to have either personal or professional experience of coping with young babies. If you do not have such experience it is worth asking the opinion of someone who does.

When faced with statements as 'I'm all right until he cries, then I just can't cope, and I feel like hitting him,' or 'When he goes on and on, something snaps,' it is important to find out if it is the quality and quantity of the crying which is distressing, or the feelings which the crying evokes; sometimes it is both. If so, it is valuable to have some idea of the relative contribution of the two aspects. Detailed information about the problem is essential before alternative ways of coping are suggested; observing a typical situation in the home and asking the mother to write a daily diary of events should be tried. Many mothers make unfortunate initial impressions with such statements as 'I feel like throwing him through the window,' or 'I could kill him.' Open-ended responses such as 'Tell me more,' 'And then what happened?' will facilitate the flow of information and often correct the initial impression.

Excessive crying

Some babies do cry more than others, particularly in the first few weeks of life, and it may be that when all the other possibilities have been excluded, reassurance that it is a passing phase is all there is to offer. However it is worth investigating the possibilities of hunger, loneliness and fear of 'spoiling'.

Many mothers expect their babies to take predetermined volumes of milk at predictable four-hourly intervals and sleep the night through very soon after birth, but it takes babies at least 6–8 weeks, if not longer, to learn to take enough milk at one feed to last for four hours, and longer at night. Most babies would prefer to suck a little, drop asleep, and wake up in half an hour and have a little more. It takes weeks of gentle coaxing to train them into more sociable habits. The whole idea of feeding schedules is unrealistic in the early weeks. The first response to a crying baby should be to pick him up and offer food. It is not easy to overfeed a milk fed baby – if he does not need the food he will either bring it back or refuse. This approach is much easier when breast feeding. If bottle feeding, the mother could make up a day's supply at the same time, provided she has a fridge in which to keep it, so that some is always available.

If the baby stops crying as soon as he is picked up or aware his mother is present, he is lonely and needs physical contact. Many babies at this age have unsettled parts of the day, and a baby sling may enable the mother to carry her baby round and get on with other things such as housework or shopping, until he drops off to sleep. The need for company is entirely normal and justifiable, and yet many mothers believe that their tiny babies are 'playing up' and will be spoilt and acquire bad habits if they 'give in'. This is simply not true, and they may benefit from reassurance that at this stage the baby's wants are the same as his needs. His needs may be very wearing, of course, and some sort of compromise will have to be reached eventually.

Crying at night may well stop if the baby is in bed with his mother. As long as she can sleep too, this may be worth trying. She will not overlay (accidentally smother) him, nor will he at this stage roll out of bed, nor is it necessarily habit forming. Dummies, much abhorred, can be very useful too. They won't placate a hungry or lonely baby, but may just comfort a tired, fractious baby enough to get him off to sleep.

As the baby's feeding and sleeping pattern become more predictable, hunger and crying should become less of a problem, but loneliness and boredom become more so. Once awake and alone he will cry. Sitting him in a baby chair watching mother, lying him in a cot full of mobiles and interesting things to watch, even putting him on the floor in view of the TV, will often stop him crying for up to twenty minutes, when a cuddle will be necessary. Encouraging mothers to cuddle and handle their babies may sound obvious and yet so often young first-time mothers feel they are indulging their babies and spoiling them.

Most babies of between 7–12 months cry when mother leaves them – 'separation anxiety'. Later they also cry if strangers approach them – 'stranger anxiety'. Explanation that this is normal, and encouraging the mother to take the baby with her from room to room, will often help.

Excessive reaction to crying

This is often due to the mother's inability to cope with the reactions provoked by the crying baby. It is essential to discuss these feelings with her. Irritation is frequently described but it may stem on the one hand from anxiety, fear and even panic with physical symptoms of anxiety, or on the other hand from feelings of anger, hurt, rejection and guilt. These two groups of feelings may suggest different underlying causes.

Feelings of anxiety often begin in anticipation of the crying and are reinforced when the baby does cry; the mother may even experience panic and physical symptoms of anxiety when the crying starts, or when handling the baby. Fear and anxiety usually stem from ignorance, unfamiliarity and lack of confidence. Young, first time mothers are especially vulnerable; mild feelings of tension and anxiety centred on the baby are very common in the first six to eight weeks after birth. The mother may be frightened that the crying means that the baby is ill, unhappy or dissatisfied, or may just feel inadequate and unable to meet his needs which seem mysterious and difficult to fathom. A bad previous experience of a seriously ill child, or a cot death, will obviously increase anxiety over subsequent children, even if they are healthy.

This is also true for the mother whose baby has been in a neo-natal unit or hospital in the first few weeks of life. The separation from the baby and the apparent efficiency and competence of the hospital staff often increase her lack of confidence, and such mothers are often frightened of their babies. It is not uncommon for the babies to be re-admitted to hospital in an attempt to alleviate maternal distress. Such admissions can provide needed respite for the parents, a chance to catch up on sleep and to recoup energy. However, admission to hospital alone, without a conscious programme involving the parents, can prove damaging. There must be work with the mother and baby together, aimed especially at helping her develop confidence and her own sense of routine. Without this, a vicious circle of repeated hospital admissions, falling self-confidence and worsening problems will probably develop. Mothers who have problems coping with crying babies, because they are anxious and frightened, frequently have difficulties with feeding as well. Explanation, reassurance and support aimed at improving the lack of self-confidence may help. However, it is reassuring to both parent and worker to realise that this kind of problem, centred on anxiety, usually occurs in the first six months of life and improves as the child gets older.

Another very common cause of being upset by a crying baby, again frequently overlooked, is embarrassment or worry about the reaction of others. A feeling of tension and resentment is generated by the crying, for example in flats, when the mother may fear the neighbours' reactions, or she may fear the baby wakening other children, or her husband, and then having to cope with their irritability. Crying in supermarkets makes other people turn and look, and she may feel criticism in their looks.

Crying may evoke feelings of anger, guilt and even hurt and rejection. This is commonly because the mother projects her own feelings on to the baby, or attributes adult-like qualities to him. She may feel that the baby does not like her, or is critical of her: 'Nothing I do is good enough for him, he won't let me comfort him'. She may feel that the baby 'knows' that she is inadequate or wicked, that he was unwanted, or the wrong sex, or that she has felt angry towards him. An over-riding sense of guilt that she is not a good enough mother is again a very common finding in the first few weeks after childbirth. Mothers in the early weeks are therefore particularly vulnerable to this kind of feeling. Many feel that their babies cry or are difficult only because they themselves are tense and depressed. The belief that babies reflect their mother's emotional state is commonly reinforced by professionals, and is probably over-emphasised.

Once a mother has given in and smacked her baby, she frequently falls prey to anticipatory fear that it is going to happen again next time, which makes the negative feelings very much worse and more difficult to tolerate. Such mothers are frequently helped by understanding the full range and complexity of normal ambivalent feelings towards small babies. They may then realise that they are not as abnormal and wicked as they once perceived themselves to be and the intensity of their negative feelings may then diminish.

It is very important to take into consideration factors that will diminish the coping resources of a mother faced with a difficult baby. These are likely to be particularly important if the difficulty is episodic rather than persistent. Tiredness is often overlooked. It may be due to excessive work, or not enough sleep, which may of course be induced by the baby himself. An overwhelming feeling of fatigue is again very common in the first few weeks after childbirth.

Many women become irritable and moody pre-menstrually. Worry about things peripheral to the child may undermine coping resources, for example concern about the financial situation, or marital problems. Serious physical illness often brings additional resources into the household, but mild illness usually passes unnoticed and the mother is expected to cope. A bad cold or headache may make it difficult for her to meet unusual demands from her baby. She may be suffering from a puerperal depressive illness and symptoms such as persistent insomnia, loss of appetite, weight loss and diminished concentration should alert the worker to ask for medical help.

Temper tantrums

The period from eighteen months to three years is aptly described 'the terrible two's'. A tantrum is an outburst of rage and frustration when the child wants to do something beyond his strength and skill, or which is prevented by an adult. Most toddlers will have at least one tantrum a week and, when very young, often one a day. They cry, throw themselves on the floor and generally rant and rave. They may be able to keep it up for some time (as long as thirty minutes) and occasionally may hold their breath or sob uncontrollably. They are not accessible to reason or comfort.

The first thing to convey to the parent is the essential normality of this behaviour and the reason for it. If you are eighteen months old and are permitted to play with water in the washing-up bowl, how can you realise that it is not acceptable to play with water in the toilet bowl? If you are in the middle of an interesting game with some toys, how would you feel if you were interrupted to do something unpleasant like getting washed?

The second is to emphasise the uselessness of confrontation, smacking and shouting. These usually exacerbate the situation. The best approach is to try to predict and avoid potential crises, particularly if the child is very tired. If mother takes something away from her child, she should do it with one hand and with the other offer something else. Precious ornaments should be moved out of reach.

Making an issue out of unimportant things like wearing gloves, or eating vegetables, is futile: better to save energy for important things like not touching plugs and the cooker, which are worth making a fuss about. In this way the frequency of tantrums may be reduced. However, when they do occur, the parent should put the child in a safe place, leave him alone, and wait until it is over. Smacking, shouting, trying to reason with him or bribe him with sweets are useless; a check should be made from time to time, so the child knows the parent is still there. Sometimes children are distractable when offered a toy, or a new experience, but often not. The child needs a cuddle when it is over. Small children are often quite frightened by the force of their own rage, and need comfort. The parent should not prolong the conflict.

Temper tantrums are very embarrassing when they happen in public – as they often do. 'I know how you must feel – isn't it awful', goes a long way.

Feeding problems

Milk-fed baby
Feeding difficulties must be observed, and the worker may need medical help in sorting out the difficulty. Some tiny babies in the first few weeks of life do not suck very easily, or tire quickly and need small, frequent feeds and a lot of patience, which can be very wearing and worrying for the mother. She may say the baby vomits. Posseting, or bringing back excess milk after a feed, is very common, but to the inexperienced mother can be very alarming. If the baby is continuing to gain weight, sympathy and support with demonstration of technique by a sympathetic health visitor are probably all that is needed. If not, a spell in hospital in supportive surroundings with mother admitted too may be the answer, particularly if the baby is vomiting or failing to gain weight.

Mixed feeding
At about four months, most babies are introduced to solids. They are often reluctant, mess about and cry. Patience and common sense are required. They often accept bland or sweet flavours more easily than savouries. The nutritional value is not different, yet many inexperienced or rigid mothers feel that savouries are good and sweet things bad. All the baby needs is extra calories; the flavour is unimportant nutritionally, and not habit-forming. They will also be more likely to accept solids if they are not too hungry, so if the mother is having difficulties, giving milk first to take off the worst of

the hunger may help. Plastic, small bowl spoons are usually more acceptable than metal ones.

Ordinary diet

'Proper mixed diet' sometimes becomes a family battle-ground ('He won't eat'), but if the child is gaining weight and normal for his age, the most important advice is to stop making a fuss. No harm will come if mother prepares food that the child actually likes, and stops forcing food on him that he hates. Large quantities of sweets and biscuits between meals will make mealtime difficult. It often helps if the mother sits down with the child and talks to him during the meal, so it becomes an enjoyable social occasion. Table manners become important from four to five years when it is appropriate to introduce knives and forks and sitting still, not at eighteen months.

Sleeping problems

Most of the problems with the small baby have already been dealt with above (see Crying). On average, in the first six months, babies sleep sixteen hours a day, which means eight hours a day awake – quite a lot, and the mother may not realise this. With an older baby, simple measures like keeping him awake during the afternoon and taking him out in the pram may help him sleep at night when mother needs her rest, rather than during the day. With the older child who is reluctant to go to bed, the problem often solves itself once he goes to school and comes home really tired. Once a child reaches three, a regular bedtime and routine become important. It is important that he does not become frightened of going to bed, and the bedroom does not become associated with angry scenes. Parents should be encouraged to make peace with their child before bedtime – no matter how cross they have been during the day. A cuddle and bedtime story will work wonders, as will lying down with the child until he drops asleep. Once the pattern of a regular bedtime is established, this will no longer be necessary.

Babies waking in the night can be very wearing indeed. If they settle in mother's bed, providing she can sleep too, it is worth trying and will not necessarily lead to problems later on.

'Spoiling'

Central to many parents' problems with their babies or small children is the concept of spoiling. The idea that small babies can want things that are bad for them and that 'giving in' (e.g. picking up crying babies, leaving lights on at night, not insisting that children eat vegetables) will somehow damage them and lead to bad personality traits later on, is very widespread, yet is a peculiarly British problem. Southern Europeans, Indians and West Indians have no such inhibitions and may even appear in British terms to indulge their small children. It is arguable at what age it is appropriate to begin expecting small children to abide by a routine and rules, but certainly in the first six to ten months of life it is inappropriate.

Picking up babies who cry, demand feeding and cuddling, removing fragile objects, giving egg custard instead of scrambled egg, will not lead to demanding self-indulgent behaviour later on. On the contrary, all the evidence suggests that babies who are picked up and fed on demand are quieter and easier to manage later. Toddlers who enjoy eating and are offered what they like have fewer eating problems, not more. Parents should be helped to identify specific issues which make them anxious about 'spoiling' and then decide which are really important. It may help to point out that allowing a baby or child to express preferences and assert his needs does not imply loss of control (letting him be 'boss'). On the contrary, in this way he is more likely to be persuaded on important issues.

Potty training

Ideas on this subject have varied tremendously from generation to generation. Health visitors and doctors currently encourage a flexible, low key approach, even discouraging attempts to train children before they are 2½ years old, yet only a decade ago babies only a few days old were sat on potties. It is therefore not surprising that many parents are preoccupied with trying to potty train their children before they are able to respond. Whatever health visitors and doctors may suggest, the influence of grannies may be stronger. Even the most competent parent is likely to feel inadequate and guilty when their two year old is still in nappies and their friend's child has been clean and dry for months.

It helps both parents and professionals to understand two important points.

Neurological control of bowel and bladder

This develops between eighteen months and 2½ years (slightly earlier in girls than boys). Before this development in the nervous system, the child cannot control and tolerate a full bowel or bladder long enough to reach a socially acceptable receptacle. Therefore training in the sense of learning from experience is impossible until about two years old.

What is possible, and is often mistaken for potty training, is to benefit from the reflex bowel emptying that some babies have shortly after eating. It is often possible to predict almost exactly when a baby is going to empty his bowels, and to 'catch' the result in a potty. There is nothing wrong with this providing it is not taken too seriously. It is convenient and saves soiled nappies and sore bottoms. However it is not training: the baby will not wait and will still soil his nappy if not caught in time.

Social training

Between 10 months and 2½ years children normally begin to acquire control of bladder and bowel by day. Where they deposit the urine and faeces is the training. There is an enormous variation in how easy it is to train them and how soon they learn, and comparison is always odious. In general, girls learn more quickly than boys and bowel potty training comes before bladder. Too much fuss, anger and distress on the part of parents will inevitably delay matters at best, and at worst produce a child with behaviour disorders and chronic bowel problems.

Children learn best by copying and it may help if they accompany their parents to the toilet. Sitting on a potty should become an enjoyable event. They should be praised with every success, but never punished if nothing happens. After potty training by day is achieved, children frequently regress to wetting and soiling if ill or upset for any reason, for example when a new baby is born.

Control at night usually comes later, between 2½ and four years. However, it must be emphasised that 10 per cent of all children are still wetting the bed at night at five years and 5 per cent at ten years. Boys are more frequently affected than girls and often the problem runs in families. Approximately 1 per cent of adult men have a problem with occasional bedwetting throughout their lives.

Bedwetting (nocturnal enuresis)

Most frequently this is a part of the normal process of acquiring nocturnal bladder control and does not necessarily mean that the child is abnormal or emotionally disturbed. If a child has become dry and then starts wetting again, it may indicate a urinary infection (especially in girls) or that the child is unhappy or anxious. Commonsense measures such as reassuring the parents and child and avoiding angry confrontations may help enormously, as will sensible restriction of fluids before bedtime and ensuring the bladder is empty before sleep. Sometimes 'lifting' the child before the parents go to bed is useful. After that, medical help such as star charts, imipramine or pad and bell (singly or in combination) are often very effective.

Soiling (encropresis)

Usually there are two types of causes, mechanical and behavioural. Mechanical types usually result from severe constipation and consequent overflow of loose stools, with little control and soiling. This is usually the result of either too much or too little training and requires retraining of bowel habits after the bowel has been cleared by laxatives or enema under medical supervision; sometimes this is best started in hospital. More rarely it is the result of a physical disease of the bowel.

The behavioural type usually results from emotional disturbances. The child is often angry and soils and smears to gain attention or to make a point. Sometimes a small child may do this out of boredom and isolation. Treatment is often most effective if done initially out of the home. Occasionally, upset and anxious children may regress to soiling, having previously been clean, particularly if afraid of toilets in strange places, or if they have experienced pain after a bout of constipation.

Conclusion

Most parents, like ourselves, will have faced some if not all of the problems discussed in this chapter and most will have discovered a way of coping by a mixture of trial and error and heeding advice. Our experiences with our own children have influenced our approach as much as the families with whom we work. There is no shortage of advice givers – relatives, friends, professionals, books – however those offering advice should avoid being didactic. In all cases, thorough discussion about and observation of the problem is essential before advice is given. As in most things, it is usually best for the family to be helped to find their own answers rather than to impose solutions which in practice are rarely followed.

17

Reaching the Abused Child

The child's right to a positive future is the primary justification for all child abuse intervention, in particular the prevention of further physical injury or death and the promotion of physical, emotional and intellectual development. In practice, most of the writing on and work with child abuse has concentrated on the parents. Since the authors have no personal involvement in specialist treatment programmes for children, this chapter will not report or advocate any new, dramatic initiatives, but the emotional consequences of physical abuse are very evident and this chapter will argue in favour of giving more direct attention to work with the children themselves.

Why children's needs have been overlooked

The emotional distress is too painful for the adults to accept

Understanding the needs of any person means getting close to him and sharing his experience. The experience of the abused child may be distressing because of the child's own distress, depression or disturbed behaviour, but equally likely because the child shows no reaction. He may see his parents' behaviour as normal and be unaware that life could be better. The injuries may be physically repulsive in themselves, but also for what they imply about what happened, and are inevitably distressing. The significance of denial as a personality defence against painful reality has been discussed in earlier chapters, and it is just as evident here. It is often easier for those involved to 'deny' the child's own needs and put energy into parental counselling, legal procedures and 'rescue' of the child to a safe environment.

The worker denies the painful consequences of intervention

Intervention has positive but also negative dimensions for the child. Sometimes the child's distress about intervention is more noticeable than that associated with the abuse, but it is difficult for workers to accept that they also hurt children, even if for a longer-term benefit. All too often adults tell children 'It will be all right soon', when the child knows that it will not. False reassurance is as damaging for children as it is for adults. Changing the physical environment is comparatively easy but consideration of the child's feelings about what has happened and is to follow is easily ignored.

Parental change is expected to benefit the children

Since the parents are usually the people with greatest contact with the child, it was thought that the main attention should be given to helping them change; the children would eventually benefit from the changed home atmosphere and improved parental care. It is now clear that parental change may be too slow for the children's needs; it is possible to prevent re-injury but not to guarantee improved care.

Parents demand all the worker's time and energy

The parents are often jealous of their children and find ways of occupying the worker so that the children have to be ignored. Often the worker has much to discuss with the parents and there are urgent problems to resolve. It is all too easy for the worker to become preoccupied with the parents and leave no time to spend with the children. The consequence is that the parents' approach to the children is reinforced: the worker's behaviour implies that children do not deserve independent consideration.

Lack of knowledge about direct work with children
A different approach is required for work with children from that with adults, and few are trained in this. Activity rather than (or as well as) discussion is the required approach: the worker has to think about what to do as well as what he wants to explore. Some of the writing about work with children seems highly analytic and awe-inspiring, particularly that in child guidance settings, and may seem too intense and off-putting for many field workers. There may also be anxiety about an unknown area of work. The consequence is that children are avoided.

Children need time
Work with children has to go at their pace; it cannot be rushed. Many workers do not, or feel they do not, have the time it takes to establish a relationship with a child, including joint activities and shared experiences.

The needs of abused children

All children have physical, emotional, intellectual and spiritual needs, especially for love and stability. Abused children share these, the difference being one of degree, although for those who have lived longest in an abusive environment the depth of the needs may be too great to be met in routine agency settings. Abused children suffer not only physical injury which can cause permanent damage, but also a violent and inconsistent environment. Many suffer from chronic family instability with frequent changes in family composition and home. It is striking how often parents who injure children, who were themselves abused, are so confused about their childhood that they cannot remember the sequence of events in their own life. There is a marked contrast between that, and the care taken by most parents to prepare their children for any unusual event, such as starting playgroup or school, going into hospital or even to stay with a relative. Abused children have often been moved around at whim and intervention usually compounds this, at least at first.

Evidence suggests that it is possible to prevent most re-injury of children, either by removal from or supervision in the home, but the emotional and behavioural consequences of living in an abusive environment are more problematic and change takes longer. In a study of fifty abused children, Martin and Beezley found evidence of the following emotional or behavioural characteristics with remarkable frequency and intensity:

Inability to have fun,
psychiatric symptoms (hyperactivity, bizarre behaviour, tantrums, enuresis, etc.),
low self-esteem,
learning problems/poor concentration/truancy,
withdrawal/depression,
opposition/defiance,
hypervigilance (frozen watchfulness),
compulsivity,
pseudo-mature behaviour,
developmental delay (especially in development of speech).

Some are survival mechanisms (ingratiation, anticipation or avoidance), whilst others are signs of inner disturbance in reaction to the experience. There is also evidence that the behaviour of abused children rarely endears them to adults and frequently provokes feelings of rejection in caregivers.

The complexity of the problem increases the older the child and the longer the abuse has persisted, but the younger the child, the more urgent is an immediate change in the emotional environment if emotional damage is to be avoided. In the first three months the baby needs food, hygiene, physical care (including handling and cuddling), loving and a feeling of security. These can be met by anybody, although the fewer the better; too many carers confuse the baby, disrupt any sense of routine, and interfere with his need to begin the identification of people who are important to him. A change from an abusing to a caring environment will produce almost instant change in the baby's behaviour.

After the third month the need for social contact and close relationships with parent-figures becomes more important. The baby needs amusement, stimulation and interest. Signs of unhappiness can develop and he may fail to thrive in the absence of adequate physical and emotional care. Abused children may show signs of passivity, anxiety and frozen watchfulness, making no response to handling or physical examination, simply staring around with a blank or anxious gaze. Change in a positive environment may not be so immediate but will happen fairly quickly.

From the eighteenth month to starting school the child needs a basis of trust and security from which to explore the world and test out his place within it. In the absence of stability he will probably develop behaviour/habit disorders and signs of deprivation. Most children will be unhappy if separated from people they know and love, even for a few days, but abused children may be so used to change that they show no reaction. Emotionally deprived children may demand attention from adults by their behaviour. Even grossly deprived children will normally change quickly and dramatically in a caring environment, but stability is paramount for future development. Frequent moves in and out of care, involving different foster or residential homes, are very damaging.

From around five onwards the child will have sufficient memory and cognitive skills for there to be conscious or suppressed reactions to the abuse, although lack of experience of any alternative may mean that the experience is seen as normal. The more disjointed and inconsistent his life, the more problems are likely to emerge. These older children are no longer the sad, pathetic toddlers who evoke sympathy from a caring adult, but annoying, disruptive nuisances causing problems for other children as well as adults. A few will be so withdrawn and passive that they merge into the background and their problems are easily missed, but they, too, often generate feelings of anger in others.

For such children, the process of change is longer and may prove impossible. There is a lack of trust and even in optimum therapeutic surroundings, loss of anxiety and fear will take time. The child may appear to get worse as he tests out his new caregivers to see if they really are more caring and accepting than his experience of adults so far. There are few instant behavioural rewards for parents, caregivers or therapists and if the child remains at home, parents will need support to live with the slow process of change. Residential and foster parents will also need considerable support, and patience will be sorely tested. For many parents, their need for immediate gratification is too great to enable them to survive this time with their child.

The child as hostage

A revealing, stark and even frightening dimension to the experience of the abused child is gained from comparison of his situation with that of hostage victims and concentration camp inmates, in a paper by Ann Fillmore. She writes:

> The abused child, like a camp inmate, is told to love and obey his warders or be injured, but at the same time given the message that he is abhorred and unworthy of love and protection. He is asked to perform acts of loyalty but at the same time psychologically and physically degraded. Most important, he is constantly threatened with life-destroying violence and often receives violence for no consistent reason or for a reason which is patently untrue. To complete the comparison, neither the abused child nor camp inmate have time-limited sentences – there seems to be no end to their situation.

> That a few days under the threat of death (as a hostage) can change the entire psyche of an adult should be a clear indication of what intermittent violence, emotional battery and intermittent kindness can do to an unknowing and inadequately verbal child.

Research into the experiences and reactions of camp inmates has suggested the following common characteristics:

amnesia about events before incarceration,
denial of experiences in the camp, or alternatively
recapitulation at length of all that happened,
low self-esteem, guilt, self-blame (internalised attitudes of
the captors),
need to fail,
inability to cope with anger/depression,
fear of therapist (perceived as a potential persecutor),
children of inmates, born later, share these self-perceptions,
latency period of up to thirty years before reactions manifest.

The following characteristics of hostage survivors are common:

inability to hate their captors,
support of captors' beliefs and objectives lasting several
months afterwards,
hatred of their rescuers,
recurrent fears/anxieties in stressful or unexpected situations,
residual guilt and sense of vulnerability,
need for reassurance,
need for repeated recapitulation of experience,
anger with captors emerges one year later (re-birth feeling),
generalised fear of strangers persists.

Many of these characteristics, known as the Stockholm Syndrome in hostages, seem to us to be personality defences against a totally inconsistent environment, alternating between threat of death and occasional kindness, with massive fear and rage which have to be totally controlled, even suppressed. Many seem to be shared by children from persistently abusing families, in particular the internalisation of the parents' attitude towards them, leading to self-blame, guilt, low self-esteem and a need to fail. Inability to express appropriate anger or depression is common, with periods of passivity followed by sudden outbursts. The children frequently act out these internalised fears, drawing violence or rejection on to themselves. Most important for those trying to help is their suspicion of the therapist. The child has no basis for trust and will expect the therapist to be as inconsistent and even as violent as his parents.

The main lesson from this comparison is that the child, especially the adolescent, is unlikely to develop a quick, positive relationship with therapists, residential or foster parents and other adults. He will expect rejection and sometimes provoke adults to fulfil his fear. He may have no trust in the intentions of his helpers. The process of change will be slow and must not rely exclusively on learning from the relationship. A behaviourist approach, including relaxation exercises, may give more scope for self-examination and change than individual therapy on its own. Many abusing parents will share these personality traits as a consequence of their own childhood abuse.

The focus of Ann Fillmore's paper was the behavioural responses of victims of specific forms of violence, and the danger in interpreting these comparisons without bearing this in mind is that abusing parents might be seen as hateful persecutors. This is usually far from the truth; they too are trapped in the consequences of their own abusive childhood. Some parents are cruel and sadistic, but most are not, as has been discussed earlier. The comparison does have the benefit of bringing home, in a different way, the frightening reality experienced by many abused children, and gives guidance for therapists.

The consequences of intervention

There is very little research into the impact of intervention on the abused child himself, including the consequences of being in care. In many cases the child resents the intervention as much as his parents do, since he has learnt to share their view of the world. The experience must be frightening, especially for the young child who has already learnt to trust nobody. He is removed from familiar surroundings, however painful they may be, and subjected to medical examination, which may seem a worse torture. He may be admitted to a hospital, placed in a residential home or driven to a strange foster home, meet many strange faces and have little idea about what is happening and how it will end. The child often feels to blame for what has happened and sees the whole process as punishment. He may also feel guilty if his parents are being interviewed by the police: 'If only I had been good, my Dad wouldn't have thrown me across the room, and all this wouldn't have happened.'

It is very easy, at the time of the incident, for those involved to see the home as all-negative and have a happy fantasy of care being the all-positive alternative. Not surprisingly, this is a common public attitude. Yet the overwhelming evidence is that care cannot guarantee perhaps the most important of all needs: stability and consistency. The high rate of foster home breakdown, especially for older children, the shift systems and high turnover of staff in residential homes, compounded by frequent changes in the field social worker (whose role, among others, is to provide a link between care and home, past and present), all contribute to this problem. The average two to three year stay in a field social work post is insignificant compared to a child's life and needs. Those with the greatest chance of success in care are young children placed in foster homes with an expectation of permanence, but for others care seems as likely to be damaging as therapeutic.

Many abused children under school age who remain at home are admitted to day nurseries. This is undeniably a safer environment, but is not in itself a sufficient therapeutic programme for the family. Unless there is concurrent work with parents, there will be no significant change in the quality of parenting. The child may also return home tired and fractious, demanding individual attention at a time when parents are themselves tired and harassed by the demands of preparing meals and getting children to bed and so perhaps unable to respond positively. Some parents are encouraged to attend the day nursery with the child, to learn about appropriate child care; this will always fail unless there are staff to spend time with the parent. Under pressure, nursery nurses will understandably give priority to the children and the parent can easily feel isolated, ignored and rejected.

Special therapies

Abused children usually have a combination of special physical, developmental and emotional needs. Like any other child, if the problem is of sufficient concern, they will be referred to specialists in hospital, child guidance, paediatric assessment unit or child psychiatric clinic, but these have very limited intake, usually with waiting lists, and there is often nothing for under-school age children. There are now adequate services for children with physical development problems but there is very little emphasis on screening for and treatment of emotional problems, which can also be disabling. Family treatment centres and therapeutic playgroups are available in very few areas, and specialist play therapists are even rarer. Few abused children have access to routine developmental screening or speech therapy; most have to rely on the basic skills of social worker and health visitor.

Child advocacy

The Child Care Act, 1980 states that a court may 'appoint a guardian *ad litem* of the child . . . [who] shall be under a duty to safeguard the interests of the child in the manner prescribed by the rules of the court' (s.7). This reflects growing awareness of the independent needs and rights of the child, but so far this discretionary power seems to have been little used by the courts. Everybody in the court claims to be speaking in the child's interests and there is no guarantee that an independent person will be more likely to understand the child's needs than any other party, or indeed the court itself, which has to adjudicate in the child's interest. There is no doubt that independent legal representation of children will increase and that there will be increasing use of guardians *ad litem*, who must have suitable qualifications and experience. 'In reaching any decision relating to a child in care, the local authority shall give first consideration to the need to safeguard and promote the welfare of the child throughout his childhood' (Child Care Act, 1980 s18 (1)). There is also a duty to seek the child's wishes, having regard to his age and understanding. In practice this is very difficult to interpret, especially when an adolescent's expressed wishes differ from the assessment of what is in his long-term interests. The matter has yet to be tested in the courts, but does establish an important fundamental principle.

Guidelines for working with abused children

The following points emerge from the discussion in this chapter:

1   Never forget the possible harmful consequences of intervention intended to be in the child's long-term interest.

2   Be honest with the child about what is happening and share his pain and fear. This may be an appropriate role for a volunteer, especially at the time of initial crisis, if the social worker is unable to spend time each day with the child. Even the youngest child needs an explanation, but, as with parents, false reassurance, although tempting, must be avoided if there is to be any hope of trust developing.

3   All abused children should have developmental screening giving attention to emotional as well as physical development. It is easy to become used to under-development and fail to recognise serious deficits. Simple

developmental tests can be performed by field workers, with basic training.

4   There should be a therapeutic plan for the families of all abused children in day nurseries.

5   Outline objectives for the future must be established before a final decision is taken to admit or keep a child in care. This must not prevent emergency Place of Safety Orders (based on an immediate assessment in a crisis), but should apply to subsequent review of such cases.

6   If the likelihood of parental change is negligible, the need for long-term plans for the child remaining in care must be faced, rather than allowing the case to drift.

7   Specialist services must be used according to the child's needs, but the number of therapists involved should be as few as possible.

8   The aim of all work with children should be to enhance stability and consistency in their lives. Cases should not be transferred for purely administrative reasons. Children should not be moved around different care placements at the slightest problem.

9   All involved, especially residential staff and foster parents, need education and support in coping with the likely hostility and rejecting behaviour of abused children.

10 Children need time. Social workers especially must make time to talk and play with them, share activities with them and get to know them in their own right, not only as parents and others see and talk about them.

18

Home from Care

The process of deciding whether to return a child from local authority to parental care differs significantly from that leading to removal from home in the first place. Certain statutory criteria have to be satisfied before a child can come into care, for example a juvenile court has to find that specified conditions have been proved if the application is made under the Children and Young Persons Act 1969, or the local authority must satisfy itself that reasonable steps have been taken to prevent the child from coming into care if there is a 'voluntary' agreement with the parents under the Child Care Act 1980 (see Chapter 14). No such statutory criteria exists in relation to the return home of a child. Whoever takes the decision, the only relevant factor is the welfare of the child.

The decision-making process is also affected by the mere passing of time. Much more should be known about the family, which should be helpful, but which often makes judgements more difficult. The child will also have been away from home for some time and it will be necessary to assess how the parents might behave and what the home would be like were he to return.

Regardless of the law under which the child has come into care, the local authority has a duty to promote his welfare 'throughout his childhood', a duty which applies equally when considering return home, but it must act within the law. Parents who requested or agreed that their child should go into care may request his return at any time (Child Care Act 1980). The authority may agree immediately or may retain the child in care for such reasonable time as is necessary to assess whether such a move is in his best interest, and after six months may insist on a transition period of up to 28 days. If the authority decides to oppose the return home, it may seek a statutory order to over-ride the parental wishes (Assumption of Parental Rights or Wardship – see Chapter 14), but if the legal grounds do not exist or the application is turned down by the court, there is no alternative but to comply.

Where the child is in care under a Statutory Order, the local authority has a moral duty to take into account the views and wishes of the parents, although they may be disregarded if they are considered to be against the child's interest. The local authority at any time may seek or agree to the return home of a child in care under a Statutory Order, without going back to court, except in Wardship cases when a judge must be consulted about all significant matters. In many cases the social worker and parents reach agreement about what is to happen and the child returns home whilst the original order remains in force. This is often known as re-turning a child 'home-on-trial', since the parental rights remain with the local authority, even though the child is living with the parents. The authority thus retains the power to decide where the child shall live and may take him back into care at any time if it so wishes without seeking additional legal powers. If all goes well, an application for the order to be revoked, rescinded or varied may be made in due course by the parents, local authority or both jointly. If the application is not opposed by any party, the court may appoint a Guardian ad Litem (usually an independent social worker) to make additional enquiries to ensure that the change is in the child's interest.

If the child is in care under a Statutory Order, the parent

and/or the child (depending on the Order) may apply to the relevant court for revocation or variation of the Order, regardless of the views of the social worker: 'The Court, in deciding that question, shall regard the welfare of the minor as the first and paramount consideration' (Guardianship Act 1973). It is therefore not sufficient to show that the parents' circumstances, attitudes and behaviour have changed since the Order was first made, although that would be necessary. Neither is it sufficient simply to assert that, all being equal, parents have a right to care for their child, nor that children are always better off with their natural parents, although such claims may form part of the argument. What must be demonstrated is that it is in the interest of the child for the Order to be changed. Thus, for example, if a child has been in care for a period and seems to be happily settled in a foster home, the court may decide that stability in that home is more significant to his future welfare than return to his parents, whatever their circumstances. This was one of the central issues in the debate on the Maria Colwell enquiry (see Chapter 4).

It will thus be clear that no court, agency or individual has sole jurisdiction over the decision to return a child home from care. In cases with Statutory Orders, considerable discretion is given, in effect, to the social worker, who has no statutory criteria to guide his exercise of that discretion, except that return home must be in the interest of the child, ultimately a subjective assessment about the future. There are rights of appeal against the Order itself and thus the social worker's use of discretion, in which case the court will consider the views of all concerned. The decision is independent and quite properly sometimes at variance with the social worker's recommendation. In practice such disagreements are rare and parents and social worker are able to work together, more or less amicably, in the best interest of the child.

There is now clear evidence that, whatever the initial hopes and intentions of parents and social worker, once a child has come into care, return home grows less likely the longer he remains there. The chances of return home after six months are statistically very low indeed, yet these first months seem to pass very quickly and court proceedings may even remain uncompleted at the end. Awareness of these comparatively recent findings has prompted many social work agencies to introduce a system of case reviews to prevent drift in case management and to ensure early return home when this seems appropriate. These seem to be having some success, but necessarily exert further pressure on social workers to make early decisions and take risks, often in the face of considerable uncertainty about family circumstances and parental attitudes.

The return of the child to parental care will always generate stress; there are inevitable risks and an uncertain outcome. It is therefore essential that, regardless of the time spent in care, a thorough assessment of family functioning is undertaken and contrasted with that made at the time of the incident. This must be based on detailed observation of the family and not only the hunches and feelings of those involved. Somebody, usually the social worker, should always spend time with the child and parents together, in order to assess the quality of their relationship by direct observation. As has been stressed throughout, behaviour is usually a better indicator of what might happen than words; most parents will say that they want their child home, but experience shows that this in itself is no guarantee of success. It is a considerable advantage if this time together can be spent in a family centre or similar facility, such as those provided in some NSPCC Special Units. The focus must be on what is best for the child and in particular the child must never be used as a therapeutic tool to help the parents with their problems.

The decision to return a child to parental care should evolve out of work with the family, sometimes only days or weeks after the abusing incident, but possibly months or even years later. It is a difficult decision, requiring the balancing of possibly conflicting needs and objectives and inevitably involving a degree of risk. It must be taken posi-

tively, with the reasons, however subjective, clearly understood by all. We have identified seventeen factors, most if not
all of which should be present before the child returns home,
assuming that such a move is felt to be in his best interest.
They can be summarised as relating to the following:

the child's physical safety and welfare;
the development of the child's full potential;
family ties, parental wishes and capabilities;
ties with substitute caregivers;
legal constraints;
the extent and acceptability of available help and support.

We now consider each point in turn.

Factors influencing the decision

A positive, trusting relationship exists between the parents and workers

This is essential. If it does not exist there is no reliable basis
for assessment. There must be evidence of a willingness to
seek help and share problems, and pleasure and happiness
when appropriate, in an open and honest way. Appointments
will be kept, fears and anxieties mentioned spontaneously
and joint plans attempted. If the early period was character-
ised by negative and hostile reactions, there should be evidence of increased accessibility and a willingness to see
helpers as a positive influence. If one or both parents are
noticeably reluctant to have any contact at all, fail to keep
appointments, and appear resentful, these indicate a failure
to establish the understanding necessary to ensure the child's
safety and welfare on return. It is important to be aware of
passive compliance masking strong negative feelings or indif-
ference, often accompanied by denial (see p. 138) or attempts
to conceal problems. The key evidence is successful attempts
to resolve problems following plans agreed between worker
and parents.

The parents are committed to rehabilitation

Assessment of the motives of the parents in seeking a return home has to be made. Sometimes the pressure will come from the social worker, perhaps following a policy to reduce the numbers of children in care or a general philosophy that children are better off with their own parents if possible. Whatever the reasoning, if the parents are not actively seeking contact with the child or responding positively to the idea of rehabilitation, the prospects for the child at home are poor; an unwanted child is an unhappy child.

In some cases the parents' desire to win their battle with authority is more significant that their attachment to the child. These parents are often under considerable family and social pressure to 'assert their rights' and win back the child. They are usually the ones who consistently deny responsibility for the original incident and resist all intervention, repeatedly threaten or initiate revocation proceedings and undermine foster or residential placements. A return to such parents will not promote the child's future safety and welfare.

In most cases however the parents will display understandable feelings of anger and pain at separation from their child, but will have co-operated to some extent with those helping. It is important to base this assessment on realistic criteria, for example it is quite unreasonable to expect a parent on a low income with other dependent children, to travel across a city to visit a foster home in a strange area, without providing an introduction and transport. In summary, there must be evidence of a consistent commitment to their child, regular contact, remembered birthdays and sensitivity to the child's feelings and needs.

The parents understand that there may be problems of readjustment when the child returns home

Discussion with the parents of the child's likely reaction to this major change in his life should begin early in the process. This can be very informative when assessing the potential for rehabilitation since it provides an opportunity to assess the growth in parental understanding of the child as an independent person with his own needs and views. Many parents assume that the child will want rehabilitation as much as they do, but this may not be so. The parents may need help to anticipate possible behavioural reactions, like bed-wetting, regression and even anger. They will need reassurance that such behaviour is normal in these circumstances and not necessarily a reflection on their parenting, and that support and advice are readily available. It is always hopeful when parents recognise the probable pain and confusion of the child, and that his feelings may differ from theirs.

The parents acknowledge explicitly that they have problems

We stated earlier that it is not essential for parents to have explicitly admitted abusing their child for there to be a hopeful prognosis, but it is important that there is an implicit, shared understanding that abuse has occurred, usually seen in acceptance that there are child care problems. Continued, absolute and implacable denial that the child has suffered and refusal to acknowledge any problems with the child are thus clearly indicative of poor prospects for return home. The acceptance of problems must not be purely verbal but must include commitment to work at overcoming them.

Reduction in personal and external stresses present at the time of the original incident

The ability to assess this will depend first on the accuracy and completeness of the written assessment at the time of the incident, often made by different people some time before, and secondly on subsequent insight derived from work with the family. It is always revealing to read early records and ask 'What has changed?'; inadequate recording inevitably puts family and workers at a considerable disadvantage. Continued contact with a family over a long period, with changes of personnel, can distort the significance of what originally happened. It is obviously inconsistent to return a child to exactly the same situation as that earlier judged unsafe.

In some cases the judgement will be comparatively easy,

for example that of a mother who had suffered a post-partum depression in adverse social circumstances and who has since responded to treatment and has improved her social situation. In others it will be more difficult, for example that of a family with chronic immaturity, disturbed family and social relationships and adverse social circumstances, with only marginal progress since the incident. It would be quite unrealistic to insist on complete resolution of all problems, but there must be evidence of emotional development in the parents such that they are unlikely to re-injure the child when under stress. This should be seen in less volatile and more stable personal relationships, especially with spouse and child.

Where environmental or financial stresses were significant, there must be evidence of significant improvements, possibly including re-housing, reduction in debts and improved financial management.

The parents are better able to anticipate crises and either cope alone or seek help

Isolation and inability to seek help with problems before they run out of control is a feature of many abusing families. There must be evidence of growth in parental insight into the nature of their problems and their reactions to them, coupled with an ability to seek help. Some families demonstrate a pathological need for conflict, disruption and turmoil, seen in persistent instability in all aspects of their lives, including marital conflict and violence; apparently insignificant events or comments can lead to major rows in minutes. Such families represent a considerable risk to any child. There must be evidence of parental ability to channel feeling and behaviour into more positive modes of expression.

No foreseeable stress or crisis

The return of the child will generate stress and so it is important to ensure, so far as possible, that it does not coincide with other upheavals or pressures, such as re-housing or the birth of another child, a parental court appearance (particularly if imprisonment might follow) or move of a significant person or source of help. We have seen cases where a child had to return to care only weeks after going home, because of the mother's confinement, the upheaval of moving house and loss of friends, or following change of social worker or other support.

Greater parental tolerance of frustration

Loss of control is found in almost all cases of child injury. There must be evidence of developing control over angry impulses, and a greater ability to cope with disagreements, momentary frustrations and arguments without losing control. This is difficult to assess when the only child is in care and was seen as the major source of frustration. A gradual process of increasing exposure to care of the child will usually provide some basis for assessment, but it is also helpful to explore other close relationships in the family and at work, where proximity often generates tension.

Realistic, non-egocentric parental perception of the child

Parents often have unrealistic expectations of their child, arising out of ignorance about child development or deeper personality problems, and they become frustrated when these are not met. For return home to be safe there must be evidence of greater parental awareness of the developmental needs of the child and some insight into their own feelings. Where the child was previously seen as an extension of themselves with no separate identity, or where the parent attributed devious motive to normal baby or toddler behaviour, there must be evidence of radical changes.

In some cases the child will have been the focus of the tension and his absence will have created a new equilibrium, reducing stress and giving the illusion that problems have been resolved. The parents may press strongly for return of the child and argue that this is now possible because problems have disappeared. For some this will now be true, but for others return of the child will renew tension and conflict. It is only possible finally to assess this by giving the parents an experience of caring for the child and observing how the child and parents react.

One young mother spent several months pressing for return of her baby who suffered a broken leg at three months: 'How can you say I can't cope when you don't even give me a chance?' There is no satisfactory answer to that and sometimes the workers have to accept that the parent will never understand and will continue to protest. In this case residential assessment/treatment was arranged and the mother took over full responsibility for care of her child, but after two weeks said that her angry feelings of nine months before were returning and frightening her. Attempts to help her come to terms with her impulses were unsuccessful and she rapidly came to accept that rehabilitation was not realistic. The child has now been in a foster home for several years with occasional visits from the mother, who has now formed a stable marital relationship and has a second baby. The mother has accepted what is best for herself and the child, but it seems unlikely that this would have happened without the residential experience.

There must be evidence of attachment to the child, sufficent to withstand the often powerful feelings of rage in the face of frustration and provocation from the child. This will usually be in marked contrast to attitudes and behaviour seen at the time of the original crisis.

The parents have more stable and satisfying marital, familial and personal relationships

Unstable, inconsistent relationships marked by conflict and often violence are typical of many abusing families. There must be evidence of a reduction in marital discord (especially violence) where this was significant, and of mutual support between parents. Where extensive conflict within the extended family contributed to the original crisis, there should be evidence either of some overall improvement or, more commonly, that the parents are better able to isolate themselves from the destructive aspects of these relationships. There should also be evidence of a capacity to make and sustain friendships, particularly in the neighbourhood, thus providing support at times of trouble and lessening feelings of isolation.

The child has been prepared for the return to parents

The return to parents will inevitably be stressful for the child, whatever his age. The social worker should discuss this with parents and alternative caregivers and they should plan together how the transition should be handled in the best interests of the child.

The law requires that decisions about a child in care must take his wishes into account, allowing for age and circumstances. If a child is forced to return home against his will, the plan will probably fail. It is therefore essential to involve the child in the planning, even if very young, although probably not before the parents have demonstrated commitment to rehabilitation. Of course this does not mean that the child's first reaction is to be taken as his final word.

Return home 'on trial' is usually preceded by days, weekends and longer periods at home when some assessment of family interaction is possible and all can adjust to the impending change. This process places strain on parents, child and substitute caregivers and should not be unduly prolonged as it can result in the child becoming increasingly confused and anxious. After the return home, the child will often wish to maintain links with the home he has just left and this should be encouraged so as to promote a sense of continuity and identity.

Siblings have been prepared for the return and their reactions anticipated

It is surprising how often this is overlooked or seen as unimportant, but sibling rivalry can sabotage the best laid plans. They must be involved in the process and their views sought and allowed for. There is a tendency for families to close up when a member is away for a long time, often seen in bedroom rearrangements: the absent member literally loses his place in the home. This is common when he has been the family scapegoat, the target for projected hostile feelings.

Family therapy sessions are often the best way to challenge such attitudes. Sometimes the return will go ahead despite sibling ambivalence, but allowing for hostile feelings. Much will depend on the nature of past relationships, the length of separation and the amount of contact whilst away.

Substitute caregivers have been prepared for the move

Substitute caregivers, especially foster parents, necessarily become close to the child living with them and are always understandably anxious about a return to the parents, whom they may rightly see as inadequate to provide as good a standard of care. There may be disagreement about the wisdom of the move, and failure to carry their commitment can undermine plans, for example they may give parents a cold reception when visiting or fail to prepare the child and unwittingly build up his anxiety. Their understanding and co-operation are therefore vital, not only for this child but also for subsequent children placed with them. The ability to separate is painful but essential.

Others professionally involved with the family have been consulted

As in the initial phase of involvement, it is important to take the views and advice of colleagues in other agencies before reaching a final decision. In most cases a case conference should be convened to assess the prospects for rehabilitation and co-ordinate the involvement of those concerned. The final decision must rest with the statutory authority but be informed by others.

There are sufficient resources to support the reunited family in the community

A realistic assessment of available support services must be made. The social worker must have sufficient skill, and time to increase commitment to the family during the build-up and afterwards. Arrangements must be made for day nursery or school place before the return. If a 24-hour lifeline is considered essential, this must exist without a need to rely on the social worker's home phone number: he may be unavailable or move away. If the reality of available, routine services does not meet the assessed need, the child should not return home.

Parents understand the conditions associated with the return

When the child is returning under a Statutory Order, it is essential for all concerned to know the basis of the agreement. Orders do not give the social worker legal right of entry to the house, nor power to compel medical examination of the child, so many social workers seem reluctant to require parental agreement to explicit conditions before the return is agreed. In our view it is appropriate and even necessary for specific conditions to be identified and the parents should be fully informed if their co-operation is to be meaningful. The only real sanction if things go wrong is return to care, but the dilemma is that if conditions are not met, it may seem inappropriate and too drastic. Conditions should therefore be drafted with foresight and there is benefit in this being done by parents and social worker jointly with a supervisor, with a final, written 'contract'. The goals must be realistic, concrete, few in number, attainable and understandable to the parents; a long list of unreasonable conditions indicates that the child should not return home.

Staff supervision and support is adequate

Recent experience has demonstrated that those involved in making child abuse case management decisions are particularly vulnerable to public and political criticism if things go wrong. Following many of the enquiries into deaths of abused children, public criticism has been directed against individual social workers, despite their being supervised by and accountable to more senior and experienced staff. The participation of supervisors in the making of key decisions, such as return from care, is essential, not only to raise the quality of judgements upon which decisions are based, but also to emphasise the shared accountability.

In most cases the final decision to allow return home

should be given status and significance for parents and workers by involving the parents in a meeting with a senior staff member, who will confirm the decision and any attached conditions. The review process and his role in it should also be outlined. Parents should be involved in reviews and senior staff should consider meeting parents in their own homes to assess progress and redefine objectives. This should reinforce the authority of the family social worker. To some this may sound heavy-handed, but a Statutory Order is significant and must be taken seriously. The parents also have a right to feedback on their efforts or inactivity. Direct involvement of the supervisor will also give the social worker the reassurance of a second opinion based on direct knowledge of the family.

Concluding thoughts

These statements provide a framework for decision but do not help resolve the major issue, namely the standard by which parental care of the child is to be judged. Work with abusing parents can prevent physical abuse but will rarely enhance parental ability to provide love and a positive emotional environment. Thus the child will probably receive less than ideal care from parents and almost certainly a lower material standard. That many others live with parents in similar circumstances is irrelevant since each decision must be made in the best interests of the individual child, and once in care the baseline changes. However the limitations of substitute care have to be recognised; placements are frequently unstable, with children moving from home to home, resulting in inconsistency and negative experiences. Many children in care express a preference for living in a 'normal' setting, regardless of how inadequate that might be.

The final judgement must be personal, reacting to the unique circumstances of the case. Careful record keeping, regular reviews, a comprehensive family history, a detailed analysis of family functioning and multidisciplinary consultation provide the best possible context within which to make these important and difficult decisions.

19

Disengagement

No agency accepts an indefinite commitment to a family, with perhaps the exception of family doctors. Some agencies, such as schools and health visitors, have a general brief which embraces all within a given age or geographic area. Their involvement ceases when the individual passes out of that category, although health visitors have a discretionary involvement (with a problem focus) beyond the fifth birthday. Other agencies, such as police, hospitals, social services and probation have a problem focus; to be referred, the patient/client must have a problem appropriate to that agency and when the problem is cured, resolved or otherwise past, the involvement ceases. The decision to cease contact typically rests with the professional or agency and is usually influenced both by the needs of the referred individual/family and by other work pressures, in particular the needs of newly referred clients/patients who are competing for attention.

Although most health and social agencies will have concern about child abuse, not all will see this problem as their prime focus and some may consider it appropriate to close a case even though the problems associated with the abusing incident are still evident. For example, the probation service is usually concerned with an adult whose offence may be unrelated to the abusing incident and so may see absence of re-offending as the criterion for closure. The psychiatrist usually ceases contact after diagnosing an absence of mental illness and the paediatrician when physical problems have been successfully treated. In many cases these agencies will expect a social services involvement to continue.

Most health services and schools also have the discretion to cease contact with an individual or family if they appear unco-operative or otherwise difficult; a family doctor may strike somebody off his list or a school may eventually expel a child. This is particularly significant in child abuse cases since the parents frequently seem resentful, aggressive and difficult and often fail to keep appointments. It is a matter of some concern to us that agencies sometimes fail to make allowances for the depth of their problems and refuse a service, perhaps at the very time of crisis when it is most needed.

The social worker is perhaps in a unique position in this context. He is also providing a problem-focused and ideally a time-limited service, but the nature of the problem frequently requires long-term intervention and follow-up. Social services departments have statutory duties in relation to child abuse and there may be a Statutory Order on the case in question. There may also be a fear of closing the case only to be faced later with serious re-injury. This chapter therefore focuses particularly on social work disengagement, but much will be relevant to other professions.

The reasons for disengagement

The focus of social work should be enabling people to cope with their lives, so that after a period of intervention the client/family will be able to manage without formal support. In some cases this goal will remain illusory because of mental, physical or personality handicap, but this ultimate objective must never be lost.

The decision to close the case should ideally emerge

naturally out of work with the family, and its approach should become evident during regular reviews with the supervisor. Reality is usually less tidy, with continuing uncertainty about the parents' capacity to manage alone, pressure of other work and also changes of staff, leaving the family sometimes without close support. The decision is made even more complex by the knowledge that intervention is unlikely to have solved all the problems. Therapeutic gains will probably be limited to changes in gross behaviour, whilst the quality of child care in many cases will remain far from ideal. Hope of progress ('therapeutic optimism') must remain alive if there is to be any chance of success, but it is unrealistic to await a total 'cure'. All that can be hoped for is marginal change in parental personality and behaviour with their children, but even this is difficult to judge.

As will have been clear from earlier chapters, child abuse is a symptom of many different family problems rather than a unitary entity. The decision to close the case must therefore be related to the original problems and treatment goals. There are dangers in seeing all child abusing families as needing long-term, high dependency involvement, but there is equal danger, perhaps even more prevalent at times of pressure on staff time, in a purely task-centred focus, ignoring the deeper personality problems which contributed to the incident and which must be modified if further incidents are to be avoided; disengagement as soon as the presenting problems have apparently disappeared is premature. However long the involvement, the process of disengagement is just as important as the handling of the original referral; how it is managed will influence the extent to which any progress will be maintained.

Basis for decision

The fundamental questions must be 'What has changed?' and 'Can progress be maintained without continued intervention?'. The answers are found by comparing the current situation and assessment with the original case profile and subsequent reviews. This will involve consideration of many of the issues discussed in the previous chapter, so comment here will be restricted to new issues.

The decision to disengage should be based on the existence of most, preferably all, of the following factors:

Reduction in personal and external stresses present at the time of the original incident (see Chapter 18)

The parents are able to anticipate problems and either cope alone or seek help

There are bound to be continuing problems – no family is free of all disagreement and stress. What is significant is evidence that the parents are able to cope alone or have reliable access to informal help from neighbours, family or community groups for example. A good way to test this is to assess how the parents coped whilst the worker was absent on leave or illness. This is discussed further below.

No foreseeable stress or crisis

Many of the families will never be settled and free from recurrent stress, but certain life-changing crises can be anticipated, such as the birth of a new baby, moving house or a court appearance with the likelihood of imprisonment. Case closure should not precede such events.

Greater parental tolerance of frustration (see Chapter 18)

Realistic parental perception of the child

The parents should have both learned something about the reality of child development and adjusted their expectations accordingly, and also have developed greater tolerance and self-control in the face of 'normal' behaviour which previously was seen as devious or provocative.

A sustained improvement in inter-personal relationships

The marital relationship should be reasonably stable and the family less socially isolated, with friendships with neighbours and others. Habitual use of violence in arguments should be absent.

Parents and children can have fun together

For many abusing parents, their children represent a constant battle and chore. There is no pleasure in the relationship. All parents and children have arguments and problems but most survive them because of shared memories of happy times together. The parents' ability to enjoy their children may be related to the age of the child, some finding it more difficult as they get older whilst others finding it easier.

Others professionally involved with the family have been consulted

By the time of disengagement, there are often very few people involved with the family apart from the social worker, family doctor and health visitor or school. Consultation is thus both less complex, but also more easily overlooked; there is no major crisis to bring everybody together. Nevertheless a full assessment from each professional perspective is essential.

It is relatively common for social workers to find other professionals expressing concern about social work disengagement and resisting it. Seeking their reaction to the proposal may reawaken anxieties associated with the original abusing incident and there may also be anxiety that the departure of the social worker will shift the burden of responsibility on to those still involved, in particular the teacher or health visitor. However it may also be that something important has been overlooked by the social worker and that there are indeed cogent reasons why social work involvement should continue.

However extensive the consultations, there will always be cases where there is disagreement about the wisdom of disengagement, perhaps because social work involvement is often seen in general and ill-defined terms with no clear objectives, or perhaps because other professions have unrealistic expectations of what change is possible in a family. We have already indicated that therapeutic gains will usually be limited and that there are dangers in perpetuating involvement without good purpose. It may thus be necessary to go ahead with disengagement in the face of opposition. In the interests of future co-operation, it is important that the reasoning behind the decisions be fully explained, even if it is not accepted.

There has been a thorough review of the case with a supervisor

Intimate contact with a family invariably leads to strong emotional feelings of attachment or dislike which can cloud worker judgement and reduce the capacity to remain objective. It is therefore worth stressing again the paramount importance of there being an objective outsider who can share the decision-making process. This decision is just as sensitive as returning the child home and accountability must also be seen to be shared.

The court will revoke the Order

Where a Statutory Order directing social work involvement is in existence, the attitude of the court is clearly relevant to any discussion about closure. There is some evidence to suggest that in the past, courts have tended not to challenge applications for revocation of Orders when they came jointly from parents and social worker. This may change with the increased use of guardians *ad litem*, appointed by the court to make enquiries on behalf of the child to ensure that his interests are protected in the application. In our view courts should give careful consideration to revocation applications, and social workers should expect to answer questions about the basis for the application just as they would when making the original applications for the Order. The formal revocation procedure will differ depending on whether the Order was made in the juvenile, matrimonial or high court.

Process of case closure

Separation, loss and rejection have been significant in the lives of many abusing parents and working towards disengagement may awaken a flood of painful memories not associated with the immediate situation. The fear of rejection and isolation may be so powerful as to induce panic. It is therefore vital that closure is handled sensitively and presented as a positive step forward as a result of progress, rather than as abandonment or convenience. It is also important to assure the family that help will still be available if there are further problems.

In some cases, long involvement will have created a strong family dependency on social work support; they may have grown accustomed to seeking the worker's advice about all major problems or decisions. In some cases this dependency will have been an explicit objective as part of the therapeutic process, but it can also develop without either side having planned or wished it. Whenever there is heavy reliance by the family on social work support, the process of disengagement must ensure progressive reduction of the dependency by a planned programme to enhance self-confidence and autonomy in the family. It is advisable to establish right at the beginning the purpose and objectives of the involvement and that it will probably be time-limited, and to structure the regular reviews of progress with the family towards eventual closure.

Disengagement may well be as difficult for the worker as for the family. Working with a family for months or years usually generates feelings of attachment with shared memories of problems faced together and even shared fun. The worker may find it difficult to envisage the family coping without him and the family may share his concern. However the worker's desire to give help and be wanted must never undermine the right of the family to manage without professional support if they can, and the supervisor has an important role in helping the social worker to assess this.

The process should start with a planned reduction in the frequency of contact, perhaps associated with a period of leave or other absence. The parents' capacity to cope without support at this time should be carefully monitored. Worker absence may reawaken fears of loss or bereavement, common in personalities of parents who themselves received inadequate parental or substitute care. If these are not talked through, they may result in manipulative attempts to prolong contact, without the parents themselves fully understanding why they are acting as they do.

Some parents will find reduced contact frightening and will try to demand more by visiting or 'phoning with problems. This always provokes anxiety for those involved since it is difficult to assess the underlying nature of the problem. There is also a wish not to be seen as unhelpful. This 'acting out' may involve re-injury of the child, but usually is less dramatic than the original incident. As far as possible such demands should be resisted, although re-injury can never be ignored. The parents should be helped to plan ahead and encouraged to cope with their problems without seeking the immediate support of the worker.

In many cases the parents will be consciously or subconsciously testing out the worker's judgement: 'Does he really think I can cope on my own?' or 'Does he really think I have made progress?' or 'Does he really trust me, and can I trust myself?'. It is important that they receive a positive response, otherwise their fragile hope and optimism may be destroyed. Anxious visiting should therefore be resisted. The emphasis must be on building the parents' belief in their own capacity to survive.

Some parents are only too pleased to see the back of their social worker but others will have warm memories of the relationship and will wish to keep in touch at a friendship level. They may send Christmas greetings, call in to visit when in the area and keep the worker informed of significant events in their life. These may be positive signs of a new ability to handle relationships at an appropriate level and also recognition of help given and progress achieved. However, such contact can be difficult for the worker who must always be alert to the possibility that it hides further problems which will need attention. The worker and his supervisor must base their judgement on knowledge of the family and, if necessary, consultation with those currently involved with them.

The worker may also wish to show that the family is still remembered by sending birthday and Christmas cards, but this must depend on the nature of the relationship with the family and the approach of the worker.

The process of case closure inevitably revolves around the ability of the parents to care for their child, and thus their feelings and attitudes, but the feelings of the children must not be ignored. They may be anxious that the departure of the worker will leave them unprotected and vulnerable once again, and they may also regret the departure of somebody who has been very important to them. They may also try to maintain the worker's involvement by making demands on his time and presenting problems. Children must therefore be personally involved in the disengagement process and time taken to explain what is happening and why.

Summary

The various agencies will have different criteria for case closure, which may have little relevance to child abuse. Social work disengagement will have child abuse as its prime focus and thus, prior to closure, there must be evidence that the child will be free from abuse and that the parents have developed trust in relationships such that they can seek help from appropriate sources and have a network of lifelines. There must be a progressive reduction of dependency and promotion of parental self-confidence and autonomy. The feelings of the children and attitude of the court must be taken into consideration. Ideally the parents will have gone a long way towards realising that we are all essentially inter-dependent and can only exist in reciprocal, sharing relationships with others.

References*

Introduction
Bloch, D, 1979
Freud, S, 1975
Watling, E F, 1947

Chapter 1
Bowlby, J, 1953, 1970
Bronfenbrenner, V, 1979
Erikson, E H, 1963, 1967
Kennel, J, 1976
Klaus, M H, 1976
Le Masters, E E, 1957
Mause, L de, 1974
Newson, J, 1963, 1968, 1974, 1976, 1980
Pringle, M L K, 1974
Richards, M P M, 1972
Wilson, H, 1978
Winnicot, D W, 1964
DHSS 1974b
Court Report, 1976

Chapter 2
Baher, E, 1976
Boisvert, M J, 1972
BASW, 1978
Castle, R L, 1972
Creighton, S, 1977, 1980
Crellin, E, 1971
Edelwich, J, 1980
Gil, D G, 1973
Giovannoni, J M, 1979
Hill, K P, 1980
Jeffrey, M, 1976
Jones, D N, 1979a, 1979b
Kempe, R S, 1978
Kessel, W, 1968
Morris, M G, 1963
Newson, J, 1963, etc.
Pickett, J, 1976, 1977
Pringle, M L K, 1966
Reavley, W, 1976

* Full references to works cited are given on pages 277–92.

Rose, R, 1976
Rosenfeld, A A, 1977
Scott, P D, 1973a, 1973b
Skinner, A E, 1969
Smith, S M, 1973, 1974, 1975
Sussman, A, 1975
Zalba, S R, 1967
DHSS, 1980

Chapter 3
Allen, A, 1961
Baher, E, 1976
BPA, 1966, 1973
Caffey, J, 1946
Court, J, 1969
Gil, D G, 1973
Griffiths, D L, 1963
Hughes, A F, 1967
Johnson, A A W, 1868
Kempe, H, 1962
Kempe, R S, 1978
Mause, L de, 1974
Newson, J, 1974
O'Neill, T, 1981
Owtram, P J, 1975
Parton, N, 1979
Pickett, J, 1979
Silverman, F, 1953
Skinner, A E, 1969
Sussman, A, 1975
West, S, 1888
Woolley, P V, 1955
Curtis Report, 1946
Ingleby Report, 1960
Registrar General, 1963
Court Report, 1976

Chapter 4
BASW, 1975b, 1978
BPA, 1966
Carter, J, 1976
East Sussex C C, 1975

Franklin, A W, 1974, 1975
Hallett, C, 1980
Hewitt, P, 1977
Jones, D N, 1979a
Maton, A, 1979
Morris, A, 1980
Parton, N, 1979
Pickett, J, 1976, 1979
Rowbottom, R, 1978
Skinner, A E, 1969
Sussman, A, 1975
Tomlinson, T, 1976
Whiting, L, 1977
Seebohm Report, 1968
Houghton Report, 1972
DHSS, 1974a, 1974b, 1975,
    1976a, 1976c, 1980.
House of Commons, 1977

Chapter 5
BPA, 1966, 1973
Burgess, A W, 1978
Caffey, J, 1946
Creighton, S, 1977, 1980
Griffiths, D L, 1963
Guthkelch, A N, 1971
Hall, M H, 1972, 1974
Hull, D, 1974
Jones, D N, 1981
Keen, J H, 1975, 1981
Kempe, H, 1962
Lorber, J, 1980
Meadow, R, 1977
Mortimer, J G, 1980
Newson, J, 1963
O'Callaghan, M J, 1978
Rogers, D, 1976
Rose, R, 1976
Silverman, F, 1953
West, S, 1888
Woolley, P V, 1955

Chapter 6
Boisvert, M J, 1972
Court, J, 1969
Creighton, S, 1977, 1980
Doyle, C, 1980
Kempe, C H, 1962, 1968, 1972
Kempe, R S, 1978
Kessel, W, 1968
Klaus, M H, 1976
Lynch, M A, 1975, 1976, 1977
Meadow, R, 1977
Morris, M G, 1963
Oates, M R, 1979
Ounsted, C, 1976
Rose, R, 1976
Rosenfeld, A A, 1977
Scott, P D, 1973
Skinner, A E, 1969
Smith, S M, 1973, 1974, 1975
Steele, B F, 1974
Sturgess, J, 1976
Zalba, S R, 1967

Chapter 7
Baher, E, 1976
BASW, 1975a, 1975b, 1978, 1980
Day, B, 1965
Doyle, C, 1980
Foren, R, 1966
Garner, H H, 1959, 1961, 1966
Haddington, J, 1979
Hallett, C, 1980
Jones, D N, 1979, 1981
Kempe, H, 1962, 1968
Lynch, M A, 1975
Manchester, 1980
McClean, R W, 1981
Morris, A, 1980
Parad, H J, 1965
Pickett, J, 1977
Rapoport, L, 1962
Wasserman, S, 1967

Wells, F, 1981

Chapter 8
Argyle, M, 1972
Baher, E, 1976
BPA, 1973
Cross, C P, 1979
Davoren, E, 1974
Goldberg, G, 1975
Pickett, J, 1977
Polansky, N A, 1971
Schneider, C, 1972
Stevenson, O, 1978

Chapter 9
Baher, E, 1976
BASW, 1975
BPA, 1966, 1973
Clarke, A, 1979
Franklin, A W, 1974, 1975
Goldberg, G, 1975
Hall, M H, 1972, 1974
Hull, D, 1974
Jones, D N, 1979b,
Kempe, C H, 1962, 1968, 1972
Lancet (editorial), 1975
McClean, R W, 1981
Pickett, J, 1977
Schneider, C, 1972
Wells, F, 1981

Chapter 10
Baher, E, 1976
BASW, 1975, 1980
Court, J, 1969
Cross, C P, 1979
Davoren, E, 1974
Doyle, C, 1980
Edelwich, J, 1980
Foren, R, 1966
Goldberg, G, 1975

Haddington, J, 1979
Harris, J C, 1980
Jones, D N, 1981
Kempe, R S, 1978
Kitchen, M, 1981
Pickett, J, 1977
Polansky, N A, 1971
Reiner, B, 1959
Schneider, C, 1972
Stevenson, O, 1978

Chapter 11
Boisvert, M J, 1972
Cross, C P, 1979
Doyle, C, 1980
Haddington, J, 1979
Hallett, C, 1980
Harris, J C, 1980
Jones, D N, 1981
Kempe, C H, 1962
Kempe, R S, 1978
Kennel, J, 1976
Lynch, M, 1975, 1976, 1977
Martin, H P, 1976
Moore, J G, 1979, 1981
Oates, M R, 1979
Pickett, J, 1977
Reiner, B, 1959
Richards, M P M, 1972
Schneider, C, 1972
Steele, B F, 1974
Storr, A, 1968
Wasserman, S, 1967
Zalba, S R, 1967

Chapter 12
Argyle, M, 1972
Baher, E, 1976
BASW, 1975a, 1975b
BPA, 1966, 1973
Carter, J, 1976
Castle, R L, 1977

Franklin, A W, 1974, 1975
Hallett, C, 1980
Hill, K P, 1980
Jones, D N, 1979b, 1981
Lancet, 1975
McClean, R W, 1981
Morris, A, 1980
Rowbottom, R, 1978
Sussman, A, 1975
Tomlinson, T, 1976
Wells, F, 1981
DHSS, 1970, 1972, 1974a, 1975,
 1976a, 1976b, 1980
House of Commons, 1977

Chapters 13 and 14
Baher, E, 1976
Court, J, 1969
Foren, R, 1966
Goldstein, J, 1973
Harris, J C, 1980
Hill, K P, 1980
Hughes, A F, 1967
Jones, D N, 1981
Kempe, C H, 1962, 1968, 1972
Kempe, R S, 1978
Leeding, A E, 1976
Lynch, M A, 1975
McClean, J D, 1980
McClean, R W, 1981
Ounsted, C, 1976
Pickett, J, 1977
Smith, S M, 1975
Wells, F, 1981

Chapter 15
Baher, E, 1976
Bean, S L, 1971
Belluci, M T, 1972
Broeck, E, 1974
Clarke, A, 1979
Court, J, 1969

Currie, R, 1981
Day, B, 1965
Doyle, C, 1980
Edelwich, J, 1980
Foren, R, 1966
Haddington, J, 1979
Helfer, R E, 1976
Hill, K P, 1980
Hutten, J M, 1977
Jeffrey, M, 1976
Jones, C, 1974
Kempe, C H, 1962, 1968, 1972
Kempe, R S, 1978
Kitchen, M, 1981
Lynch, M A, 1975
Moore, J G, 1979, 1981
Ounsted, C, 1976
Pickett, J, 1977
Polansky, N A, 1971
Reavley, W, 1976
Rees, R van, 1977
Reid, W J, 1972
Reiner, B, 1959
Storr, A, 1968
Wasserman, S, 1967

Chapter 17
Baher, E, 1976
Bean, S L, 1971
Bender, B, 1976

Berry, J, 1972
Fillmore, A V, 1981
Goldstein, J, 1973
Helfer, R E, 1976
Hyman, C, 1978
Jones, C O, 1978
Jones, D N, 1981
Kempe, R S, 1978
Kinnard, E M, 1980
Martin, H P, 1976, 1977
Page, R, 1977
Pringle, M L K, 1974
Rowe, J, 1973
Rutter, M, 1975

Chapter 18
Baher, E, 1976
Hill, K P, 1980
Kempe, C H, 1962, 1968
Kempe, R S, 1978
Page, R, 1977
Pickett, J, 1977
Thoburn, J, 1980

Chapter 19
Fox, F E, 1969
Hill, K P, 1980
Pickett, J, 1977
Reiner, B, 1959

Bibliography

Allen, A and Morton, A (1961) *This is Your Child: The Story of the NSPCC*, London, Routledge and Kegan Paul.

Argyle, M (1972) *The Psychology of Inter-personal Behaviour*, Harmondsworth, Penguin.

Baher, E, Hyman, C, Jones, C, Jones, R, Kerr, A and Mitchell, R (1976) *At Risk: An Account of the Work of the Battered Child Research Department, NSPCC*, London, Routledge & Kegan Paul.

Bean, S L (1971) 'The Parents' Centre Project: a Multi-service Approach to the Prevention of Child Abuse', *Child Welfare*, 50: 277–82.

Belluci, M T (1972) 'Group Treatment of Mothers in Child Protection Cases', *Child Welfare*, 51: 110–16.

Bender, B (1976) 'Self-chosen Victims: Scapegoating Behaviour, Sequential to Battering', *Child Welfare*, 55, 6: 417–22.

Berry, J (1972) *Social Work with Children*, London, Routledge & Kegan Paul.

Bloch, D (1979) *'So the witch won't eat me': Fantasy and the Child's Fear of Infanticide*, London, Andre Deutsch.

Boisvert, M J (1972) 'The Battered Child Syndrome', *Social Casework*, 53: 475–80.

Bowlby, J (1953) *Child Care and the Growth of Love*, Harmondsworth, Penguin.

Bowlby, J (1970) *Attachment and loss* (Vol. 1), London, Hogarth Press.

British Association of Social Workers (1975a) *Confidentiality in Social Work*, Birmingham, BASW.

British Association of Social Workers (1975b) 'Code of Practice for Social Work with Children at Risk', *Social Work Today*, 6, 11: 345–50.

British Association of Social Workers, *Code of Ethics*, Birmingham, BASW.

British Association of Social Workers (1978) *The Central Child Abuse Register*, Birmingham, BASW.

British Association of Social Workers (1980) *Clients are Fellow Citizens*, Birmingham, BASW.

British Paediatric Association (1966) 'The Battered Baby', *British Medical Journal*, 1: 601–03.

British Paediatric Association and British Association of Paediatric Surgeons (1973), 'Non-accidental Injury to Children. A Guide on Management', *British Medical Journal*, 4: 656–60.

Broeck, E (1974) 'The Extended Family Centre', *Children Today*, 3, 2: 2–6.

Bronfenbrenner, U (1979) *Two Worlds of Childhood*, Harmondsworth, Penguin.

Burgess, A W, Groth, A N, Holmstrom, L L and Sgroi, S M (1978) *Sexual Assault of Children and Adolescents*, Lexington, Mass., Lexington Books.

Caffey, J (1946) 'Multiple Fractures in the Long Bones of Children Suffering from Chronic Subdural Haematoma', *Amer. J. Roentgenology*, 56: 163.

Carter, J (1976) 'Co-ordination and Child Abuse', *Social Work Service*, 9: 22–8.

Carver, V (ed.) (1978) *Child Abuse: A Study Text*, Milton Keynes, Open University Press.

Castle, R L and Kerr, A M (1972) *A Study of Suspected Child Abuse*, London, NSPCC.

Castle, R L (1977) *Case Conferences: A Cause for Concern?*, London, NSPCC.

Clarke, A (1979) 'Ante-natal Problems and Health Care in Abusing Families', *Child Abuse and Neglect*, 3, 3: 1027–32.

Court, J (1969) 'The Battered Child: Historical and Diagnostic reflections', *Medical Social Work*, 22: 11–20.

Creighton, S and Owtram, P (1977) *Child Victims of Physical Abuse: A Report on the Findings of NSPCC Special Unit Registers*, London, NSPCC.

Creighton, S (1980) *Child Victims of Physical Abuse, 1976*, London, NSPCC.

Crellin, E, Pringle, MLK and West, P (1971) *Born Illegitimate*, London, National Foundation for Educational Research.

Cross, C P (1979) *Interviewing and Communicating in Social Work*, London, Routledge & Kegan Paul.

Currie, R and Parrott, B (1981) *A Unitary Approach to Social Work: Application in Practice*, Birmingham, BASW.

David, C A (1974) 'The Confrontation Technique in the Battered Child Syndrome', *Am. J. Psychotherapy*, 28, 4: 543–52.

Davoren, E (1974) 'The Role of the Social Worker', in *The Battered Child* (2nd edn), Helfer, R E and Kempe, C H (eds.), 135–50, Chicago University Press.

Day, B (1965) 'Supportive Casework in an Authoritative Setting', *Case Conference*, 11, 9: 289–93.

Doyle, C (1980) 'Effective Methods for Tackling Child Abuse', *Social Work Today*, 12, 15: 13–14.

Doyle, C and Oates, M R (1980) 'Child Abuse: When to Tread a Careful Path between Parent and Child', *Social Work Today*, 12, 5: 12–15.

East Sussex County Council (1975) *Children at Risk. A study into Problems Revealed by the Report of the Inquiry into the Case of Maria Colwell*, Lewes, East Sussex County Council.

Edelwich, J and Brodsky, A (1980) *Burn-out: Stages of Disillusionment in the Helping Professions*, New York, Human Sciences Press.

Erikson, E H (1963) *Childhood and Society* (2nd edn.), New York, Norton, (Harmondsworth, Penguin, 1965).

Erikson, E H (1967) 'Growth and Crises of the Healthy Personality', reprinted in *Child Abuse and Neglect: A Reader and Sourcebook*, ed. C M Lee, Milton Keynes, Open University Press.

Fillmore, A V (1981) 'The Abused Child as Survivor', unpublished paper presented to the Third International Congress on Child Abuse and Neglect.

Foren, R and Bailey, R (1966) *Authority in Social Casework*, Oxford, Pergamon Press.

Fox, F E, Nelson, A M and Bolmar, M W (1969) 'The Termination Process: A Neglected Dimension of Social Work', *Social Work*, 14, 4: 53–63.

Franklin, A W (1974) 'The Tunbridge Wells Study Group on

Non-Accidental Injuries to Children', *Social Work Service*, 4: 28–39.

Franklin, A W (ed.) (1975) *Concerning Child Abuse: Papers Presented by the Tunbridge Wells Study Group on Non-Accidental Injuries to Children*, London, Churchill Livingstone.

Freud, S (1975) *Psychopathology of Everyday Life*, Harmondsworth, Penguin.

Garner, H H (1959) 'A Confrontation Technique used in Psychotherapy', *Am. J. Psychotherapy*, 8: 18.

Garner, H H (1961) 'Passivity and Activity in Psychotherapy', *Arch. Gen. Psychiatry*, 5: 411.

Garner, H H (1966) 'Intervention in Psychotherapy and Confrontation Technique', *Am. J. Psychotherapy*, 20: 391.

Gil, D G (1973) *Violence against Children: Physical Child abuse in the United States*, Cambridge, Mass., Harvard University Press.

Giovannoni, J M and Becerra, R M (1979) *Defining Child Abuse*, London, Collier Macmillan.

Goldberg, G (1975) 'Breaking the Communication Barrier: The Initial Interview with an Abusing parent', *Child Welfare*, 54, 4: 274–82.

Goldstein, J, Freud, A and Solnit, A J (1973) *Beyond the Best Interests of the Child*, London, Collier Macmillan.

Goode, W J (1971) 'Force and violence in the family', *Journal of Marriage and the Family*, 33, 4: 624–35.

Griffiths, D L and Moynihan, F J (1963) 'Multiple Epiphyseal Injuries in Babies (Battered Baby Syndrome)', *British Medical Journal*, 5372: 1558–61.

Guthkelch, A N (1971) 'Infantile Subdural Haematoma and its Relationship to Whiplash Injuries', *British Medical Journal*, 2,5759: 430–1.

Haddington, J and Truckle, B (1979) *Non-accidental Injury: The Shared Task of Caseworker and Supervisor in Practice and Theory*, unpublished paper presented to 2nd International Congress on Child Abuse.

Hall, M H (1972) 'Non-accidental Injuries to Children', in *79th Annual Congress*, London, Royal Society of Health.

Hall, M H (1974) 'The Diagnosis and Early Management of Non-accidental Injuries in Children', *Police Surgeon*, October: 21–2.

Hallett, C and Stevenson, O (1980) *Child Abuse: Aspects of Interprofessional Co-operation*, London, Allen & Unwin.

Harris, J C and Bernstein, B E (1980) 'Lawyer and Social Worker as a Team: Preparing for Trial in Neglect Cases', *Child Welfare*, 59, 8: 469–77.

Helfer, R E and Kempe, C H (eds.) (1976) *Child Abuse and Neglect: The Family and the Community*, Cambridge, Mass., Ballinger.

Hewitt, P (1977) *The Information Gatherers*, London, National Council for Civil Liberties.

Hill, K P (1980) *Decision Making in Child Abuses: A Retrospective Study of 200 Cases of Non-accidental Injury to Children in Nottinghamshire*, unpublished thesis, CCETSW, London.

Hughes, A F (1967) 'The Battered Baby Syndrome – A Multidisciplinary Problem', *Case Conference*, 14, 8: 304–08.

Hull, D (1974) 'Medical diagnosis', in *The Maltreated Child*, Carter, J (ed.) 55–66, London, Priory Press.

Hutten, J M (1977) *Short-term Contracts in Social Work*, London, Routledge and Kegan Paul.

Hyman, C A (1978) 'Some Characteristics of Abusing Families Referred to the NSPCC', *British Journal of Social Work*, 8, 2: 171–9.

Jeffrey, M (1976) 'Practical Ways to Change Parent-child Interaction in Families of Children at Risk', in Helfer, R E and Kempe C H (eds.), *Child Abuse and Neglect: The Family and the Community*, 209–23, Cambridge, Mass., Ballinger.

Jenkins, R (1979) 'Social Services for Children', in *Seebohm across Three Decades*, Cypher, J (ed.), 27–34, Birmingham, BASW.

Johnson, A A W (1868) *Lectures on the Surgery of Childhood*, London.

Jones, C and Jones, R A (1974) 'Treatment: A Social Perspective', in *The Maltreated Child*, Carter, J (ed.), 89–99, London, Priory Press.

Jones, C O (1978) 'The Predicament of Abused Children', in *Child Abuse: A Reader and Sourcebook*, Lee, C M (ed.), 96–110, Milton Keynes, Open University Press.

Jones, D N , Hill, K P and Thorpe, R (1979a) 'Central Child Abuse Registers: The British experience', *Child Abuse and Neglect*, 3, 1: 157–66.

Jones, D N, McClean, R and Vobe, R J (1979b) 'Case Conferences on Child Abuse: The Nottinghamshire approach', *Child Abuse and Neglect*, 3, 2: 583–90.

Jones, D N (1981) 'Child Abuse – Three Perspectives on Confidentiality: A Social Work Perspective', *Concern*, 39, 20–5.

Kaplan, D M and Mason, E A (1960) 'Maternal Reactions to Premature Birth, Viewed as an Acute Emotional Disorder', reprinted in *Crisis Intervention*, Parad, H J (ed.), 118–28 (1965), New York, Family Service Association of America.

Keen, J H, Lendrum, J and Wolman, B (1975) 'Inflicted Burns and Scalds in Children', *British Medical Journal*, 4,5991: 268–9.

Keen, J H (1981) 'Normal Bruises in Pre-school Children', (letter), *Archives of Diseases in Childhood*, 56: 75.

Kempe, H *et al.* (1962) 'The Battered Child Syndrome', *Journal of the American Medical Association*, 181,1: 17–22.

Kempe, C H and Helfer, R E (eds.) (1968) *The Battered Child* (2nd ed. 1974; 3rd ed. 1981), Chicago University Press.

Kempe, C H and Helfer, R E (1972) 'Innovative Therapeutic Techniques', in *Helping the Battered Child and His Family*, Kempe, C H and Helfer, R E (eds.), Philadelphia, Lippincott.

Kempe, R S and Kempe, C H (1978) *Child Abuse*, London, Fontana/Open Books.

Kennel, J, Voos, D and Klaus, M (1976) 'Parent-infant Bonding', in *Child Abuse and Neglect*, Helfer, R E and Kempe, C H (eds.), 25–53, Cambridge, Mass., Ballinger.

Kessel, W (1968) 'Self-poisoning', *British Medical Journal*, 7965: 1265–70, 1336–40.

Kinnard, E M (1980) 'Mental Health Needs of Abused Children', *Child Welfare*, 59, 8: 451–62.

Kitchen, M (1981) 'What the Client Thinks of You', *Social Work Today*, 11, 37: 14–19.

Klaus, M H and Kennell, J H (1976) *Mother-infant Bonding*, New York, C V Mosby.

Lancet editorial (1975) The battered . . ., *The Lancet*, 31 May, 1228–9.

Lee, C M (ed.) (1978) *Child Abuse: A Reader and Sourcebook*, Milton Keynes, Open University Press.

Leeding, A E (1976) *Child Care Manual for Social Workers*, London, Butterworths.

Le Masters, E E (1957) 'Parenthood as crisis', reprinted in *Crisis Intervention*, Parad, H J (ed.), 111–17 (1965), New York, Family Service Association of America.

Lorber, J, Reckless, J P D and Watson, J B G (1980) 'Non-accidental Poisoning: The Elusive Diagnosis', *Archives of Diseases of Childhood*, 55, 8: 643–7.

Lynch, M A, Lindsay, J and Ounsted, C (1975) 'Tranquillisers causing aggression' (letter), *British Medical Journal*, 1: 266.

Lynch, M A, Steinberg, D and Ounsted, C (1975) 'Family Unit in a Children's Psychiatric Hospital', *British Medical Journal*, 2: 127–9.

Lynch, M A (1975) 'Ill-health and Child Abuse', *The Lancet*, 7929: 317–19.

Lynch, M A (1976) 'Child Abuse: The Critical Path', *Journal of Maternal and Child Health*, 1, 3: 25–9.

Lynch, M A and Roberts, J (1977) 'Predicting Child Abuse: Signs of Bonding Failure in the Maternity Hospital', *British Medical Journal*, 1: 624–6.

McClean, J D (1980) *The Legal Context of Social Work*, London, Butterworth.

McClean, R W (1981) 'Child Abuse – Three Perspectives on Sharing Information: A Police Perspective', *Concern*, 39: 20–5.

Manchester (1980) *Child Abuse Procedures. City of Manchester Guidelines*, City of Manchester, Social Services Department.

Martin, H P and Beezley, P (1977) 'Behavioural Observations of Abused Children', *Devel. Med. Child Neurol.*, 19: 373–87.

Martin, H P (ed.) (1976) *The Abused Child – A Multidisciplinary Approach to Developmental Issues and Treatment*, Cambridge, Mass., Ballinger.

Maton, A and Pickett, J (1979) 'Central Registration of Child Abuse in Manchester: An Evaluation', *Child Abuse and Neglect*, 3, 1: 167–74.

Mause, L de (1974) *The History of Childhood*, London, Souvenir Press.

Meadow, R (1977) 'Munchausen Syndrome by Proxy: The Hinterland of Child Abuse', *The Lancet*, 1977, ii: 343–5.

Moore, J G and Day, B M (1979) 'Family Interaction Associated with Abuse of Children over Five Years of Age', *Child Abuse and Neglect*, 3, 1: 391–400.

Moore, J G, Galcius, A and Pettican, K (1981) 'Emotional Risk to Children Caught in Violent Marital Conflict: the Basildon Treatment Project', *Child Abuse and Neglect*, (forthcoming).

Morris, A, Giller, H, Szwed, E and Geach, H (1980) *Justice for Children*, London, Macmillan.

Morris, M G and Gould, R W (1963) 'Role Reversal: A Concept in Dealing with the Neglected Battered Child Syndrome', in *The Neglected Battered Child Syndrome*, 26–46, New York, Child Welfare League of America.

Mortimer, J G (1980) 'Acute Water Intoxication as another Unusual Manifestation of Child Abuse', *Archives of Diseases in Childhood*, 55, 5: 401–03.

Newson, J and Newson, E (1963) *Infant Care in an Urban Community*, London, Allen & Unwin.

Newson, J and Newson, E (1968) *Four Years Old in an Urban Community*, London, Allen & Unwin.

Newson, J and Newson, E (1974) 'Cultural Aspects of Childrearing in the English-speaking World', in *The Integration of a Child into a Social World*, Richards, M P M (ed.), 53–82, Cambridge University Press.

Newson, J and Newson, E (1976) *Seven Years Old in the Home Environment*, London, Allen & Unwin.

Newson, J and Newson, E (1976) 'Day to Day Aggression between Parent and Child', in *Violence*, Tutt, N (ed.), 90–109, London, HMSO.

Newson, J and Newson, E (1980) 'Parental Punishment Strategies with Eleven Year Old Children', in *Psychological Approaches to Child Abuse*, Frude, N (ed.), 64–80, London, Batsford.

Oates, M R (1979) 'A Classification of Child Abuse and its Relation to Treatment and Prognosis', *Child Abuse and Neglect*, 3, 3: 907–17.

O'Callaghan, M J and Hull, D (1978) 'Failure to Thrive or Failure to Rear?' *Archives of Diseases in Childhood*, 53, 10: 788–93.

Oliver, J E, Cox, J, Taylor, A and Baldwin, J (1974) *Severely Ill-treated Young Children in North-East Wiltshire*, Oxford Regional Health Authority.

O'Neill, T (1981) *A Place Called Hope*, Oxford, Blackwell.

Ounsted, C, Oppenheimer, R and Lindsay, J (1976) 'Aspects of Bonding Failure: The Psychopathologic and Psychotherapeutic Treatment of Families of Battered Children', *Developmental Medicine and Child Neurology*, 16: 447–56.

Owtram, P J (1975) 'NSPCC Special Units', *Social Work Service*, 8: 8–11.

Page, R and Clarke, G A (1977) *Who Cares? Young People in Care Speak Out*, London, National Children's Bureau.

Parad, H J (ed.) (1965) *Crisis Intervention: Selected Readings*, New York, Family Service Association of America.

Parton, N (1979) 'The Natural History of Child Abuse: A Study in Social Problem Definition', *Brit. J. Social Work*, 9, 4: 431–51.

Pickett, J (1976) The Management of Non-accidental Injury to Children in the City of Manchester', in *Violence in the Family*, Borland, M (ed.), 61–87, Manchester University Press.

Pickett, J (1976) 'Registers of Non-accidental Injuries and their Potential in the Prevention of Repeated Injury', *Der Praktische Arzt*.

Pickett, J and Maton, A (1977) 'Protective Casework and Child Abuse: Practice and Problems', in *The Challenge of Child Abuse*, Franklin, A W (ed.), 56–80, London, Academic Press.

Pickett, J and Maton, A (1979) 'The Multi-disciplinary Team in an Urban Setting: the Special Unit Concept', *Child Abuse and Neglect*, 3, 1: 115–21.

Polansky, N A, Borgman, R D, De Saix, C and Shlomo, S (1971) 'Verbal Accessibility in the Treatment of Child Neglect', *Child Welfare*, 50, 6: 349–56.

Pringle, M L K, Butler, N R and Davie, R (1966) *11,000 Seven Year Olds. First Report of the National Child Development Study*, London, Longmans.

Pringle, M L K (1974) *The Needs of Children*, London, Hutchinson.

Rapoport, L (1962) 'The State of Crisis: Some Theoretical Considerations', in *Crisis Intervention*, Parad, H J (ed.), 22–31, New York, Family Service Association of America.

Reavley, W and Gilbert, M T (1976) 'The Behavioural Treatment Approach in Child Abuse Cases: Two Illustrative Case Reports', *Social Work Today*, 7, 6: 166–8.

Rees, R van (1977) *Five Years' Experience with Child Abuse as a Symptom of Family Problems*, Amsterdam, Socio-Therapeutisch Institut De Triangel.

Reid, W J and Epstein, L (1972) *Task-centred Casework*, Columbia University Press.

Reiner, B and Kaufman, I (1959) *Character Disorders in Parents of Delinquents*, New York, Family Service Association of America.

Richards, M P M and Bernal, J F (1972) 'An Observational Study of Mother-infant Interactions', in *Ethological Studies of Child Behaviour*, Blurton Jones, N (ed.), Cambridge University Press.

Rogers, D, Tripp, J, Bentovim, A, Robinson, A, Berry, D and Goulding, R (1976) 'Non-Accidental Poisoning: An Extended Syndrome of Child Abuse', *British Medical Journal*, i: 793–6.

Rose, R, Owtram, P, Pickett, J, Marran, B and Maton, A (1976) *Registers of Suspected Non-accidental Injury: A Report on Registers Maintained in Leeds and Manchester by NSPCC Special Units*, London, NSPCC.

Rosenfeld, A A and Newberger, E H (1977) 'Compassion *vs* Control: Conceptual and Practical Pitfalls in Broadening the Definition of Child Abuse', *Journal of the American Medical Association*, 237: 2086–8.

Rowbottom, R and Hey, A (1978) *Collaboration between Health and Social Services*, London, Brunel Institute of Organisation and Social Studies.

Rowe, J and Lambert, L (1973) *Children who Wait*, London, Association of British Adoption and Fostering Agencies.

Rutter, M (1975) *Helping Troubled Children*, Harmondsworth, Penguin.

Schneider, C, Pollock, C and Helfer, R E (1972) 'Interviewing the parents', in *Helping the Battered Child and his Family*, Kempe, C H and Helfer, R E (eds.), 55–65.

Scott, P D (1973a) 'Parents who Kill their Children', *Medicine, Science and the Law*, 13: 120–6.

Scott, P D (1973b) 'Fatal Battered Baby Cases', *Medicine, Science and the Law*, 13: 197–206.

Silverman, F (1953) 'The Roentgen Manifestations of Unrecognised Skeletal Trauma in Infants', *American Journal of Roentgenology*, 69, 3: 413–27.

Skinner, A E and Castle, R L (1969) *78 Battered Children: A Retrospective Study*, London, NSPCC.

Smith, S M (1975) *The Battered Child Syndrome*, London, Butterworths.

Smith, S M and Hanson, R (1974) '134 Battered Children: A Medical and Psychological Study', *British Medical Journal*, 3: 666–70.

Smith, S M , Hanson, R and Noble, S (1973) 'Parents of battered babies. A Controlled Study', *British Medical Journal*, 4, 388–91.

Steele, B F and Pollock, C B (1974) 'A Psychiatric Study of Parents Who Abuse Infants and Small Children', in *The Battered Child*, (2nd edn.) Helfer, R E and Kempe, C H (eds.), 89–131, Chicago University Press.

Steinmetz, S K and Strauss, M A (eds.) (1974) *Violence in the Family*, New York, Harper Row.

Stevenson, O (1978) 'Obtaining and Communicating Good Information', in *Child Abuse: A Study Text*, Carver, V (ed.), 170–8, Milton Keynes, Open University Press.

Storr, A (1968) *Human Aggression*, Harmondsworth, Penguin.

Sturgess, J and Heal, K (1976) 'Non-accidental Injury to Children under the Age of Seventeen', *Social Work Service*, 9: 39–49.

Sussman, A and Cohen, S J (1975) *Reporting Child Abuse and Neglect: Guidelines for Legislation*, Cambridge, Mass., Ballinger.

Thoburn, J (1980) *Captive Clients: Social Work with Families of Children Home on Trial*, London, Routledge & Kegan Paul.

Tomlinson, T (1976) 'Inter-agency Collaboration: Issues and Problems', in *Violence in the Family*, Borland, M (ed.), 136–45, Manchester University Press.

Wasserman, S (1967) 'The Abused Parent of the Abused Child', *Children*, 14, 5: 175–9.

Watling, E F (transl.) (1947) *Sophocles: The Theban Plays*, Harmondsworth, Penguin.

Wells, F (1981) Child Abuse – Three Perspectives on Sharing Information: A Medical Perspective', *Concern*, 39: 20–5.

West, S (1888) 'Acute Periosteal Swellings in Several Young Infants of the Same Family, Probably Rachitic [rickets] in Nature', *British Medical Journal*, 1, 856.

Whiting, L (1977) 'The Central Registry for Child Abuse Cases: Rethinking Basic Assumptions', *Child Welfare*, 56, 4: 761–7.

Wilson, H and Herbert, G W (1978) *Parents and Children in the Inner-city*, London, Routledge and Kegan Paul.

Winnicott, D W (1964) *The Child, the Family and the Outside World*, Harmondsworth, Penguin.

Woolley, P V and Evans, W A (1955) 'The Significance of Skeletal Lesions in Infants Resembling those of Traumatic Origin', *Journal of the American Medical Association*, 158, 7: 539–43.

Zalba, S R (1967) 'The Abused Child: a Typology for Classification and Treatment', *Social Work*, 12: 70–9.

Government Reports and Papers

Report of the Committee on the Care of Children (*Curtis Report*) (1946) London, Cmnd 6922, HMSO.

Report of the Committee on Young Persons (*Ingleby Report*) (1960) London, Cmnd 1191, HMSO.

Registrar General (1963) *Statistical Review of England and Wales*, London, HMSO.

Report of the Committee on Local Authority and Allied Personal Social Services (*Seebohm Report*) (1968) London, Cmnd 3703, HMSO.

Department of Health and Social Security (DHSS) (1970) *The Battered Baby*, London, HMSO.

Department of Health and Security (DHSS) (1972) *The 'Battered Baby' Syndrome: An Analysis of Reports Submitted by Medical Officers of Health and Children's Officers.*

Report of the Departmental Committee on the Adoption of Children (*Houghton Report*) (1972) London, Cmnd 5107, HMSO.

Department of Health and Social Security (DHSS) (1973) *Report of Tunbridge Wells Study Group*.

Department of Health and Social Security (DHSS) (1974a) *Memorandum on Non-accidental Injury to Children*, LASSL (74) 13, CMO (74) 8.

Department of Health and Social Security (DHSS) (1974b) *Maria Colwell*, LASSL 74 (25).

Department of Health and Social Security (DHSS) (1974c) *The Family in Society: Preparation for Parenthood*, London, HMSO.

Department of Health and Social Security (DHSS) (1975) *Prisoners Convicted of Offences against Children in the Home: Release on Licence under Section 60(1) of the Criminal Justice Act, 1967*, LAC (75)3.

Department of Health and Social Security (DHSS) (1976a) *Non-accidental Injury to Children: Reports from Area Review Committees*, LASSL (76)2, CMO (76)2, CND (76)3.

Department of Health and Social Security (DHSS) (1976b) *Health Visitors and Home Nurses and the Legal Problems of their Clients*, HN (76)4.

Department of Health and Social Security (DHSS) (1976c) *Non-accidental Injury to Children: The Police and Case Conferences*, LASSL (76)26, HC (76)50, HO 179/76.

Report of the Committee on Child Health Needs, *Fit for the Future, (Court Report)* (1976) London, Cmnd 6684, HMSO.

House of Commons Select Committee on Violence in the Family (1977) *Violence to Children*, Vol. 1: Report, London, HC 329 – i, HMSO.

House of Commons Select Committee on Violence in the Family (1977) *Violence to Children*, Vol. 2: Minutes of evidence, London, HC 329 – ii, HMSO.

Department of Health and Social Security (DHSS) (1980) *Child Abuse: Central Register Systems*, LASSL (80)4, HN (80)20.

Enquiry Reports

Published reports into the death or ill-treatment of a specific child are usually referred to by the child's name. Reports are listed in chronological order of publication

O'NEILL (1945) *Report by Sir Walter Monckton on the circumstances which led to the boarding out of Dennis and Terence O'Neill at Bank Farm, Misterley and the steps taken to supervise their welfare*, London, Cmnd 6636, HMSO.

BAGNALL (1973) *Report of working party of social services committee inquiry into circumstances surrounding the death of Graham Bagnall and the role of the county social services*, Salop County Council.

BAGNALL (1973) *Report of a committee of the hospital management committee into the circumstances leading up to the death of Graham Bagnall insofar as the hospital authority were concerned*, Shrewsbury Group Hospital Management Committee.

NASEBY (1973) *Report of the committee of enquiry set up to enquire into the circumstances surrounding the admission, treatment and discharge of baby David Lee Naseby, deceased, at Burton-on-Trent General Hospital from February to May 1973*, Staffordshire Area Health Authority.

COLWELL (1974) *Report of committee of enquiry into the care and supervision provided in relation to Maria Colwell*, London, HMSO.

PIAZZANI (1974) *Report of the joint committee set up to consider co-ordination of services concerned with non-accidental injury to children*, Essex Area Health Authority and Essex County Council.

AUCKLAND (1975) *Report of the committee of inquiry into the provision of services to the family of J. G. Auckland*, London, HMSO.

CLARK (1975) *Report of the committee of inquiry into the considerations given and steps taken towards securing the welfare of Richard Clark by Perth Town and other bodies or persons concerned*, Scottish Education Department, Social Work Services Group, HMSO.

COLWELL (1975) *Children at risk. A study into the problems revealed by the report of the inquiry into the case of Maria Colwell*, Lewes, East Sussex County Council.

GODFREY (1975) *Report of the joint committee of enquiry into non-accidental injury to children with particular reference to Lisa Godfrey*, Lambeth, Southwark and Lewisham Health Authority (Teaching), Inner London Probation and After-Care Committee, London Borough of Lambeth.

MEURS (1975) *Report of the review body appointed to enquire into the case of Stephen Meurs*, Norfolk County Council.

COLWELL (1976) *Children at risk. Joint report of the County Secretary and Director of Social Services*, Lewes, East Sussex County Council.

HOWLETT (1976) *Joint enquiry arising from the death of Neil Howlett*, City of Birmingham District Council and Birmingham Area Health Authority.

BREWER (1977) *Report of the review panel appointed by Somerset Area Review Committee to consider the case of Wayne Brewer*, Somerset Area Review Committee.

'H' family (1977) *The H. family: report of an investigation by the Director of Social Services and the Deputy Town Clerk*, Surrey County Council.

BROWN (1978) *Paul and L. Brown. Report of an inquiry held at Wallasey*, Wirral Borough Council and Wirral Area Health Authority.

MENHENIOTT (1978) *Report of the Social Work Service of the DHSS into certain aspects of the management of the case of Stephen Menheniott*, Department of Health and Social Security, London, HMSO.

PEACOCK (1978) *Report of committee of enquiry concerning Simon Peacock*, Cambridgeshire County Council, Suffolk County Council, Cambridgeshire A.H.A. (Teaching), Suffolk A.H.A.

SPENCER (1978) *Karen Spencer*, Derbyshire County Council.

BROWN (1979) *An inquiry into an inquiry*, British Association of Social Workers, Birmingham.

CHAPMAN (1979) *Lester Chapman inquiry report*, Berkshire County Council.

CLARKE (1979) *The report of the committee of inquiry into the actions of the authorities and agencies relating to Darryn James Clarke*, Department of Health and Social Security, London, Cmnd 7730, HMSO

BROWN (1980) *The report of the committee of inquiry into the case of Paul Stephen Brown*, Department of Health and Social Security, London, Cmnd 8107, HMSO.

HADDON (1980) *Report of the Director of Social Services to the Social Services Committee, Claire Haddon born 9.12.78*, City of Birmingham Social Services Department.

TAYLOR (1980) *Carly Taylor: report of an independent inquiry*, Leicestershire County Council and Leicestershire Area Health Authority (Teaching).

MEHMEDAGI (1981) *Maria Mehmedagi. Report of an independent inquiry*, London Borough of Southwark, Lambeth, Southwark and Lewisham Area Health Authority (Teaching), Inner London Probation and After-Care Service.

PAGE (1981) *Malcolm Page. Report of panel appointed by the Essex Area Review Committee*, Essex County Council and Essex Area Health Authority.

PINDER/FRANKLAND (1981) *Child abuse enquiry sub-committee report concerning Christopher Pinder/Daniel Frankland (born 19.12.79, died 8.7.80)*, Bradford Area Review Committee.

Reports of the Commission for Local Administration in England

Report into complaint No. 1064/H/77 against Berkshire County Council, 1979.

Report into complaint No. INV 172/3/78 against the London Borough of Camden, 1979.

Report into complaint No. 235/C/78 against the Metropolitan Borough of Bury Council, 1979.

This section of the bibliography was compiled with the indispensable assistance of the NSPCC National Advisory Service Library.

Relevant Legislation

Offences Against the Person Act, 1861.
Prevention of Cruelty to Children Act, 1889.
Children Act, 1908.
Infant Life (Preservation) Act, 1929.
Children and Young Persons Act, 1933.
Infanticide Act, 1938.
Children Act, 1948.
Sexual Offences Act, 1956.
Homicide Act, 1957.
Mental Health Act, 1959.
Matrimonial Proceedings (Magistrates Courts) Act, 1960.
Children and Young Persons Act, 1963.
Children and Young Persons Act, 1969.
Family Law Reform Act, 1969.
Local Authority Social Services Act, 1970.
Guardianship of Minors Act, 1971.
Guardianship Act, 1973.
Matrimonial Causes Act, 1973.
Children Act, 1975.
Child Care Act, 1980.
Foster Care Act, 1980.

Index

Main page references are given in bold type